The Battle Stalin Lost

ALSO BY
Vladimir Dedijer

Tito: A Biography

Beloved Land

The Road to Sarajevo

THE
BATTLE
STALIN
LOST

Memoirs of
Yugoslavia
1948-1953

Vladimir Dedijer

The Viking Press NEW YORK

First published in 1971 by The Viking Press, Inc.
625 Madison Avenue, New York, N.Y. 10022

Published simultaneously in Canada by
The Macmillan Company of Canada Limited

SBN 670-14978-0

Library of Congress catalog card number: 79-119780

Printed in U.S.A.

ACKNOWLEDGMENT: To Doubleday & Company, Inc.: From
The Eagle and The Roots by Louis Adamic. Copyright
1952 by Doubleday & Company, Inc. Reprinted by permission of the publisher.

TO THE MEMORY OF
Jan Palach

Contents

FOREWORD

ix

1.

Dark Clouds Gather

3

2.

Stalin and the Yugoslav Communists

31

3·

The Key Question: Economic Relations

73

4·

The Opening Gambit

97

5·

The People—the Only Source of Resistance

133

6.

Alone in a Hostile World

167

7.

Inquisition in Eastern Europe   *217*

8.

Breaking Through the Russian Blockade   *249*

9.

The Painful Road to the Truth   *291*

INDEX   *335*

Foreword

This book grew from a series of articles published in the Slovenian newspaper *Delo* in the winter of 1968–1969. I was moved to write these articles—and eventually the book—by the armed aggression of the Soviet Union and four other East European countries against Czechoslovakia. In August 1968, while that aggression was in progress and it appeared that Yugoslavia might suffer the same fate, I talked with some young friends on the editorial board of the Ljubljana student newspaper *Tribuna* about Stalin's attempts to destroy Yugoslavia in 1948–1953. I realized that they did not know very much about those earlier events, which were remote history for them, so I left off what I was doing at the time and started on the articles. My intention was to make available to them materials that would, among other things, enable them to perceive more clearly and in depth the new dangers hovering over not only Czechoslovakia but other countries as well, including their own. Although Stalin is dead, neo-Stalinism is gaining ground in the U.S.S.R.

This is not a history of the events between 1948 and 1953 but rather the story of my own personal experiences during that period. I also wanted to show how the struggle against Stalin affected my own thinking about social development.

In writing this book I used documents I had collected for my projected history of the Yugoslav revolution and my own unpublished diaries from that period. The book first appeared in *Delo* and was also serialized in several other papers and journals in Yugoslavia and Czechoslovakia. (The serialization in Czechoslovakia was stopped after Dubček's fall in April 1969.)

I finished writing *The Battle Stalin Lost* in late January 1969, when the news came of the sacrifice of Jan Palach, the Czech student who burned himself to death in protest against Soviet occupation of his country. That is why I decided to dedicate this book to his memory.

Vladimir Dedijer

The Battle Stalin Lost

I.

Dark Clouds Gather

Tito Tells the Incredible News ★

In January 1948 I was supposed to leave for China to try to write a book about the Chinese revolution. Tito had given me the idea. One winter's night I had gone to give him the first copy of my book on the 1946 Paris Peace Conference, and at one point in our conversation he had suddenly said, "What about writing a book like this one on the Chinese revolution? So little has been written on it in this country."

The suggestion had astonished me. I stammered something about having lots of work to do. Just a few days before, I had taken over the post of director of the newly formed Government Information Office; I was also head of the Press and Agitation Section of the Agitation and Propaganda Administration in the Yugoslav Communist Party's Central Committee, and a regular Yugoslav delegate to the United Nations General Assembly (the Economic and Social Council, which dealt with humanitarian, social, and scientific problems). From time to time I lectured on international relations at the Higher Party School; I was president of the Physical Culture Association of Yugoslavia; editor of the monthly magazine *Thirty Days*. . . .

"Well, as you like. Actually you could let all that go for a while. China is extremely important, and you like to write.

The only thing that worries me is your health. Last year in Moscow you had that Jacksonian epileptic fit from your head wound. I'm afraid your health wouldn't stand up to the strain of a long journey, and then you might find yourself in conditions very like those of a partisan war. And there's your family to consider."

I started to feel ashamed. I was always being pulled in two directions, it seemed—on the one hand toward my old profession of writing and on the other toward my Party and government work. True, I had published four books since the end of the war and kept up my diaries. Had I done so out of personal ambition, or out of a feeling of responsibility to those of us who had lost their lives in the war? I seemed to be working off a debt to them by describing that struggle as best I could. But I also did my government work out of a feeling of duty. Or was there something else involved—the public acclaim and recognition, the flattery, in holding top posts?

As I thought about it, I realized that Tito was doing me a great personal service, enabling me to do the work I had the greatest inclination for. Writing suited me emotionally, too, for through it I could re-experience the days I had spent with the partisans. I remembered 1941, after the first enemy offensive, when I could not get my bearings in my new role as political commissar. Tito had noticed it and suggested that I keep a diary of the war. Now again he was giving me good advice—to write about a great, living revolution.

But I could not find words to express what was going through my mind. I tried to cover my discomfiture with a clumsy joke. Usually my jokes were aimed at others (I had been nicknamed President of the Bulls in the China Shop Club), but this time I trained my guns on myself. "Don't worry about my health. It's true I'm a ninety-per-cent disabled veteran, but that means I'll be doing silly things with only ten per cent of my capacity. Imagine if I were completely healthy!"

So I pulled myself together and agreed to go to China. When I left Tito's house and went out into the cold night, I wondered how I could have been so deaf and blind as to resist the suggestion. It would be far more exciting to go on a long journey with lots of adventure than to pore over the rules and regulations stipulating that employees in the Information Office had to lock their drawers each evening.

The next morning I went straight to the Ministry of Foreign Affairs to see Ivo Vejvoda, head of the Eastern Department, to ask him to get me a transit visa through the Soviet Union so that I could get to northern China, where Mao Tse-tung's headquarters were.

After that I set about organizing the materials I already had about China and looking for new information. In Belgrade, just before the war broke out, I had published, under semi-legal conditions, a book about China and the Chinese communist guerrillas, with the help of Milovan Jakšić—who happened to have been the best goalkeeper at the world championship soccer games in Uruguay in 1930, and was otherwise the owner of a bookstore. (There were a great many progressives among Yugoslavia's athletes, with whom I had worked closely. We had, for instance, been successful in boycotting the 1936 Olympic Games in Berlin thanks to the help of Dr. Milutin Ivković, the famous back on the state soccer team; another well-known player, Aleksandar Tirnanić; and Dragoš Stevanović, a school chum of mine and Balkan light athletics champion.) Jakšić had agreed to publish my book in his "White Bear" series—which also included books about Stakhanov, the Dean of Canterbury's memoirs about Russia, and Colonel Mahin's book about the Red Army. For this book on China I had used material from Edgar Snow, Agnes Smedley, and Anna Louise Strong, as well as from *Inprecor,* the illegal organ of the Comintern. The book was banned, but with Jakšić's help and the assistance of the Party apparatus we had managed to sell about three thousand copies in Yugoslavia. (During the war I was happy to come across a copy of the book in a partisan detachment in Bosnia.) I had wanted particularly to present the experience of the Chinese guerrilla fighters themselves, and I had also noted down some of their sacred guerrilla rules—"The people are the water, and the guerrilla fighters are the fish"—which applied to all liberation movements, no matter where.

After the war General Sreten Žujović and I had been the first Yugoslav partisans ever to meet with a Chinese guerrilla. Our meeting took place in April 1945, in the Fairmont Hotel in San Francisco, where the constituent assembly of the United Nations was being held. The Yugoslav delegation was headed by Dr. Ivan Šubašić, and Žujović and I were delegates; Chiang Kai-shek's delegation included Tung Pi-wu, member of the Politburo of the Chinese Communist Party. Those were the days when the three great Allied powers thought they could settle conditions in various countries where revolutions were raging by making agreements among themselves, but the effect was often absurd, as this shows.

I was not then aware of these things, however, nor did I imagine them possible. We met Tung Pi-wu for the first time at a reception given by Soviet Foreign Minister Molotov, head of the Soviet delegation, whom I was also seeing for the first time that evening and who introduced us (Žujović in a general's uniform and I in my colonel's) to the Chinese official. Some Poles and, as I recall, some Czechs were also present, and Molotov started praising the Yugoslav partisans for having put up such a great fight against the Germans. He was echoed with even greater vehemence by Dimitri Manuilsky. A white-haired man of unusually vigorous gesture, Manuilsky kept patting me on the chest while saying to the Poles, "Now when the Germans tried to capture Tito at Drvar, this colonel stuck out his chest and saved the Commander in Chief, but he got three bullets in the attempt."

I wrung my hands, begged him to stop. "It wasn't quite like that . . ."

Manuilsky patted me on the shoulder. "See how modest the Yugoslav partisans are? They refuse to talk about their exploits." He winked, pulled me aside, and whispered, "I am saying these things on purpose. These Poles and Czechs should have an idea of how *they* should have fought when the going was tough." Manuilsky could not have known that he had hit a sensitive spot—the feeling I had that my best comrades had laid down their lives and that I had been condemned to live on after them.

The elderly Chinese stood by, a man of proud bearing, observant and attentive. Before leaving, he gave me his visiting card and expressed the hope that he could see Žujović and me again.

I continued the evening in the company of Orson Welles. As early as 1942 he had defended the partisan cause and written the truth about Draža Mihailović and his Chetniks. That evening Welles wanted to attend a press conference I was having with a group of American newspapermen.

The newsmen were good-humored, shooting questions at me about the Germans, or Fritzes and Huns, as they called them. Sergeant York, who had captured 124 Germans single-handed toward the end of World War I, was a native of Tennessee, and their questions seemed to suggest they thought I was some sort of reincarnation of him.

"Colonel, did you kill a hundred Germans?"

"If each partisan had killed a hundred Germans, the war would have been over long ago!"

"Well, did you kill at least fifty?"

I did not answer, and a third journalist asked, "Did you kill at least ten?"

I collected my wits. I told them I had participated in a number of battles but that I had no idea how many Germans I had killed. They were not satisfied, and one of them snapped, "But your biography says you were wounded three times."

"Yes, I was wounded three times," I answered, seething, "but all three times the bullets struck me in the back as I was fleeing the battlefield. Partisans were good at not allowing themselves to become enemy targets."

Welles began to guffaw. Nobody else caught on to what I was trying to say.

The next day, Žujović informed me that Novikov, secretary of the Soviet delegation, had come with an invitation from Molotov to drive around the countryside with him.

We drove to Palo Alto, where, during lunch, the other diners recognized Molotov and began applauding him. An old man called out, "Look at the Russian! He still has snow on his boots." When the restaurant owner, a vivacious lady in her forties, came up with the menu and recognized Molotov, she cried, "Oh! gee!" and rushed to hug him. She had a son in the Pacific, she told us, and hoped the Allies would win a quick victory so that he could come home.

In the evening, Žujović and I met with Tung Pi-wu. In beautiful Russian he told us about his life. (I was surprised he did not try to hide his family and social background: "I come from a family of big landowners and finished my studies in Japan.") A founding member of the Chinese Communist Party who had taken part in the First Congress of the CCP in 1921, he had previously been a member of the Kuomintang leadership.

He had also been a delegate to the Sixth Comintern Congress in Moscow in 1928 and had spent a number of years in Russia studying at Lenin University. After 1930 he returned to China, to the free region of Kiangsi, where he was elected to the Central Committee. He described the communists' struggle against Chiang Kai-shek, the Long March, and his work in northern Shansi, where he had been head of the Party school. In 1937 he was appointed a member of the CCP delegation formed to negotiate an agreement between the United Front and the Kuomintang for a joint struggle against Japan. Between then and his arrival in San Francisco, he had been a member of the communist delegation in Chungking headed by Chou En-lai.

We in turn told him about our war—about the guerrilla activities in the countryside, about the resistance in the towns. Both Žujović and I were amazed at how many strategic and tactical features the Chinese and Yugoslav revolutions had in common, although there had been no direct contact between them.

Tung Pi-wu told us that he would send us materials from the Seventh Congress of the CCP, scheduled for the near future. He also gave me a memorandum on the liberated areas of China and asked if I could get it published in Yugoslavia. I promised him we would. (When I returned, my friend Vili Jager helped me write an introduction for this memorandum, and it was duly published in the November 1945 issue of *Thirty Days*.)

Only news agency accounts of the Seventh Congress of the CCP were published in Yugoslavia, and the Russian press and magazines did not carry the main reports submitted at the congress. But through some English communists Tung Pi-wu sent me a copy of Mao Tse-tung's report, and the text was published in *Thirty Days*.

Time passed, and no answer was forthcoming from the U.S.S.R. about my visa. Vejvoda explained that the Soviet diplomatic machine ground slowly and that patience was necessary. I recalled Milovan Djilas' opinion that diplomacy was an obsolete instrument in relations between socialist countries.

Then came a letter from the executive of the Communist Party of India which made me change my plans. It was an invitation to the Central Committee of the Communist Party of Yugoslavia to attend the Second Congress of the Indian Party in Calcutta.

The head of the International Department of our Central Committee, an old Montenegrin communist named Nikola Kovačević, suggested that I go and afterward try to get through Burma to southern China, where the guerrilla movement was flaming up again. This proposal was accepted by the Central Committee and two of us were appointed delegates: myself and Radovan Žogović, a Montenegrin poet. Žogović was a rather unbending person, strict with others and even more so with himself.

I had told none of my family where I was going or why. Somehow we still maintained the habits of secrecy that had marked our prewar and wartime revolutionary work. My wife, Vera, for instance, for a long time had had no inkling that

I was working in the "Agitprop" section of the Central Committee. Sometimes she would come to pick me up at the Madera Building on Revolution Boulevard—the Central Committee headquarters. There was no name on the building, and she was reluctant to ask what it housed, but one day she could stand it no longer.

"This evening when you came out I heard you tell that messenger boy, 'Tie him up, or he'll wreak havoc around here.' What kind of place are you working in?"

I laughed uproariously. Someone had sent the Central Committee the gift of a large police dog, which had started wandering about in the building, and I had asked the messenger to tie the dog up until we decided what to do with him. But I did then tell my wife I was working in Agitprop and that I was off for India and perhaps other countries as well. She looked at me sadly as I talked. "You know, in a way we are still revolutionaries. The Party comes first, and then one's personal life, family, and so on. If anything happens to me, you will be taken care of."

I had a tremendous amount of work to get through before leaving, and I was reading everything about India that I could get my hands on. Before the war I had translated a book by R. Palme Dutt about the struggle of the Indian people and the Communist Party of India, published by the Left Book Club. Excerpts had also been printed in the prewar *Thirty Days*. So I needed only to refresh my memory about India's political history.

Two days before our departure, Branko Vučinić, Tito's secretary, called to ask me to go up to Tito's that evening.

It was about five in the afternoon when I started for Tito's house. Dusk had already fallen. It was a rather unusual February—warm, mild weather, instead of the usual heavy snows. Slowly I made my way to No. 15 Rumunska Street. The officer opened the gate and I walked up the long, familiar path through the big garden. The walk is flanked on both sides by trees whose branches make a green canopy overhead. It was always pleasant to walk along that path, with the ivy-covered garden walls behind one.

Tito's home is a simple but spacious two-story house which had belonged to an engineer before the war and which had nothing to differentiate it from the other houses in the neighborhood. In October 1944, when our units were liberating Belgrade, the headquarters of one of our corps had been set up there; later the Supreme Headquarters of the People's Liberation Army had moved in and, when the war was over, Tito had remained there.

The front door opened onto a large hall whose paneled walls were covered with quotations from folk poems carved in medieval Serbian lettering. A wooden staircase led to the second floor. To the left was the dining room and to the right a spacious study. Tito's writing desk was in one corner of the study, and in the middle were twelve leather chairs around a long conference table.

As I entered, Tito was working at his desk. He left the reports he had been reading and waved me to the sofa. He seemed tired. This surprised me, as he usually showed no fatigue. How familiar his fresh, tanned face was—the high forehead, strong cheekbones, and mass of hair. Once again I thought how I had never been able to describe him faithfully when people asked me what he looked like—perhaps because his face reflected such a strange mixture of determination and gentleness, the latter particularly evident in his smile and penetrating blue eyes.

I had expected that he would talk about my forthcoming trip. He lit a cigarette and, as was his habit, placed it in his silver-rimmed holder. He began to smoke. He crossed his legs. He had about him the look of a man who wanted to discuss something complex and wished to assess his listener's mood first. I knew that look well.

This all took only a few seconds. Although I had known Tito fully ten years and had been with him frequently, I had not the faintest idea what he was about to say to me. I was more than a little astonished when, instead of talking about my journey, he started on another topic.

"Have you seen what happened in Rumania? They have had orders to remove all photographs of me! You didn't read about it in the foreign news reports?"

His serious tone took me aback. I had seen the reports but was certain there was no truth to them.*

I always felt very clumsy in my talks with Tito. Usually I could not formulate my thoughts as I wanted to, and ended up saying the first thing that came to mind. I did so this time too. "How's that? Aren't those the usual lies?"

A shadow came over his face. I looked at him more carefully and realized then how much his appearance had altered. His face seemed darker, with deep worry lines etched in it, and hollows under his eyes showed how little he had slept. At once it was clear to me that my first impression upon entering had been the right one. Tito was tired. I realized something serious was up—something that was causing him a great deal of worry.

Tito crossed his legs nervously. He took a deep pull on the cigarette and, apparently ignoring my confused question, continued, "You're a lucky man—that means you don't know yet! How wonderful it was in the war, when during the Fifth

* A report published in the Yugoslav news agency Tanjug's Red Bulletin on February 13, 1948, read:

THE FRENCH PRESS ON THE REMOVAL OF MARSHAL
TITO'S PICTURES FROM BUCHAREST SHOP WINDOWS
Paris, February 12

Tanjug's correspondent reports:

Under the title "Tito's Portraits Removed from Bucharest's Shop Windows," today's *Figaro* carries the following report from its Vienna correspondent:

"According to reports from Bucharest, the Rumanian Communist Party has ordered Marshal Tito's portraits removed from all displays where the head of the Yugoslav government appeared in company with Marshal Stalin, Dimitrov, and Groza. All kinds of rumors are circulating in Bucharest about Marshal Tito, whose position does not seem as secure now as is generally believed. He appears to have lost Moscow's confidence. These rumors cannot be verified for the moment, but are worth recording."

Offensive, we were surrounded on all sides by the Germans. Then we knew we were alone and did the best we could. And now, when the Russians could help us, they are obstructing us."

My skin turned to gooseflesh. For a few minutes I was speechless. Thoughts flashed through my mind like lightning, causing almost physical pain. I recalled a talk I had had a few days ago with the new Soviet cultural representative in Belgrade, Kalinin. He had told me that there was no love for the Soviet Union in Yugoslavia; that Russian was hardly being studied, whereas French and English were popular; that things were different in Bulgaria, where the Society for Friendship with Russia had almost a million members. I had thought him silly, and could not imagine this unimportant Soviet bureaucrat preaching to Yugoslavia. I had laughed and said, "It's quite clear why it's that way in Bulgaria. They were unable to like the U.S.S.R. during the war, when the going was tough, so they want to make up for it now."

But what Tito told me meant that the zealous civil servant, fresh from Moscow, had been following instructions from above. I remembered his boast that "Zhdanov personally" had sent him to Yugoslavia. How impertinent it had seemed to babble such nonsense about us! But now I linked his words up with what Tito was telling me. That had been no babbling, then, but a sign of conflict with the Soviet Union, a conflict with Stalin. But surely that was impossible! Who in this country did not like the Soviet Union? How could we possibly quarrel with Stalin? It was as though someone had said we were at war with ourselves. All this raced through my mind.

Tito noticed the impression his words had made on me. Slowly, and it seemed to me gently, as though he wanted to let me know only gradually what lay ahead of us, he continued speaking. The reason for his fatigue soon became clear. A fateful decision was being made, perhaps the most fateful in Yugoslavia's recent history. It was not only individuals who were involved, but the future of Yugoslavia, the future of the whole country.

My feverish thoughts were interrupted by Tito's voice. "We'll see what the future holds. Kardelj, Djilas, and Bakarić are in Moscow."

"But didn't they go to discuss military assistance and aid for Yugoslav industries?"

"No, not only that. Much more serious matters are at stake. We expect them back any moment."

That was all. We went on to talk about India, and then I took leave of him. Thoughts about what Tito had told me preoccupied me for the remaining two days before my departure.

The Trip to India ★

In my youth, when I was fifteen and went abroad for the first time to Poland, I learned how to protect myself from the emotional toll taken by contact with other cultures, other people, other impressions, that might have prevented me from doing what I had set out to do. I found it necessary always to have with me something private, something that represented my own world, so I took my favorite books along. This habit persisted in later life; when in preparation for a trip I would always pack some books I had enjoyed as a boy. As I traveled I would leaf through their pages, and days long past would spring to life. Thus when I left for India on February 15, 1948 (via Prague, Amsterdam, and Rome, this being the only route by which Yugoslavs could then reach India), I took along Matavulj's *Bakonja fra Brne* and Janko Kersnik's *Peasant Portraits*.

Years later, when I read the works of Jovan Cvijić about the social psychology of Montenegrins, Bosnians, Herzegovinians, and other mountain peoples from my part of the world, I realized the true significance of my curious habit. Was I not, in some way, what the scientists called a "violent Dinaric mountaineer type?" Cvijić attributes some fine characteristics to them, but also some dreadful ones. I loved reading his criticism of the personality cult as practiced by Dinaric types—that is, their self-love. As soon as a Montenegrin learns to walk, for instance, he begins to speak in decameters and to think of himself as the hero of his village. Was not this youthful travel habit a cult of my own, as though I were carrying an image of myself around with me, polishing it up and admiring it all day long?

This time the books dear to me did not seem necessary. I was completely absorbed in Tito's revelations about our conflict with the Russians, and wondering for the nth time whether it was not all just a nightmare.

I could not shake off the dark thoughts. My gloom deepened. How could a misunderstanding have arisen? We had given no cause for it. Still, take a good look once again! Could Stalin be right? After all, the U.S.S.R. was the land of the October Revolution—a socialist state already in existence for thirty years, whose people had amassed a tremendous amount of experience. Had not our Party been leading us toward the same goal for many years? Had it not taught us boundless affection for the first land of socialism, and respect for Stalin as a great leader and teacher? How could Kalinin, that tiny cog in the Soviet machine, lie so brazenly about us (and by order, at that, as I was to see later)? Had the Party not taught us that to love the Soviet Union meant to respect the truth? A progressive revolutionary movement could not resort to falsehoods. Its strength lay in telling the people the objective truth about society at every level of life.

After twenty-eight hours of flying, we were in Calcutta. For the first time in my life I realized that Western Europe was an island of plenty in a global sea of human misery and poverty. We had left Amsterdam and its canals—a town so clean that "you could lick honey from the sidewalk"—and disembarked in the vast anthill of Calcutta, where thousands upon thousands of undernourished people were sleeping in the streets, urinating, bathing, eating, gathering rain water to wash, dying in inhuman poverty.

The people were scrawny; the cows dragging along the streets were bony, hungry, and tottering; the trees were gaunt —everything seemed degenerated, human beings and animals and plants. All Calcutta, with its five, six, seven, or eight million inhabitants, looked like a myriad gypsy shantytowns intersected by asphalt streets. In the center were buildings symbolizing the power of the British Empire—official residences in Georgian style, a magnificent hippodrome, and hotels in front of which doormen with great bamboo sticks kept off the unfortunate mobs.

As the beginning of the congress had been postponed from February 22 to February 28, we found ourselves with free time on our hands. Uninterested in the museums and unable to read the materials sent us by the Indian Party, I spent most of the time wandering around the streets looking at the suffering people. Strange ships like Noah's ark plied the rivers. There were differences to be observed even among the people who slept on the sidewalks. One fortunate man among them—one in twenty—would have found newspapers to lie on; the others lay on the bare asphalt. Among the bodies laid out in rows stood a single bed with a fat man reclining on it; he owned a pair of shoes, but, fearful that someone might steal them, he had stuck them under the legs of his bed, so that anyone trying to take them would have to lift the bed and awaken him.

A little farther on, a smith with an anvil sat under a branchless tree. He had a cat on a leash and sat leaning against the tree, gazing at the starry skies and enjoying himself—just like a Dutch bourgeois in his well-lit, curtainless rooms.

I had read dozens of books about imperialism, but nothing had ever brought it home to me as did that afflicted mass of people. Britain had ruled India for more than two centuries and had conserved all the social relationships intact. It had not permitted social forces to develop, but had rather protected what was narrow and backward in the society. The poverty of the people, the general degeneration of man and nature, were not the product of inborn characteristics but the fruit of centuries of hunger. The black eyes of the children crawling in the dust seemed to shine with a sorrow from time immemorial, as though all the suffering of past generations found expression in a single pair of dark, almond-shaped eyes.

Our comrades in the Central Committee of the Indian Party had told us that Calcutta had the highest death rate in the world. Here the average life span was twenty-six; in Britain and Holland it was seventy. How many potentially great writers, musicians, and scientists did that mass slaughter carry off each year? How terrible the consequences of imperialism and inequality!

I had read somewhere that in the Napoleonic wars alone, we lost 11 per cent of the population and one-eighth of our lands in the Military March. How many people had we lost in the Bosnian-Herzegovinian revolt in 1875–1878, during which an estimated quarter of the population had to flee their homes? And what had World War I cost us? According to some statistics, we lost 1,900,000 men between Doberdob and Kajmak-čalan. And in the last war almost two million. That is what imperialism had cost us.

Epidemics of cholera and smallpox raged in Calcutta. Our friends begged us to get vaccinated against these diseases. The papers said that hundreds of people were dying daily. After my injections, I got a high fever.

It was very hot. Through the hotel-room window I saw great birds hovering in the air with wings outspread. It seemed to me that one of the birds was carrying a human hand. When I recovered my senses, I told an Indian communist what I had seen, but he assured me it was only a dream: there are no Parsees in Calcutta who leave their dead in high towers, having broken their bones; this is done only in Bombay, where scavenger birds descend upon the corpses and carry away parts in their beaks.

We visited a village some twenty miles from Calcutta. The tiny houses were made of mud. We called on some peasant activists—about a dozen men and women. Within their clean and whitewashed houses we were offered exotic fruit. Our peasant host was a vigorous man, bearing his poverty with pride. We talked about the big landowners. Something in the way these peasants moved reminded me of our Macedonians. If they agreed with what a speaker was saying, they shook their heads from left to right.

Returning to Calcutta we ran into a young Yugoslav, Dušan Puhalo, who had participated in the Southeast Asian Youth and Student Conference. The Indian Actors' Association was giving a tea for the delegates to the youth conference, and Zogović and I were also invited. But just as we were about to leave, we received a message that Joshi wished to talk to us. We arrived at the party a half-hour late and found police cars and ambulances in front of the building.

An unknown group of men armed with machine guns and grenades had made its way into the building and opened fire on the guests, who were standing along a wall quietly drinking tea. The hosts had leaped in front of the murderers. Not one of the guests was wounded, but two Indian Party members—both of them professional actors: Sushil Mukherjee and Bhadmadhab Ghese—had been killed, while another seven people had been injured.

No one knew who had hired the murderers. There were rumors to the effect that they belonged to the Chandra Bhose movement. Chandra Bhose had once been a disciple of Gandhi and even at one time president of the Congress Party. In the 1930s he had visited Europe and in 1936, Yugoslavia. The editor of the Belgrade newspaper *Politika,* where I was working at the time, had sent me to interview Bhose. He spoke of the misdeeds of British imperialism in India and I had written a long interview (which the censors banned). Afterward Bhose left the Congress Party and during the war joined the Japanese in the hope that Japanese troops in Burma would liberate the Indians from British rule. He had even organized an Indian army. But in 1945 he disappeared and was rumored to have died in an airplane crash. He still had influence in Calcutta, however; people said he was alive and would come one day to liberate India.

It was never discovered whether it was his men who had

made the assault. I was called to the police station that same evening to talk with an English police sergeant. (Although India was already independent, the police force had not yet been taken over by the Indians.) Very politely, he told us that they could not be responsible for our security. I thanked him and left.

The next evening we attended the funeral of the murdered men. A red flag at half-mast was borne at the head of the procession, in which thousands of workers marched. The coffins were covered with the banners of the World Federation of Democratic Youth and the International Students' Union, brought by a representative from Vietnam.

Is it only poverty that impels people to rebel? Is spontaneous rebellion sufficient for a revolution or does ideology also play an important role? I pondered these questions as I sat in Mehmed Ali Park under an enormous tent where the Second Congress of the Communist Party of India was in session. The delegates were sitting cross-legged on mats or on the ground; there were few workers among them and even fewer peasants, most of them being from the middle classes. They had come from all parts of the Indian subcontinent.

My thoughts turned homeward to Yugoslavia's experience with spontaneity and ideology. In Bosnia and Herzegovina alone there had been some thirty spontaneous peasant insurrections between 1806 and 1910, but without ideology all of them had failed; they had lacked progressive social forces capable of directing the uprising and inspiring it with purpose. At the end of World War I spontaneous resistance had occurred in all parts of the country—the people wanted changes, wanted a new class to take power; but it all fell through as there was no real ideology. Full-fledged revolution can result only from the combination of spontaneity and revolutionary organization.

But every revolution in this century has produced something new: new forms, new possibilities for a transition to a higher degree of social organization. No two revolutions are alike in form. That was the crux of the problem: how could subjective revolutionary forces find forms best suited to the given conditions in a particular country? Also involved, therefore, was a *revolutionary instinct.*

Many communist parties failed the test on this question. It seemed to me that the Indian Communist Party was grappling with the same problem. In any case, I had the impression that the Indian communists had not delved deeply enough into their own reality, into the historical conditions of their own country; in the most fateful hours of their recent history they had waited for directives from without. When World War II began, they proclaimed it an imperialist war and clung to that attitude even a full six months after Hitler's Germany attacked the Soviet Union. Later, when the Central Committee of the ICP had rectified its position on this question, it blindly joined hands with representatives of its own *haute bourgeoisie,* renouncing all struggle for the hegemony of the proletariat and even going to the other extreme, helping the British bourgeoisie unreservedly while prominent members of the Congress Party languished in jail. It was therefore the communists' own fault that they lost influence over the masses.

The French Party, too, or at least one wing of it, made similar mistakes between August 1939 and the German attack on the U.S.S.R. The case of the Norwegian Party was even worse: on May 1, 1940, its official paper, *Arbeiderer,* welcomed Hitler's invading troops as saving Norway from the Western imperialists. After June 22, 1941, when the Party appealed to the Norwegian masses to rise up against Hitler, hardly anyone was ready to follow its lead.

I think the Communist Party of Yugoslavia succeeded in retaining its prestige among the masses as a patriotic force in the critical period between the Soviet-German pact in August 1939 and June 22, 1941. We criticized the Western powers bitterly but did not spare Hitler either. It was no wonder that Ribbentrop, in his note of June 22, 1941, explaining why Germany had attacked the U.S.S.R., used as one of the "proofs" of Soviet bad faith a proclamation issued by the Communist

Party of Slovenia criticizing Germany, and another issued by the Yugoslav Communist Party. Our broad approach helped us retain influence over the masses and enabled us to develop the people's liberation struggle. But one had to be a revolutionary to gauge the pulse of the masses accurately—neither too much nor too little. How skillful as revolutionaries were our Indian comrades? It was precisely this congress that was to bring about a change in Party line.

The principal report was submitted by B. T. Ranadive, head of the left-wing faction. He condemned "the opportunism of the secretary-general," J. P. Joshi, during the past three years, and castigated him for not seeing that the Indian bourgeoisie was playing a treacherous role when it struck a compromise with the American and British imperialists. Joshi's line had been aimed directly against the struggle of the Indian masses for complete independence, and made it easier for Indian capitalists and large landowners to continue terrorizing and exploiting Indian workers and peasants.

A tremendous ovation followed the address by the peasant delegate Jivandam, from the area of Telingana, in Hyderabad. He brought the congress greetings from the rebellious peasantry of Hyderabad, where an armed uprising had been in progress since 1946, under the leadership of local Party organizations, against the terrorism of the Nizam of Hyderabad. The peasants of Telingana, headed by the communists, had cast off the Nizam's yoke, organized Party detachments, and established the first liberated area in India, with a population of five million. Police stations and county administrations had been liquidated in more than two thousand villages. Though the Nizam had mobilized a large armed force, the insurrection continued to advance. In the freed area the landed estates were being broken up, the land was being distributed to the peasants, and people's committees were being formed.

During a recess I talked with Jivandam and his comrades. They were interested in hearing how we had set up our government in the liberated areas, kept our wounded concealed from the enemy, and set up proletarian brigades.

I spoke on the second day of the congress, transmitting to those present the greetings of the Communist Party of Yugoslavia. When I took the floor the audience thundered their greetings to Tito, and I started to get stage fright. This always happens whenever I give a speech or lecture—the aftereffect of a traumatic experience in my younger days. In 1936 I had just returned to Belgrade from London, where I had spent a year as the correspondent of the newspaper *Politika*. My articles had been published on the front page and everything had gone to my head; I was conceited and thought the Danube came up only to my knees. Some of my friends from Herzegovina—Miro Popara, Avdo Humo, and Čedo Kruševac—asked me to give a lecture in the main hall of the Law Faculty in Belgrade. I agreed and considered it unnecessary to make any preparations. The Party had organized a large audience, and as soon as I got to the podium I saw that the hall was crammed. I opened my mouth, but only croaks came out. My grandmother, mother, and aunt in the front row started to wring their hands. I could get nothing out. Popara leaped to the podium and said, "Let's invite Dedijer to come back in three days with a written lecture. He writes better than he speaks."

That taught me a good lesson. Three days later I came back with a written text about England and spoke calmly, again before a full auditorium, without even glancing at the text.

How wonderful it is to be young, when everything seems possible and simple.

As I had planned in Belgrade, I sounded out the possibilities for getting to China via Burma. Among the delegates to the congress (and there were only three foreign delegations: Australian, Burmese, and Yugoslav) was the secretary-general of the Communist Party of Burma, Thakin Than Tun. When I told him about my plan, his reaction was negative. Burma itself was in a state of upheaval and Chiang Kai-shek's guards were posted the length of the Burma-China boundary.

One morning, while we were reading that fine newspaper

the *Statesman,* which regularly informed its readers of the fighting in China, we were joined by the Chinese newspaperman Chang Han-fu, editor of the *New China Daily News,* who was covering the congress. He had the latest copies of New China News Agency bulletins from Hong Kong, with lots of news about the fighting in China and life in the liberated areas. I asked him for advice on getting to China via Burma, but he too shook his head. It seemed clear now that my plans for going to China would have to be scrapped.

Among the other foreign delegates to the congress was a fascinating personality, the president of the Communist Party of Australia, L. Sharkey. (On his way to Calcutta he had talked with communists in Malaya and brought their greetings to the Indian comrades.) Sharkey loved theoretical discussions, and one afternoon during recess a few of us debated Marx's theory on absolute and relative pauperization.

Sharkey contended that all Southeast Asia was caught up in a process of absolute pauperization, that the poor were getting poorer and the small handful of exploiters of every kind was getting richer. According to him, a profoundly revolutionary situation existed in Southeast Asia, especially as American imperialism was endeavoring to fill the vacuum created by the decline of British, French, and Dutch imperialism. We should not shut our eyes to the population explosion in this part of the world, he reminded us, which even the high mortality rate could not mitigate. He was particularly pessimistic about the Indian bourgeoisie's ability to solve this problem.

There was another question on which we could not see eye to eye. A discussion had developed between the Indian leader Ranadive and a peasant communist from Telingana over where the shock units of a revolution should be based: in the villages or in the towns. Ranadive asserted that the communist movement had to have the strongest roots among the urban proletariat; he criticized the comrades from Telingana for having based their activities on the peasantry. Sharkey was one hundred per cent on Ranadive's side, while I had other arguments to put forward. The ideology, I granted, had to be that of the workers, who would provide the firm core, but India was still not industrialized, and the overwhelming majority of the people were peasants. The revolution could not be carried out unless the suppressed masses participated, and in this case they were predominantly peasant. Sharkey invoked the Comintern resolutions, while I recalled Lenin, the first to succeed in bringing about a revolution in a predominantly peasant country, because his revolutionary instinct told him where social antagonisms were the greatest. He had to rely on the nucleus of the working class and working-class ideology, but he could not divorce himself from the peasant masses.

Sharkey told us that the situation in Malaya was tense and that a popular uprising could break out any moment. Thakin Than Tun also described the situation in Burma as highly explosive. Sharkey asked us what we would do if we were communists in Malaya and Burma; would we work toward a revolution or not? The answer, of course, was that everyone had to work out his own assessment of the internal situation, the antagonisms in society, the subjective factors. It was hard for outsiders to give advice. In 1941, when the Yugoslavs launched their revolution, they asked no one for advice.

But we agreed that all Southeast Asia was being pauperized to the extreme; that the class in power was holding onto it by the cruelest use of force; that the imperialists were not only not losing their grip, but even stepping up efforts to restore the state of affairs existing before the war. In the face of the whole system of violence and suppression, the people had no way out but to reply in kind: by force, by revolution.

Since those talks of March 1948, it has been reported from various quarters that "the Yugoslavs doled out adventuristic advice in Calcutta." Several contemporary historians have asked me to give a more precise answer as to whether this is true. With Aneurin Bevan once in 1957 I had a long talk about the positions of the Indian Communist Party in 1948.

downhill fast. They are withdrawing their experts and claim they are surrounded by antipathy."

I had nothing to say. All my hopes had been in vain.

I went back home to find some childhood friends waiting for me, the athlete Dragoš Stevanović and the painter Lale Ivanović. In high school we had all run together in cross-country races each fall and spring. Now they were in gym suits, ready to run from my house on Senjak Hill over Banovo Brdo and Košutnjak Park. Although not in particularly good condition, I was only too happy to join them, and ran with them all the way, trying to flee from the terrible news Djilas had communicated.

But there was no getting away from it. During the next few days I realized there was no way out.

The editorial offices of the Cominform newspaper *For Lasting Peace, For People's Democracy* were located in Belgrade. The editor-in-chief was a Soviet official named Pavel Yudin; Boris Ziherl of Yugoslavia was his deputy. Zogović and I had written a report on the Indian Party congress, and I was also urged to write an article for Yudin's paper. I finished one posthaste and went over it with Zogović, whose useful suggestions I agreed with. I then handed the article in, but it was never published. Ziherl told me that Yudin had raised certain objections, and I got my manuscript back.

I wondered why Yudin had not wanted to publish it. It was true that no Soviet Party representative had attended the congress in Calcutta, nor had the Soviet press reported the proceedings except in the most perfunctory manner. I read the article again and then it dawned on me why Yudin had rejected it. Moscow had taken offense at the fact that the Yugoslav revolutionary experience was held in such high esteem in India. Here are a few passages from that article, now published for the first time:

This self-critical report was elucidated, on behalf of the Central Committee of the Indian Communist Party, by Ranadive, a member of the Politburo of the Central Committee and head of the faction that had on several occasions, especially during the past few years, opposed the opportunist line of J. P. Joshi. He observed that after a long struggle the entire Central Committee had agreed that that line had been wrong. Ranadive further stated that theoretical materials from the Central Committee of the Yugoslav Communist Party, Tito's address at the Second Congress of the Front, and Kardelj's article entitled "Notes on Some Questions of Internation Development" in *Kommunist* (January 1947) had helped the Central Committee perceive that its line had been opportunistic. Speaking in the name of the Indian Communist Party, Ranadive thanked the Central Committee of the Yugoslav Communist Party for its assistance, and added that the principal theoretical materials of the Central Committee of the Yugoslav Communist Party had been translated into the Indian languages and were on the "must" list of reading matter for members before the congress. . . .

After two days of discussion the congress adopted a general resolution pertaining to the new line to be followed by the Indian Communist Party. The resolution called for the creation of a democratic front in the struggle against the American and British imperialists, and against the Indian upper middle class, which had betrayed the interests of the nation and struck a compromising bargain with the imperialists. The resolution referred to the program of the democratic front which contains the following points:

First, complete secession from the British Empire and the establishment of full and complete independence for India.

Second, the creation of a democratic government to represent the will of the people and not the will of the capitalists —a government which would oppose collaboration with the Anglo-American imperialists and form an alliance with the democratic states for the purpose of strengthening peace and international cooperation.

Third, the promulgation of a Constitution based on universal adult suffrage and proportional representation, guaranteeing full freedom and democracy to the people and securing full economic power for the working masses.

Fourth, the right of self-determination for the various nations, including the right to secession. The creation, on a voluntary basis, of an Indian Federation with autonomous linguistic provinces. . . .

One point of the program calls for abolition of the big landed estates, liquidation of British capital in India, nationalization of the basic branches of industry, and a purge of reactionary elements from the army and government. . . .

The congress closed with a public session attended by fifty thousand Calcutta workers. Representatives of the Communist Parties of Australia and Yugoslavia spoke. Their addresses were followed by speeches by Bovanisen and Dange, members of the Central Committee of the Indian Communist Party, who outlined to the masses the new line of the Indian Communist Party.

2.

Stalin and the Yugoslav Communists

At the beginning of January 1948 a military delegation had gone to Moscow to discuss military aid for Yugoslavia. At the same time the Russians sent Tito a telegram asking for a member of the Yugoslav Politburo, preferably Milovan Djilas, to come to Moscow to discuss a number of foreign-policy matters, with special reference to Albania. Consequently, Djilas went with the military delegation.

The delegation spent over a month in Russia, but with no results. At their first meeting Stalin told Djilas that Yugoslavia "should swallow up Albania" and asked him to cable Tito along these lines. (Later, in Belgrade, Stalin's move was interpreted as an attempt to compromise Tito's government as having imperialistic designs on Albania.) Stalin also promised that the military delegation would get everything it was asking for, but the stalemate did not break.

At about this time, toward the end of January, Georgi Dimitrov, Prime Minister of Bulgaria, visited Rumania and at a press conference answered questions as to whether a Balkan federation or confederation would be formed. Dimitrov said the question was premature, but added, "When it comes to creating such a federation or confederation, our people will not ask the imperialists and will not heed their opposition, but will solve the question themselves, guided by their own interests bound up with the interests of other peoples and the international cooperation necessary to them and to other nations." On January 29, however, *Pravda* openly attacked Dimitrov: "Those countries do not need a questionable and fabricated federation or confederation, or a customs union; what they require is the consolidation and defense of their independence and sovereignty by mobilizing and organizing internally their people's democratic forces, as was correctly stated in the well-known declaration of the nine communist parties."

A few days later Stalin invited high-ranking representatives of Yugoslavia and Bulgaria to an urgent meeting in Moscow. Actually, this was the first phase in his open attack on the independence and sovereignty of Yugoslavia, but it was not the fate of our country alone that was at stake. By putting Yugoslavia in harness, the Soviet Union could increase its control over all the East European countries and re-establish in the international workers' movement the kind of total obedience to Moscow that had existed up to the dissolution of the Comintern in 1943.

Bulgaria's most prominent leaders—Dimitrov, Vassil Kolarov, and Traiche Kostov—hurried to Moscow at Stalin's call. Stalin had let it be known that he hoped Tito would also come. But Tito's native instinct—the instinct of the oppressed but rebellious peasants of his area—told him that the Kremlin wished not a comradely exchange of opinions but unreserved obedience to its orders. Therefore he did not respond to the suggestion. In any case, he was not in good health and was beginning to have trouble with gallstones. The Russians did not bother to hide their dissatisfaction. I noted in one of my diaries that Aleksandar Ranković had said: "The Russians expected Tito would be in the delegation and were furious when he did not come."

Tito's intuition had been right. The Yugoslav delegates to

Moscow—Edvard Kardelj, Milovan Djilas, and Vladimir Bakarić—were treated to an angry monologue by Stalin. Although ostensibly venting his main fury on Dimitrov, he was also aiming at us. He criticized the Yugoslavs for not responding to Albania's request for military units to protect its southern borders, and for not consulting with the Soviets on these and other foreign-policy matters. And then, all of a sudden, Stalin asked that a federation between Yugoslavia and Bulgaria be formed "tomorrow." Actually, he was playing a game. The Yugoslav delegates were unanimous in concluding that there was something else behind Stalin's demands (see p. 101). Dimitrov had come to the same conclusion. After the meeting he told our delegation in confidence, "This is not just a criticism of my statements, something else is afoot. . . . It will be far easier for us and for you to progress, because our level of productive forces and the educational level of our populations are higher than they were for the Soviet Union."

At the Soviet government's request, an agreement was signed on February 12, two days after the meeting with Stalin, providing for mutual consultation on foreign-policy questions between the Soviet and Yugoslav governments. The treaty was canceled by the Soviets on April 24, 1948.

After the delegation returned to Belgrade, Djilas wrote a report on that historic meeting, adding his own personal observations. The Central Committee met on March 1 and approved the position taken by the Yugoslav delegation at the Moscow talks.

That is how Stalin lost the first round. But events posed a more general question transcending the framework of Soviet-Yugoslav relations. Stalin's attitude toward Yugoslavia must be regarded against the background of Stalin's plans vis-à-vis all the countries of Eastern Europe entered by the Soviet army at the end of the war and recognized by the Western powers as within the Soviet sphere of influence.

There are signs (to be mentioned later) that early in 1948 Stalin thought all Eastern Europe should be included in the

Soviet Union. Yugoslavia had a special place in this plan. In many ways she had been the most faithful follower of Soviet foreign policy, even of the internal Soviet system. On the other hand, she had had the most autonomous revolutionary development: in 1944 and 1945 government teams trained in Moscow had taken power in Poland, Czechoslovakia, Hungary, Rumania, and Bulgaria, but not in Yugoslavia, whose leadership was a symbol of the significant war effort made by the Yugoslav people toward their own liberation and the common victory over Hitler.

Still, the evidence reveals that it was Stalin's desire to subjugate Yugoslavia and that he anticipated an early victory. It is hard to say whether he had had a complete strategic and tactical plan worked out in advance for bringing Yugoslavia to heel. The Soviet archives of 1948 are still not accessible, and without them a complete historical assessment cannot be made. But from what we do know *now*, from eyewitness accounts and what was learned in the Soviet Union and other East European countries after Stalin's death, it appears that he had not worked out such a plan for Yugoslavia. He was above all a pragmatic politician: he had set a trap, certain he could spring it, and when he could not, he went about setting more cunning and dangerous traps for his opponents. The struggle went on a full five years, from January 1948 up until Stalin's death in March 1953.

Stalin's offensives can be described as follows:

1. "Silent strangulation," by way of direct pressure brought to bear at the meeting in Moscow on February 10, 1948, for the purpose of forcing capitulation. This fell through at the very inception.

2. An attempt to provoke conflict within the Central Committee of the Yugoslav Communist Party, with the Russians relying on Andrija Hebrang and Sreten Žujović, the so-called "sound forces" inside Yugoslavia. These measures were combined with "black propaganda" and the dissemination of reports that Tito was in disgrace through bourgeois newspapers

and news agencies in Western Europe. Stalin was confident that this second phase would succeed, for he had also threatened Yugoslavia with economic blockade. In the spring of 1948 he said in the Kremlin, "As soon as I move my little finger, Tito will be thrown out." But this offensive, too, failed to bring the desired results.

3. A more broadly conceived phase of attack involving the ideological excommunication of the Communist Party of Yugoslavia, with the world Communist movement bringing pressure to bear on Yugoslavia in the name of socialism to save the country from counterrevolution. In March, April, and May, Stalin sent a number of letters to the Yugoslav Central Committee to that end; supposedly confidential, they were likewise distributed to all other communist parties, which also started to pressure Yugoslavia.

4. Public anathema through the Cominform. Stalin tried to get representatives of the Yugoslav Central Committee to attend the Cominform meeting in Bucharest on June 28, 1948, where the Yugoslav Communist Party was openly anathematized.

5. Tightening the economic blockade. At the same time Moscow tried to organize the (abortive) escape of Yugoslav General Arso Jovanović, former chief of staff of the Yugoslav Armed Forces, whom Soviet intelligence meant to use in organizing some sort of pro-Russian political center outside of Yugoslavia.

When all these steps proved futile, Stalin declared an all-out economic blockade; threatened aggression; accused Yugoslavia of aggression and fascism; staged public trials of high officials in other East European countries, accusing them of treasonable acts committed at the behest of Yugoslavia; provoked border incidents; and persecuted Yugoslav diplomats and minorities in other countries. He stopped short only of open armed aggression, for he was, after all, wise enough to know he could not predict the outcome of such a step—a mere local war or a world-wide conflict.

The Enigma of Stalin ★

There is nothing more difficult than to be writer and actor in one's own drama. Even today, after more than twenty years, I cannot think coolly about those days in the spring of 1948, so highly charged with significance for the history of Yugoslavia. Testimony of this kind is colored by the writer's own bias and errors in judgment. The conflict between the new Yugoslavia and the Soviet Union in 1948 was fraught with passion, with a strange kind of fire, like the disputes between medieval Christian sects. The feverish feeling of those times is with me still.

Moreover, the participants and witnesses were not immediately aware of, and even later often did not know exactly, what was going on. Major state secrets were in question, and the archives of only one party to the dispute have been opened for examination since. Nor was it immediately realized, even by those in key government positions, that the clash was inevitable. I noted the following words of Tito in my diary in the spring of 1948: "Only *then* did everything become clear to me. All those elements I had considered accidental, for which I had found a thousand excuses, came together to form a whole, took on their true meaning. . . ."

As I have said and am not ashamed to admit, until the spring of 1948 conflict between the new Yugoslavia and the Soviet Union had seemed impossible to me. This was the consequence both of my education and of errors in judgment. I had even clashed with those closest to me over this matter. My father-in-law, Lado Križman, is what they call a "stubborn highlander"; he always has his own opinion of things and states it candidly. (Indeed his whole family is like that. His father, Ivan Križman, editor of the *Young Slovene* in Kranj before World War I, had held on to his convictions and was persecuted for them, the entire family suffering as a result.) Sometime in 1947 he had said to me, "I just wonder if those Russians are always going to help us. And I have my suspicions about the

Bulgarians." I blew up and read the riot act to the old man, calling him all sorts of names. He only shook his head. During the war he had sent materials to partisan detachments in Slovenia, and his daughter had been sentenced to six years in prison for having tacked up signs around Ljubljana on May 1, 1942, reading "Long live the U.S.S.R." But if he had sided with the partisans and Russians then, he was having second thoughts. He said to my wife, Vera, "I had no idea that husband of yours was such a nut. You can't even have a normal conversation with him." When the conflict with Russia broke out in 1948, my father-in-law said nothing to me.

I have often thought about the reasons for my convictions about the Soviet Union before 1948, about the roots of my prejudices. I and my friends who in the thirties had realized just what the social realities were, had had only two alternatives. On one side was imperialism, with all the evils it had wrought: the Yugoslavia of King Alexander, with its inhuman relationships, its suppression of the people, its unfortunate Macedonians, not even allowed to speak their mother tongue, the murders of the Croat leaders in parliament, the arrests and torture of my best friends. On the other side was the country where Lenin had effected a revolution in the face of enormous difficulties—the first socialist country in the world. We looked starry-eyed upon the Soviet Union; she seemed the only hope and guide. Assaults on her by the most stupid and backward social forces in our country and abroad had only convinced us further that we were in the right.

There was no other alternative. If we were to live on and fight we had to have an ideal—not a Utopian one, but something real, something that actually existed, that was developing.

I never visited Russia before the war, but when news came in 1937 of the Stalinist purges, I was confused and upset. I was not yet a member of the Party, although my house in Belgrade had been used as a hiding place by Tito and other high-ranking Party leaders. I felt that I was not ready to be a communist, which required outstanding courage, strength, and perseverance. The news about the trials and purges had an adverse effect on the difficult struggle we were waging against dictatorship in Yugoslavia, and on our efforts to help Spain and Czechoslovakia in their fight against fascism. But instinctively I refused to believe that a lasting distortion was involved, and clung to the hope that all would be well in the end. Sometime in 1938 Sydney and Beatrice Webb published a new edition of their great study of the Soviet Union. The subtitle to the first edition had been "A New Civilization?" whereas the second edition was printed without the question mark. I castigated myself, thinking: "Look what a suspicious intellectual you are. You are being taught a lesson—and by social democrats at that, by the most dogmatic among them, the British—that there should be no doubt about the prospects of development in the Soviet Union."

I was tortured by thoughts about my professional and general background. I told myself: "You are not in the movement, in the revolution, because you are hungry, because you are oppressed by social conditions, but because you are an idealist and you want to achieve your ideals. But are you as stanch in your belief as a true proletarian, as a worker or peasant?"

I once had a long discussion about this with the leader of the Young Communists of Yugoslavia, Ivo Lola Ribar. He developed the idea that we professionals and intellectuals were not simply interested in achieving our ideals, but also were threatened in Yugoslavia because of our very social position, especially the younger among us. A young Macedonian, for instance, could not get a job unless he entered into a compromise with the regime against the interests of his own people. We were all threatened by the prospect of war, of dying before we began to live. Finally, pure reason left us no choice but communism. In the chaos we lived in, the only rational answer seemed to be a new society where there would be no wars and no exploitation whatsoever, and the intellectual's source of strength was his ability to perceive in greater depth the historical inevitability of this.

I was, however, much more emotional about such matters than Lola Ribar. Before I finally joined the Party in 1939, I again had long talks about these matters with a number of Party members. I remember being particularly saddened by a talk with Veselin Masleśa, who said that in journalism the surplus value was created by the manual laborers—the printers, paper binders, newsboys—while we writers were nothing, only parasites.

These recurrent attacks of anxiety about my professional and intellectual status—about my being a sort of black sheep in the Party and therefore in a far worse position than my comrades of proletarian background—were constantly with me, even during the war itself. As soon as I opened my eyes in the morning, I would think: "Today you must prove your loyalty to the Party, your fidelity to your comrades." And in the evening I would ask myself, as in evening prayer: "Have I done all I could, have I betrayed any of my principles?"

I recall a terrible inner crisis on Piva Mountain in Montenegro, while I was in the partisans' Supreme Headquarters. It was May 1942, and I had been told to write my curriculum vitae. I wrote it, just as I am writing this, with an open heart and with no attempt to make things sound better than they were or to conceal anything. But when I handed it in, I was asked, "Have you been entirely candid, have you put everything down, won't you have another try at it?" I wrote it again, tearfully; I had not been believed the first time.

But the great events of the war pushed all this to the background. Whoever experienced the horrors of that war will have to admit that the Soviet Army held out the greatest hope that Hitler would be beaten in the end. The Soviet Union bore the brunt of the war, and the main fascist forces met their end on the Eastern Front. After the war, I carefully collected data about the losses suffered by individual countries:

The Soviet Union: 7,000,000 fighting men and 13,000,000–18,000,000 civilian dead.
Poland: 6,000,000 dead, both army and civilians.
Yugoslavia: around 2,000,000 dead.
China: 2,000,000.

The United States: 295,904.
Great Britain: 265,770.

The number of war dead is not the sole criterion for measuring the war effort of the Allied countries, but it is the most painful. Factories and homes and other material things have been rebuilt, but the dead can never be brought back to life. This factor of massive violent death is a powerful link among people on the scales of history and cannot be forgotten overnight.

This is all the more true in Yugoslavia since our losses, relative to the size of the country and its population, were among the highest in the world. Moreover, when Hitler launched his attack on the U.S.S.R. in 1941, we developed a nationwide resistance to the German occupation forces. When Hitler's divisions reached the outskirts of Moscow, large parts of Yugoslavia had been liberated and were under the partisan flag.

An unselfish code of ethics developed, as happens only during great mass efforts and in fateful hours. On March 9, 1943, when the main partisan forces were surrounded in the Neretva River valley with four thousand wounded, I wrote the following in my diary:

The airplanes are the worst. They began at dawn and did not let up until dusk. The bombers flew low, machine-gunning everything in sight, and one bomb load after another was dropped on Prozor. This has been the worst day.

The village of Duge, with four hundred wounded, was also bombed . . . but despite everything our drivers have managed to get the wounded through. . . . One of our messenger boys, Mico, put it very nicely: *"Every bomb they drop on us means one less for Russia.* Victory will come soon. And if we had surrendered to Hitler, they would have sent us to the Eastern Front, and at least half a million of us to German factories; they would have looted everything we have. We would have been slaves forever. But Tito has made a miracle out of nothing."

Mico was a peasant from the Sandjak; there were thousands upon thousands of such Mico's, with their epic way of looking at life and death—all over Yugoslavia, from the mountain of Triglav in the north to the border station of Djevdjelija in the south.

In the autumn of 1943, after the battle of the Sutjeska, I walked all the way from Montenegro to liberated territory in Slovenia. One evening in Rog, when we were sitting around the fire, the Slovene poet Edvard Kocbek told a group of us the story of a peasant from Dolenjska who was taken into custody by the Germans for having helped wounded partisans. When he faced the German firing squad, the Slovenian peasant shouted, "Listen, your Germans, I am dying for your sake, too."

I was thinking about Mico and that peasant from Dolenjska the other day, when I met a talented young Slovenian dramatist. For him Stalin was simply the personification of the terror perpetrated against intellectuals and the terrible trials of 1936–1938, and nothing more. For me he was that, but also something else. As the leader of the Soviet Union in World War II, he was the symbol of resistance to Hitler not only for Soviet citizens but for fighting men far beyond the borders of Russia. How many partisans in our country had gone to their death with his name on their lips! The young dramatist had not the faintest idea of what was going through my mind, or of what I had experienced in the war. "The people should not be lied to," he brusquely declared; the whole truth must be told.

I spoke to him disconnectedly, saying whatever came to mind. Then I hurried home, took my war diary, and read again, probably for the thousandth time, something I had written on June 9, 1943, at the Sutjeska, when the same bomb that fatally wounded my first wife, Olga, also wounded Tito and a host of others.

Had scarcely closed my eyes, when there was a crash of bombs. About fifty meters away a reconnaissance plane was

bombing a battalion of the Fourth Brigade. Trees were coming down on our heads, but the column of Montenegrins did
not break, merely quickened the pace. No one was injured.
Then came nine dive bombers over Milinklade and the
valley of the Hrcavka. And then the bombers appeared.
Being bombed in a forest is extremely unpleasant—the bombs
disperse on the trees and shrapnel flies all over the place. We
stretched out in a damp gully, the stream wetting our feet.
We kept looking at our watches and wondering when this
horrible day would end. Our stores of drugs took a direct hit.
A little after twelve a courier brought a letter from Ranković
for Moša Pijade: "Tito has been wounded and the English-
man is dead. The Germans are coming. Send an escort
battalion."

The escort battalion left for Milinklade and a new wave of
bombers came at us. I heard someone calling from a distance: "Comrade Vlado, Dedijer . . ."

A nurse from my wife Olga's medical unit came running
up, breathless and flushed, her hair disheveled. "Comrade
Vlado, Olga is calling for you. She has been seriously
wounded."

Pijade told me to go. The nurse Ruška spoke quickly.
"A bomb fell near the surgical team. Olga's shoulder is
smashed. She is so good, that doctor of ours. She told us, 'Go
away and leave me alone. Don't let the Germans catch you
because of me.' She's only worried because all our medical
supplies have been destroyed."

We climbed rapidly up the slope of Milinklade. The
wounded were coming down in large numbers. Ruška told
me that over a hundred fighting men from the Fourth Bri-
grade had been killed or wounded that morning at the top
of the hill where the planes found them in a clearing.

Again a wave of bombers. The wounded came down the
slopes in groups. The dive bombers flew down to the very
treetops unloading their bombs. They were followed by
small reconnaissance planes bombing the groups of men.
Suddenly we were deafened by the sound of airplane engines.
Ruška and I fell to the ground. Seven or eight bombs fell
around us. The stink of gunpowder suffocated us. It was
pitch dark. When the air cleared, I saw lying next to us a

comrade from the Sixth Bosnian Brigade, a young man with big dark eyes, both his legs torn away. His blood gushed out in a stream, carrying away the young beech leaves the explosion had shaken from the trees. We could do nothing to help him. He was dying. He waved to me and whispered: "Long live Stalin!"

The young man's name was Kozomara. He was a worker from Sarajevo and had joined the partisans in 1941. Millions of people like him breathed their last in World War II with Stalin's name on their lips, and the fact remains that for them Stalin was *the* symbol of resistance to Hitler. Even now he remains that for me, though I could tell my young dramatist friend a few things about Stalin and perhaps even persuade him that I was a thoroughly destalinized Stalinist.

Olga was in agony for eleven days. Her right shoulder gone, she accompanied the partisans from the Sutjeska all the way to Romanija Mountain, sometimes on foot, sometimes on horseback, always without food, in the pouring rain and cold mountain wind. She died on June 20, a day after I was wounded in the head. I was running a high temperature the night we buried her. I wrote about her burial in my diary:

I stood at the very edge of Romanija Mountain, against the cliffs, on the path leading from Stejna-Medaković to Mokro. It was already night. The wind howled, bending the enormous pine trees. We dug Olga's grave with our hands and knives, as we had no spades. I had a platoon with me, the rear guard of our column. All the others had gone on ahead. The village was only two hours away, and the Germans were probably already there.

Olga lay wrapped in a white blanket, her black hair almost covering her face. The wind blew harder, bending the trees even more. Laza, a miner from Sekević, in Serbia, who had joined the partisans in 1941, was digging with his hands. "Vlado, we've reached rock," he said.

The last clump of soil was dug out by a man whom Olga had operated on. "She saved my life. All of us loved her." We laid her in the shallow grave, covering it with stones to make a mound, eight yards from where the path comes out on Romanija Mountain, next to the southeast slope. Saša Božović, Stanojko Djurič, and three other comrades from the platoon took off their caps with me. "Glory to Comrade Olga!" shouted Laza, and we all repeated his words.

We made off into the dark forest and caught up with a battalion of the Second Proletarian Brigade. In the gloom we tramped silently through the dense, marshy woods. Olga had given her life for her people, died as a member of our Party. I clutched her watch, which I had taken for our daughter Milica, and the tears ran—one, two, a whole stream.

That night is etched in my memory forever. When I had my first epileptic attack, as a result of my head wound, sometime in the spring of 1944, I dreamed of that night, of my hands wet with blood that dripped from my head wound and mixed with the earth I was digging out for Olga's grave. When I had a similar attack in March 1947 in Moscow, during the Big Four foreign ministers' conference discussing the treaty with Austria and the problem of Carinthia, they took me to the Kremlin Hospital, where I was examined by a team of doctors. When a psychiatrist asked me about my mental state, I told him how haunted I was by that terrible night, how I could not sleep because I always leaped up disturbed whenever the grave appeared in my dream.

Then came 1948 and the conflict with Russia. Because of the post I held, I had to make public statements about Soviet policy toward our country at Information Office press conferences, in my books and articles, and in speeches at the United Nations. And so Moscow launched attacks on me. I took them philosophically at first, and even started a notebook entitled "The Anthology of Curses and Slanders about Vladimir Dedijer," in which I entered all epithets with the exact date. But all of a sudden they started attacking Olga. I was stunned. Had they found my file in the Kremlin Hospital and discovered the story of my personal loss and resulting trauma? Were they now trying to destroy me psychologically by striking at my most sensitive spot? The culminating slander came in a book by Orest Maljcev called *The Yugoslav Tragedy*, published in Moscow in 1952, for which the Council of Ministers of the U.S.S.R. gave Maljcev the Stalin Award of the Second Degree for 1951. The book said we were all Gestapo members, American or British spies. Olga was described as having sat out the war in a luxury villa on Dedinje Hill in Belgrade in the company of Gestapo officials, carrying out various espionage tasks for them against the fighting men of the people's liberation war!

This was not just my own personal tragedy. It set me thinking about the tactics Stalin had used in his struggle against Yugoslavia from the very first day the conflict came out into the open. In letters to the Yugoslav Central Committee in April and May 1948 Stalin made a special effort to play down the contribution of the people of Yugoslavia and the Yugoslav Communist Party in World War II, denying that there had ever been a revolution. These attacks later developed into slanders about the leaders of the uprising being in the pay of the Gestapo. For the great majority of Yugoslavs, this was the main reason why they took a stand against Stalin in 1948; they wanted the truth about historical events. Once again Stalin had resorted to the principle that the end justifies the means, thus revealing to the world that he did not recognize the need for a code of ethics in relations between revolutionary movements and communist parties, or in relations between peoples or states.

But there can be no revolution without ethical principles. By his behavior Stalin revealed the crisis of society in the Soviet Union. History has taught us that any progressive movement which neglects ethics is sowing the seeds of its own degeneration. Charnishevsky had written this in one of his books and Svetozar Marković, after reading it, had coined the slogan: "In small nations, ideas are worth only as much as the people who implement them." The Slovene writer Ivan Cankar had also taken a similar view.

Even if we try to abide by those revolutionary ethics, however, we cannot assess Stalin only on the basis of the purges of 1936–1938 or his attack on Yugoslavia in 1948. His entire historical development must be considered, and all the periods of his activity.

In judging Stalin I tried not to use Stalinist yardsticks. Even the terrible pain I felt when my dead wife, a good and honest intellectual, was accused of being a Gestapo spy did not make me hate Saint Nicholas because of Nicholas, as they say in Yugoslavia—did not make me curse the idea of communism as such because of the form of Stalin's society in the Soviet Union.

I made an effort also to see myself in historical perspective. When they changed the name of Stalingrad to Volgograd a few years ago, my reactions were mixed. Although enthusiastic about the process of destalinization in the Soviet Union, I felt that perhaps they should not have changed the name of Stalingrad. I leafed through my diary again and read what I had written in February 1943 about how our suffering people, then in the midst of the Fourth Offensive, had reacted to the news of the victory at Stalingrad—the beginning of the end of Hitler's tyranny.

In an article for the *Times Literary Supplement* in 1966 on the problem of historiography in the Soviet Union, I made public my feelings about Stalingrad. I reproached the Soviet leaders for applying Stalinist methods against the dead Stalin. I felt he should be condemned for all that he was guilty of, but that he should also receive his due for his accomplishments —for instance, his contribution to his own homeland during the war and to the struggle against Hitler.

The First Misunderstanding with Stalin ★

There seems to be some sort of fateful schedule whereby a crisis in relations between Moscow and the Yugoslav communists breaks out every ten years.

In 1938 the Comintern almost adopted a decision to dissolve the Communist Party of Yugoslavia. Those were hard times for Yugoslav communists in the Soviet Union, for Stalin's purges also affected them. This period in history has not been examined yet, so we don't know exactly how many were killed, but guesses run to several hundred (one report mentions eight hundred). Danger threatened *all* Yugoslav communists in Russia, and many of them only by a hair's breadth avoided execution, or being packed off to the concentration camps in Siberia and Kamchatka, from which men rarely returned.

The new Yugoslav Party leadership returned to their country, however, to break new ground. Young people joined the Party. Then Hitler attacked in 1941 and the people's liberation struggle was launched. The peoples of the Soviet Union and Yugoslavia came closer together than they had ever been before. But as soon as the Yugoslav revolution gained momentum, a conflict with the Comintern, or rather with Stalin, arose.

During the war, although I was close to the Supreme Headquarters, I knew nothing of any kind of disagreement with Moscow. True, we were always waiting for Soviet paratroopers and for help in armaments, but when they did not come we reasoned that the Red Army was still almost three thousand miles away, the intervening territory in the hands of Hitler's troops, and the technical difficulty involved in landing Soviet planes or parachuting medical supplies and ammunition to liberated areas in Yugoslavia insuperable.

Only after 1948 did I have the opportunity, together with Moša Pijade, to read carefully through all the radio messages in Tito's files, at which point certain matters became clear. I realized there had been disagreement during the very first days of the uprising as to the nature of the Yugoslav revolution, the relations between the two revolutions, and the path to socialism.

These documents proved to me that, owing to distortions in Soviet society, Soviet hegemony had been strengthened, and in the process an attempt had been made to subordinate the Yugoslav revolution to Soviet ideas. Stalin put up a "theoretical" defense of his concepts, summed up in slogans stressing the need to "build socialism in only one country": "Socialism can be achieved only by expanding the state boundaries of the Soviet Union, and not by equal cooperation among countries in which the revolution has triumphed."

Every revolution is a combination of ideology and spontaneous action by the masses: if the goals toward which the masses aspire are not clearly established, even the fiercest rebellions will fall through. At a consultation of the Yugoslav Central Committee in May 1941 in Zagreb, Tito, speaking of the preparations for armed resistance to the occupation, stressed the need to create a new government from the very first day. There was no other way for the struggle to succeed. How could anyone have appealed to the peoples of Yugoslavia to rise up against the German, Italian, Bulgarian, and Hungarian occupiers without telling them clearly that they were also fighting for a new kind of government; for a republic and not a monarchy; for equality among all the nationalities of Yugoslavia; for the complete independence of the country from foreign capital; for the industrialization of the economically backward areas; for ending the exploitation of man by man; for equal participation by women in society; for the right of young people to have a say on key problems?

The decisions adopted at that plenum in May were radioed secretly to Moscow, but the reply arrived only on July 4, after war had broken out between Russia and Germany, when the Comintern sent the following message: "The present stage is one of liberation from the fascist yoke and not of socialist revolution." Dimitrov signed the message, but actually it had come from Stalin. I learned later from the Bulgarian revolutionary Ivan Karaivanov, an old Comintern hand who had moved to Yugoslavia in 1945, that Dimitrov had lost all influence in the Comintern as early as 1936 and was only a figurehead; all decisions were made by Stalin and carried out to the letter by Manuilski and other Comintern officials.

But the development of the uprising in Yugoslavia followed

its own laws. The people had to be told that they would have a new government. Tito informed the Comintern on August 21 that "probably a kind of central people's government would be formed."

Toward the end of 1941 and in the first few weeks of 1942, the radio between the Supreme Headquarters and the Comintern did not function regularly. The uprising was then in full swing. Only in March did the Comintern reply to letters from Yugoslavia and assess the situation critically; its position was that the fighting was too revolutionary, that in essence the struggle should be a struggle against fascism. Accordingly, the Soviet government recognized the royal government-in-exile in London and its Minister of War, Draža Mihailović, who was openly at war with the partisans. In the autumn of 1941 Radio Moscow referred to Mihailović as the head of the resistance movement in Yugoslavia and refused to condemn him for his attack on liberated territory in western Serbia, or for his collaboration with the Germans against the People's Liberation Army.

It was only in late spring that the Free Yugoslavia radio station, which broadcast news to Yugoslavia from the Soviet Union and received news from the Supreme Headquarters, made public the first news reports about Draža Mihailović's betrayal.

It was stressed in Moscow that the revolutionary development of events in Yugoslavia should not be allowed to obstruct cooperation with the United States and Britain. However, during the entire war there was not a single serious conflict among the Allies because of Yugoslavia, so this argument was of only secondary significance. What Stalin really feared was a revolution generated by the people of Yugoslavia themselves, beyond his control and against his wishes.

In the autumn of 1942 conditions were ripe for setting up the Anti-Fascist Council of the People's Liberation of Yugoslavia, the provisional government of the new Yugoslavia. On November 12 Tito informed Moscow by radio of the founding of the People's Liberation Army and of the intention to proclaim the establishment of the National Committee for the Liberation of Yugoslavia when the Anti-Fascist Council met at Bihać on November 26.

The Comintern was quick to reply. It did not agree with the establishment of a provisional government, or with the abolition of the monarchy and proclamation of a republic, and stated that the National Committee should be a general political body, anti-fascist in character. "At this stage, do not pose the question of abolishing the monarchy. Do not raise the slogan of the republic. The question of the regime in Yugoslavia, as you conceive of it, will be solved after the disruption of the Italo-German coalition and the country's liberation from the occupiers."

This directive was carried out. Moscow's intervention made it impossible to abolish the monarchy and proclaim a provisional revolutionary government. But in a three-page radio message sent on November 29, Tito took the Comintern to task for its attitude. After submitting all the necessary information about the proceedings and decisions of the first session of the Anti-Fascist Council (the partisans' parliament), he said:

> I must inform you that it is precisely the noncommunist activists in Yugoslavia who have condemned the Yugoslav government-in-exile as a traitorous one, as does the entire nation. Although we do not consider the Executive Committee of the Anti-Fascist Council as any kind of a government, it will nevertheless have to look after affairs of state and the front, in which it will be assisted by the people's liberation committees set up in virtually all areas, liberated and unliberated. There is no other government here except those committees and the military government which looks after the fighting.

Stalin could not or would not grasp the fact that in multinational Yugoslavia, where exploitation had been rife, the struggle could not be restricted to fighting the occupiers. The masses could be mobilized only around a platform that promised a general solution of of internal antagonisms.

Stalin: I Was Stabbed in the Back ★

In looking over the messages Tito exchanged with the Comintern during the war, I came to the conclusion that the gravest conflict with Stalin took place at the end of 1943, when the Anti-Fascist Council met for the second time and the foundations for a new Yugoslav state were laid.

Stalin was consistent in implementing a policy based not on the interests of the liberation struggle and revolution in Yugoslavia, but rather on the immediate situation and tactical interests of the Soviet Union. And he wanted to force the Yugoslav revolution into that mold.

In the course of 1943 the People's Liberation Army won victories in all parts of Yugoslavia. Hitler failed in his attempt to smash the main partisan forces in the Fourth and Fifth Offensives. Draža Mihailović suffered a resounding defeat at Jablanica. It was clear to friend and foe alike that the partisans were the only real force in the country.

Simultaneously, conditions were ripening for the establishment of a supreme people's authority, for initiating the development of Yugoslavia along democratic federal lines as a community of equal peoples. The royal government-in-exile had to be deprived of all the prerogatives of legitimacy, and King Peter II prohibited from returning home.

Decisions on these matters were drafted for the Second Session of the Anti-Fascist Council to pass. But this time the Politburo did not wish to allow any interference from the outside, as had been the case a year earlier at the First Session. On the eve of the meeting in Jajce, in the autumn of 1943, a Soviet plane dropped paratroopers into liberated territory, among them one Šterija Atanasov-Viktor, of Bulgarian descent. The mission was headed for an intelligence assignment in Bulgaria. At Jajce, Viktor was told that the Anti-Fascist Council would be holding a session, but he was not given detailed information about the proposals to be submitted. On November 28 he used the partisans' radio station to send a report to the Comintern, signed Georgijev, which Tito initialed. Moscow was informed of all the decisions of the Anti-Fascist Council by radio on November 30. The text was written out longhand by Moša Pijade, in Serbo-Croatian (in the Latin alphabet), to which Tito added "Translate into Russian." Tito also initialed all three pages of the text and added the date, which Moša Pijade had forgotten. The next day Pijade wrote yet another report, of four pages, in which he enumerated the names of the members of the Presidium.

Vlatko Velebit, recently appointed chief of our military mission to Allied headquarters for the Middle East, took with him a copy of all the Anti-Fascist Council's decisions, and the Allied military mission was also informed.

I learned later how the decisions had been received in Moscow from Veljko Vlahović and Djuro Salaj, who had been in the Soviet capital at the time—Vlahović as Yugoslavia's representative and head of the Free Yugoslavia radio, Salaj as a member of its editorial board and an announcer. I made the following notes of my talk with Vlahović:

Moscow learned about the Anti-Fascist Council's decisions, including the decisions to strip the royal government-in-exile of its legitimacy and forbid King Peter to return, after they had been passed, that is, from the message of November 30, 1943. The first reaction in Moscow was sharp. The Free Yugoslavia radio station got orders not to broadcast the resolution forbidding King Peter to return to Yugoslavia; moreover, Veljko Vlahović was reprimanded and all his broadcasts for Free Yugoslavia were placed under censorship. Manuilsky delivered Stalin's message to him: "Hazyayin [Stalin was known to a small circle in Moscow as Hazyayin, which means "the host"] is extremely angry. He considers this a knife in the back of the Soviet Union and a blow to the Teheran decisions."

And my diary contains this passage about Salaj:

All of us in the editorial office [he told me] were enthusiastic when we got the news about the decisions passed at the Second Session. It was the greatest victory of our revolution. We worked with great spirit to prepare the text for broadcast, for although we were far away from our homeland we realized the historic significance of the event.

I remember vividly how Veljko Vlahović read the various decisions to me and the other members of the office. . . . His face glowed with joy. For years we Yugoslav communists had been waiting and suffering silently in Moscow, and now our hour had come, an hour of recognition of what our people had achieved.

But then came the bolt from the blue. We were told that the Soviet Foreign Ministry had issued orders forbidding the broadcast of the Anti-Fascist Council's decisions. We used pull to try to get the orders rescinded, but in vain.

The only thing we could do was point out to Soviet officials that the London radio was broadcasting the decisions while we were not. A concession was then made. We were told we could broadcast the news that the session in Jajce had been held, but not a word about the decisions. All they allowed us to do was repeat the decisions of the First Session!

We persisted in trying to prove our point, that the struggle being waged by our people would only suffer if the decisions were not broadcast, but the Soviet bureaucrats were adamant.

When we finally thought we had succeeded, we were in for another big disappointment. Molotov personally issued an order that we could broadcast the decisions, with the exception of the resolution forbidding King Peter to return to Yugoslavia.

Then we really blew up. Was Free Yugoslavia supposed to defend the monarchy? Only after the London radio had broadcast all the decisions did Molotov relent.

That, then, is how the top Russian circles looked upon the decisions of the Second Session, the greatest achievement of the Yugoslav peoples in the course of the liberation war.

This case demonstrates that the Soviet government took very little account of the aspirations of our peoples. It was governed exclusively by the interests of its own foreign policy.

In the messages exchanged between Tito and Moscow, I found proof of everything Vlahović and Salaj had told me. I later also looked over the texts of the Free Yugoslavia broadcasts. Although Moscow had been informed on November 30 of the decisions passed by the Second Session, Free Yugoslavia was allowed to broadcast them only on December 15.

Moša Pijade commented, "Stalin's revolutionary days are over. He has become a statesman and is no longer sensitive to the needs of a revolution. He is worried about the boundaries of great states and agreements on spheres of influence."

The First News About Secret Treaties on Spheres of Influence ★

Stalin's implacable fury at the decisions of the Second Session of the Anti-Fascist Council was not surprising. He considered the Yugoslav revolution not as an independent process but as something to be accommodated to his own policies. At the end of 1943 it was already clear that Hitler would lose the war. Discussions began among the major states in the anti-Hitler coalition about postwar policy, new boundaries, and spheres of influence.

We knew nothing of this during the war. And I must admit, since we had been taught to have boundless faith in the Soviet Union, it seemed impossible to us that the first land of socialism could make such arrangements with other states.

Documents and eyewitness accounts revealed to us much later that we, the partisans of Yugoslavia, and the entire struggle of the peoples of Yugoslavia, had been the subject of bargaining and haggling among the big powers even during the war. While all that was going on, the partisan Supreme Headquarters had been situated in an inaccessible part of eastern Bosnia, virtually cut off from the rest of the world except for radio connections with the Comintern.

Although we had established a people's government over a large part of Yugoslavia and had a considerable military force, we had no real contacts with East or West until the capitulation of Italy in the autumn of 1943, when we sent our first missions to Italy, the Middle East, and Moscow. But we still had no diplomatic or consular services, and no information media—all that was yet to come.

At the end of November 1943 I underwent surgery in Cairo, and again early in 1944 in Naples. From there I went to Bari, where a partisan base was located which sent supplies to our army, took care of our wounded, and disseminated information about our liberation struggle. I worked with my comrades there in these various activities.

On one occasion in the summer of 1944 I met a progressive American newspaperman who considered himself a Marxist, and we became good friends. He told me in the greatest confidence that Russia and Great Britain had concluded a secret treaty dividing up the Balkans, particularly Yugoslavia, into spheres of influence, and that British propaganda organizations in Italy had already adjusted their work to the new situation.

I refused to believe it. I told him that the Soviet Union was not an imperialist country and could never do such a thing. We had a heated discussion. I had been reading Stalin's wartime addresses and showed him one dating from November 6, 1941, which we had published in the Užice edition of *Borba*:

> We do not and we cannot have any war goals like imposing our will and our regime on the Slav and other peoples of Europe who expect assistance from us.
>
> It is our purpose to help those peoples in their struggle for liberation from Hitler's tyranny and then to allow them full freedom to organize life in their countries as they see fit. There is to be no interference in the internal affairs of other peoples.

The American replied that circumstances had changed, that Stalin was not the same person, but I stuck to my arguments. After a few days I went to Naples for a medical checkup, and we continued our talk there on the same subject. With us was another liberal American, my own age, who had an excellent knowledge of European and Balkan history and had been a member of the progressive youth movement before the war. He also told me that he had heard something about such negotiations and that the Americans were also involved. He knew very well, he said, how much the Yugoslavs had suffered in World War I as a result of secret diplomatic maneuvers and treaties about spheres of influence. In April 1915 Great Britain, France, and Russia had concluded the secret London Treaty with Italy, ceding to Rome the Slovenian littoral, Istria, half of Dalmatia, half of Albania, and even a part of Asia Minor inhabited by Turks and Greeks.

I reacted sharply and pointed out that it was Lenin who in 1917, only one month after the October Revolution, had ordered the publication of that agreement and issued an official communiqué to the effect that the new Soviet government abrogated it, since it did not wish to participate in the plundering imperialist policy of dividing countries up into spheres of influence.

My American friend knew history very well. He observed that Marx had been among the first to appeal to the working class of the world to exercise vigilance over the activities of governments, particularly as concerns secret diplomacy and the bargaining of bourgeois diplomats at the expense of the people, without their knowledge and against their vital interests. He quoted Lenin's peace decree of November 1917, in which the Soviet government said that it opposed secret diplomacy and would work in the open for all to see. "But," he said, "under Stalin all that has changed."

I asked him to cite at least one concrete proof of the Soviet Union's being party to a secret agreement. He referred to the Soviet-German pact of August 1939.

I reacted violently. "The Munich treaty between Hitler and the Western countries was a typical spheres-of-influence agreement. The European bourgeoisie talked Hitler into attacking Russia and all the East European countries—the same bourgeoisie that in 1918 organized an unsuccessful expedition of nine different armies, under the single banner of anti-communism, to suppress the young Soviet republic. The Soviet-German pact was a reply to the West's foul play. Stalin had to defend himself. He was engaged in a real war with the Japanese militarists. He needed breathing space—security on the western border while he dealt with the East. Imagine what would have happened if Hitler had started at the old Soviet borders rather than the new ones, if he had had a head start of several hundred kilometers. Moscow would have fallen!"

I lost my head completely and almost walked off in a huff. I began to storm at the two Americans and stopped discussing the issues we disagreed on. I told them they were under the influence of their own bourgeoisie and could not understand the essence of communism.

They fell silent. It was not easy for them, as they looked up to me as a partisan lieutenant-colonel wounded three times and just emerged from the whirlpool of revolution. The journalist started to waver, but the historian stuck to his guns.

"Never mind. I would rather the news were not true. I see how deeply it affects your idealistic view of the Soviet Union."

I got up and left without saying good-by.

Things changed with the times. Later, through my own experience and Yugoslavia's—on my own skin, one might say— I learned to assess Stalin's behavior more realistically, and naturally began to perceive the true and essential motives behind the Soviet-German pact of 1939. History will be the final judge, and I believe it will deal most critically with Stalin's policies. The principal victims of Stalin's miscalculations were the people of the Soviet Union: documents reveal that Stalin believed Hitler blindly, and this impaired his country's defenses. He simply did not wish to believe that Hitler's Germany would launch a treacherous attack on the Soviet Union.

But in 1944, at the height of our liberation war, and with what I then knew, I defended that pact as though I myself had signed it.

Randolph Churchill Gives the Secret Away ★

In June 1944 I went back to headquarters on the island of
Vis. Never had we lived under such non-partisanlike conditions. We had always been on the move, our pack horses ready
to push on as soon as the shooting started, which it did practically every day. And now here we were at the seaside! (True,
there was no drinking water, but we drank wine instead,
because there was not enough rain water for all.) When work
was done we went swimming, but even then made up a game
of battle which included dunking one another. As a former
water-polo player, I was a past master at this. Once I was
attacked by four Montenegrin generals: they had me cornered,
but I started shouting insults against various Montenegrin
clans—one of them was a Katunjanin, a Montenegrin "aristo-
crat," while another was from somewhere in the Scutari plains,
a "fukara"; they set about arguing among themselves and I
got away scot-free.

Our beach became very international. We were joined by
several Western statesmen who came to see Tito, among them
Robert Murphy, a special political adviser to General Eisenhower. We barely escaped a serious diplomatic incident, the
first in a series of mishaps with the American government. As
I was recognized king of the sea as far as dunking was concerned, the minute I entered the water everyone made for the
shore, trying to avoid provoking me. That day, however, I saw
a redheaded man swimming toward me, splashing as he approached. That was supposed to be a terrible provocation;
I started for him to punish him for his brashness, but Tito
yelled from the beach, "Stop it, he's a guest!" And so Robert
Murphy was spared a plunge into the depths of the blue
Adriatic.

The same day some partisan commanders from Croatia
arrived at headquarters. They had many things to tell us,
including a talk with Randolph Churchill, son of the British

Prime Minister, who had been parachuted into liberated territory as a member of the British military mission.

Randolph Churchill had inherited his father's courage, but
he was rather short-tempered and at some headquarters or
other had once become very angry when they did not immediately give him a horse. One of our officers, a Dalmatian,
had been with him and tried to calm him down. But Churchill's temper showed no signs of waning. In his fury he said:
"My father wrote to me that he has made an agreement about
division of spheres of influence in Yugoslavia with Uncle
Joe [Stalin], and then we'll show you partisans a thing or
two."

I immediately linked this up with what I had heard from
my American friends in Italy, but again it all seemed impossible, like a joke Stalin was playing on old Churchill. Five or
six years had to pass before we got a clearer picture—from
statesmen's memoirs and the archives of the big powers—of
the real intentions of the three Allied powers, and particularly
the U.S.S.R., toward Yugoslavia during the war.

In assessing these agreements dividing Yugoslavia into
spheres of influence, it is necessary to ascertain whether they
pertained to division of *territory* or of *influence,* and also what
internal forces in Yugoslavia aided and abetted the powers in
their plans.

As we know, Hitler dismembered Yugoslavia in April 1941,
piecing it out to Germany, Italy, Bulgaria, Hungary, and
Albania, while at the same time setting up the "Independent
State of Croatia" under Ante Pavelić, and of "Serbia" under
General Milan Nedić. The Soviet government recognized this
subjugation, as it broke off diplomatic relations with the
Yugoslav government after Hitler's invasion (as it had done
with Norway under similar circumstances). After June 22,
1941, when Hitler attacked the Soviet Union, the latter withdrew this unfortunate decision.

According to documents known so far, the wartime governments of the Soviet Union and Great Britain adhered for the most part to the principle of Yugoslavia's integrity, but at times the American government did not. In the personal archives of President Roosevelt in Hyde Park, there is a note about a talk with British Foreign Secretary Anthony Eden at the end of March 1943, during which Roosevelt took the view that "it would be absurd to force the Croats and Serbs to continue living together in one state. Eden thought differently, that is, that they could and should live together." In Robert E. Sherwood's book *Roosevelt and Hopkins,* a somewhat more complete version of Roosevelt's views on the future Yugoslav state is presented:

> *Serbia.* The President expressed his oft repeated opinion that the Croats and Serbs had nothing in common and that it is ridiculous to try to force two such antagonistic peoples to live together under one government. He, the President, thought that Serbia, itself, should be established by itself and the Croats put under a trusteeship.

During the war, Louis Adamic and Savica Kosanović publicly opposed these views of Roosevelt's, which the President did not try to conceal. He had some queer explanations for his attitude, to the effect "that he had collected Serbian stamps as a small boy and had become accustomed to calling Yugoslavia Serbia!"

I once talked with Mrs. Roosevelt about the reasons for the President's attitude and was able to delve a little deeper into the whole matter. It seems he was under the influence of Konstantin Fotić, onetime Yugoslav ambassador to Washington. Fotić held the view—deeply imbedded among the most conservative Serbian politicians, who went into exile during the war—that a greater Serbia should be formed; that it should break off completely from the Croats, not only territorially but culturally; that they were two separate worlds, two religions, and two languages. Roosevelt was also influenced by a number of right-wing Roman Catholics, headed by Otto Hapsburg, who wanted to create a central European Catholic federation which would include Slovenia and perhaps Croatia. Thus

the most chauvinistic Serbs, Croats, and Slovenes found themselves in agreement as to the disruption of Yugoslavia, although they hated each other bitterly and could not agree
at all on the boundaries of their mutual pretensions!

However, the spreading of the people's liberation war, waged
equally in all parts of Yugoslavia by all nationalities, was
paralleled by the growth of a new Yugoslavia based on federation and equality among the various parts. This made it impossible to dismember the country, though even late in 1943
some of the big powers proposed that partisan and Chetnik
zones of influence be set up. There was a widespread opinion
to the effect that the partisan movement was "Croatian" and
the Chetnik "Serbian." Even some Russians had accepted this
idea. (When I was in the hospital in Cairo, a Soviet military
mission which had been at our headquarters in Drvar came to
visit wounded partisan officers. To my amazement, a Soviet
general asked us if there were any Serbs among the partisans.)

There is another mystery. In the autumn of 1942 the Chetniks in western Yugoslavia distributed leaflets saying that the
partisans were Trotskyists and not recognized by Stalin as true
communists! These reports were spread about by Mihailović's
deputy for western Yugoslavia, Ilija Birčanin, who was also
responsible for contacts with the government-in-exile in London. And again in London, members of the royal Yugoslav
government were told by people close to the Soviet embassy
that the partisan movement was Trotskyist. Tass's Red Bulletin
No. 32 of February 1, 1944, carried a news report from London
to the effect that a group of "Yugoslav Trotskyists" was active
there, allegedly as "police agents"; mention was made of Peko
Dapčević, Blagoje Nešković, and Kosta Nadj. Veljko Vlahović,
upon reading this, sent a letter of protest to Molotov on
February 9:

The three comrades mentioned by the reporter are members
of the Communist Party of Yugoslavia and not a single one
of them is in London. All of them have so far been honest
fighters and communists.

Peko Dapčević, as is known, is commander of the II Corps of the People's Liberation Army. Blagoje Nešković is a member of the Presidium of the Anti-Fascist Council, and Kosta Nadj is commander of the III Corps of the People's Liberation Army.

I should like to call your attention to these stupidities fabricated in London and ask you to intervene to correct such inaccurate assertions.

History has not yet explained these relations between Moscow and certain circles around the government-in-exile and Mihailović. Were they intelligence contacts? Or an attempt to grasp at the straw of "ancient Slav ties and sacred relations between the Serbian and Russian peoples?" Or was it simply that Stalin wanted to have an egg in every basket, to win at the end of the war no matter what happened?

In any case, the idea of dividing Yugoslavia up into Chetnik and partisan zones proved untenable. Partisans were all over Yugoslavia. Negotiations were stepped up among the Big Three for spheres of influence in Yugoslavia. The consequence was the Tito-Šubašić agreement, an attempt to restore the monarchy through the back door and to disavow the decisions passed by the Second Session of the Anti-Fascist Council.

Winston Churchill Confirms the Fifty-Fifty Agreement ★

Did Stalin and Churchill conclude an agreement for division of spheres of influence in Yugoslavia? Is the fifty-fifty thesis based on historical sources or not?

In January 1951 Milovan Djilas went to Great Britain on an official mission, and I accompanied him. On January 31 we visited Prime Minister Clement Attlee at No. 10 Downing Street. The next morning Churchill's secretary telephoned with a luncheon invitation from Churchill for the same day. We said we were sorry, but had accepted an invitation to lunch from the British government. The secretary then suggested we come at eleven a.m., which we agreed to do.

This was the first meeting between Churchill and any Yugoslav partisans since the conflict over Trieste in 1945, when he had addressed many harsh words to us, especially to President Tito.

Churchill's wife was waiting for the three of us—Djilas, Jože Brilej, and myself—at the door to Churchill's house in Hyde Park Gate. We were surprised at the modesty of the house. I whispered to Djilas, "Your villa on Dedinje is more luxurious, though you cannot claim a Duke of Marlborough as an ancestor."

I was rather out of sorts that day and had been arguing with Djilas since dawn. I had bought some old English books about Yugoslavia in a secondhand bookshop, among them the *Annual Register* of 1875, which stated that the Herzegovinian uprising against Turkish rule had begun not at Nevesinje, but right near the home of my ancestors in the village of Čepelica, not far from Bileća. Djilas had made fun of me for my local patriotism and claimed jokingly that the Herzegovinian uprising would have failed had it not been for the Montenegrin commanders who led it. That morning we had also gone to Westminster Abbey, where we saw the tomb of Disraeli, the Prime Minister who had sided with the Sultan against the Herzegovinian insurgents. Djilas had said that I ought to spit on his grave.

"I would have good reason to, because it was precisely in 1875 that my grandfather's home was razed while the Hajde-hodžić beys, whose vassals we were, prayed in the mosque at Trebinje for the health of Disraeli." I was like a bad-tempered dog who is not satisfied with biting his victim once but goes back to snap again. Djilas laughed.

Lady Churchill told us nonchalantly that Churchill worked in bed every day until two, so he would receive us in his bedroom. It was a spacious room with a large bed and several tables piled with books and manuscripts. A green candle was burning on the bedside table, which Churchill used to light his cigar. When I looked at him in his voluminous white night-shirt, edged in red, and took in the whole atmosphere, I re-called a picture from early childhood: that is how I had imagined the wolf in "Little Red Ridinghood," dressed in the grandmother's clothing and waiting for his victim. All that was lacking was the nightcap. I was just about to whisper this to Djilas and Brilej when Djilas, who knew me and could imagine what I was about to say, kicked me under the table.

The talk began with formalities. Churchill offered us some-thing to drink—port, I think. He poured it himself, his hand steady. When he got to my glass, I said, "Sorry, but I don't drink. I'm an athlete."

Churchill, glass in hand, gave me a hard look. Never had I been regarded with more scorn. "You don't drink? Strange!" In confusion, I started looking around at the walls, on which some of Churchill's paintings hung. Churchill noticed this and said, "It seems it's not only my liquor but also my paintings that you don't like."

It was true. I was almost on the point of saying that they reminded me of the works of Dejneka and Gerasimov, the most important Soviet socialist realists. But I checked myself in time from uttering such sinful thoughts—Churchill was very proud of his paintings.

Churchill began to recollect his meeting with Tito. Djilas interjected, "In 1945 you said that Tito had tricked you. We Yugoslav partisans considered that a great compliment."

Churchill liked that kind of talk. He winked and said with a laugh, "I don't remember having used those words, but I was so angry at all of you that I could have said something worse." Laughing again, he continued, "It was a mistake to say that and it shall never happen again."

I stared at a pile of proof sheets on one table, straining to see if I could read anything. They were Churchill's memoirs, precisely the ones in which he refers to his meeting with Stalin in the autumn of 1944, when, according to many sources, the arrangement had been concluded on spheres of influence in

Eastern Europe (about which tentative agreement had been reached in late 1943). When we had set out for Churchill's house, I had told Djilas that I would be compelled to ask the statesman if that information had been accurate.

The conversation about affairs of state was drawing to an end, and Djilas noticed my impatience. He steered the conversation towards Churchill's relationship with Stalin. Churchill said, "I don't think there will be war. Stalin has grabbed enough and would not want to risk anything now; besides, he is afraid of the atomic bomb. I do not believe he will attack Yugoslavia—he is not so foolish as to stir that hornet's nest. He would more likely turn west, where the way is open."

Churchill stressed that he did not want war with the Russians, but that if he were in power he would force Stalin into an agreement by not laying down his arms. He added that already he had once come to an agreement with him about Greece, Rumania, and Bulgaria.

Djilas broke in, "And Yugoslavia?"

Churchill calmly replied, "Fifty-fifty. Naturally in terms of influence, not territory."

For a long time the Soviet Union kept silent on the matter of these agreements about spheres of influence. In recent years there have been vehement denials of Stalin's ever having made such bargains. But the facts argue that such an agreement was indeed concluded. Moša Pijade was in Moscow during that time in 1944 to which Churchill referred; in an undated letter in 1952, he wrote to me:

It is unfortunate that I cannot find the press report of my speech in which I described the scene with Molotov. Briefly, here is how it went:

In October 1944, when Churchill and Eden were in Moscow and when they made the fifty-fifty agreement about Yugoslavia, I and Stanoje Simic were invited to a reception Molotov gave for them. He immediately whisked the prominent guests to a separate salon so that I did not come into contact with them. But Molotov, after seeing them out, passed near me, tapped me on the shoulder and smiling in a friendly way said that all would be well for Yugoslavia. I was happy to hear that, of course, but I had not the faintest idea they had divided the country up into spheres of influence.

Yalta, Yugoslavia, and China ★

Yugoslavia was not the sole victim of the Soviet Union's foreign policy of blocs and spheres of influence. In settling his accounts with the powerful statesmen of the world, Stalin wanted to use other countries too for purposes of bargaining, from China and Korea to Europe.

Stalin began this kind of negotiating with Churchill. British diplomats had a wealth of experience along these lines dating from World War I, when certain territories had been offered to two or three partners. But in World War II the British Empire had dwindled, and there were only two real partners left at the gambling tables when the fate of nations hung in the balance: the Soviet Union and the United States.

Toward the end of the war the ailing Roosevelt was losing his grip on and influence over world policy. Mrs. Roosevelt told me that he had once complained about the growing role of hegemony and spheres of influence in international relations; he felt such an approach was obsolete and clashed with the realities. But no matter how powerful personalities are, they do not make history, but rather are carried along by the social forces behind them. The rule applied to Roosevelt and it applied to Stalin.

By concluding a secret sphere-of-influence agreement, Stalin demonstrated that he had stopped being a revolutionary. The 1917 Decree on Peace had represented the principle upon which the entire foreign policy of the Soviet state was based. Lenin had appealed to all peoples and states of the world to

conclude a just peace with no annexations or indemnities.*
In 1925 Stalin too had spoken up against spheres of influence,
and in 1930 the *Little Soviet Encyclopedia* had stated:

Spheres of influence are areas in semi-colonial countries in
relation to which competing states conclude agreements for
mutual concessions to their political and economic interests
in those areas. Spheres of influence are the product of the
colonialistic policies of the imperialist states, as, for instance,
the agreement between imperial Russia and England on
spheres of influence in Persia.

But that was the past, the distant past, of the revolutionary
Soviet Union. When Stalin was up to his neck in secret
diplomacy and spheres of influence, his propagandists made the
following admissions in a book called *The History of Diplomacy,* published in Moscow in 1945: "Parallel with open,
public, and published agreements, states also conclude secret
and confidential treaties with each other."

Actually, Stalin was trying to justify his arrangements with
Western statesmen not only concerning Yugoslavia but all
eastern and southern Europe. Yugoslavia was divided into
spheres of influence, but in Rumania, Hungary, Bulgaria, and
other countries in the region Stalin had full sway, while in
Greece, for instance, he ceded all rights to Western powers.
These secret agreements with the leading statesmen of the
West were concluded completely in the spirit of Webster's
definition of "sphere of influence": "a territorial area within
which the political influence or the interests of one nation are

* After all the secret treaties entered into by imperial Russia had been
published and annulled, a sailor, Markin, wrote the following in 1917, in
the preface to the book containing them:

The working people of the whole world must know how their diplomats,
working in luxurious offices, traded secretly in human lives . . . how they
concluded disgraceful treaties. . . . Everyone must know how the imperialists, with one stroke of the pen, annexed whole provinces. How they
soaked the fields of battle with the blood of human beings. Every published
document is a weapon against the bourgeoisie.

held to be more or less paramount." This is rather indefinite, but it is typical that no formal protectorate or abolition of the sovereignty of the victim is sought.

There was a gentlemen's agreement among the signatories of the spheres-of-influence agreements in World War II: the word of honor given by each that they would divide their booty honestly.

As early as December 1944 Stalin and Churchill had occasion to test the value of their secret bargains. The Greek partisans had liberated most of the country from the Germans, but Churchill decided to establish power in his sphere of influence and reimpose the monarchy and the old social system on the Greek people. British tanks took possession of Athens, and Stalin didn't lift a finger. In the House of Commons Churchill tendered Stalin public recognition: the British government was extremely grateful to Marshal Stalin for not taking an excessive interest in Greek affairs, for offering assurances that he had no intention of criticizing British behavior in Greece or of interfering in the affairs of that country. Stalin had stated, said Churchill, that he had full faith in British policy in Greece.

But in 1947 a popular uprising led by the old partisans broke out in Greece. On February 10, 1948, in the presence of Dimitrov and other Bulgarians, Stalin told Kardelj, Djilas, and Bakarić: "For instance, we do not agree with you that Yugoslavia should give further assistance to the Greek partisans. We think we are right and not the Yugoslavs. True, we too have made mistakes. For instance, after the war, we invited the Chinese comrades to Moscow. We told them that we felt conditions were not ripe for an uprising in China and that they should seek a modus vivendi with Chiang Kai-shek and disband their army. The Chinese comrades agreed with their Soviet comrades, but when they went back to China they did just the opposite. They rallied their forces, organized their armies, and now they are beating Chiang Kai-shek. There, in the example of China, we made a mistake. It turned out that the Chinese comrades were right and not the Soviet comrades. But that is not the case with you in the Balkans. That is not the case with the Greek partisans."

Stalin had concluded a number of secret agreements with the big powers on China and the Far East, one of them being the decision adopted at Yalta on February 11, 1945, when Roosevelt and Churchill agreed to Stalin's demand that the Soviet Union get back all parts of China and all concessions lost by imperial Russia in the Russo-Japanese War of 1904–1905, as well as certain Japanese territories. Stalin had pledged that the Soviet Union would go to war against Japan and provide armed assistance to Chiang Kai-shek "for liberation from the Japanese yoke," although Chiang Kai-shek was at that time waging open war against the Chinese units under Mao Tse-tung.

As far as Korea was concerned, the three statesmen agreed that the thirty-eighth parallel should divide the country into two spheres of influence—which was a division of territory nonetheless. (It is interesting to note that the imperial Russian government in 1903 informed the Japanese government that the Russian sphere of influence in Korea was the territory above the thirty-ninth parallel.)

The dimensions of Soviet hegemony in that part of the world are best reflected in addresses by Stalin and Malenkov after the victory over Japan. On September 3, 1945, Stalin declared, "The defeat of the Russian Army in 1904, in the Russo-Japanese War, left our people unpleasant memories. It lay on our land like a dark stain. Our people believed the day would come—and waited for it—when Japan would be defeated and that stain removed. For forty years we, the older generation, waited for that day."

On February 7, 1946, Malenkov went even further: "In the East the Soviet Union has won back what the Czar lost. This has eradicated the disgraceful stain of the defeat of the Russian Army in 1904. . . . In brief, we won because of Stalin's wise leadership, and now the Soviet Union has gathered under its powerful wing all those whose fate it is to be within its borders."

The Yalta meeting and the decisions made there by Stalin, Roosevelt, and Churchill jeopardized all the achievements of the people's liberation war in Yugoslavia. Those decisions read:

> It was agreed to recommend to Marshal Tito and to Dr. [Ivan] Šubašić:
> (a) That the Tito-Šubašić agreement should immediately be put into effect and a new government formed on the basis of the agreement.
> (b) That as soon as the new government has been formed it should declare:
> (I) That the Anti-Fascist Council of the People's Liberation of Yugoslavia will be extended to include members of the last Yugoslav National Assembly who have not compromised themselves by collaboration with the enemy, thus forming a body to be known as a Provisional Assembly, and
> (II) That legislative acts passed by the Anti-Fascist Council of the People's Liberation will be subject to subsequent ratification by a Constituent Assembly. . . .

On one occasion in 1952 Tito said to me, "The Russians told us nothing about the Yalta decisions, although they were a real crime against Yugoslavia. They *forced* us to accept deputies from the prewar Stojadinović parliament in the Anti-Fascist Council."

Mankind came out of World War II with a growing awareness of the right of peoples to self-determination, to equality among states. The terrible differences imperialism had drawn between various parts of the world were eventually wiped out. In a letter to me of May 22, 1944, Edvard Kardelj had speculated on the tasks of Yugoslavia's foreign policy:

> I am thinking above all of the need for a clearer foreign-policy orientation, particularly for the forging of links with movements and states with which we shall have closer contact in the future.
> This refers not only to the Soviet Union and the other

allies, but for instance to Czechoslovakia, France (the French must naturally be told that the methods France formerly used in relation to the Little Entente, etc., are impossible for all time), and the freedom-loving forces of Greece, Italy, and our other neighbors.

Establishing links with such forces would undoubtedly facilitate our position later on—all the more so as in such a case Yugoslavia would not face the peace negotiations alone but as a force with consolidated international relations.

There was a postscript to his letter:

Stari* has read the letter and agrees.
He also sends you greetings!
Send the enclosed letters to the addressees.
And write.

* "The Old Man"—Tito's nickname.

3.
The Key Question:
Economic Relations

In 1945 Yugoslavia lay in ruins. The revolution had triumphed, and now thinking had to be directed toward modernizing the economy in the quickest way possible, toward transforming the land from a backward agricultural society into an industrialized one. The conditions for this transformation existed, as Yugoslavia had a wealth of natural resources.

Before 1941 foreign capital had kept Yugoslavia in a state of total economic dependence. With great hope and faith, Yugoslavia in 1945 turned to the Soviet Union for advice and cooperation in putting through its economic development program. But the very first step in that direction brought disagreement and disillusion.

At that time I did not concern myself with economic problems except to the extent required by my regular work, for which I had to know some concrete facts about our general financial and economic relations with foreign states.

It was not until 1952 that I set myself the task of establishing just exactly what sort of economic relations had existed between the Soviet Union and Yugoslavia in the years after the war. The Yugoslav archives were then in very bad shape indeed. Owing to the danger of Soviet aggression, many of them had been transferred to the western part of the country, and others destroyed. In the summer of 1952 I had a lengthy talk with Boris Kidrić, head of the Economic Council, about these problems. He gave me a general outline of the history of 1945–1948 as he knew it, and spoke of his meetings with Stalin and other Soviet leaders. At his request, his associates Zvonko Morić and Kiro Gligorov drew up a report for me incorporating the available documentation. I also corresponded with Vlatko Velebit, who had conducted the first negotiations with Soviet representatives in 1945, and talked with Tito, Kardelj, Ranković, and Vlado Popović about their meetings with Stalin concerning major economic issues.

It is on the basis of all this material, and information about the economic relations between the U.S.S.R. and Yugoslavia and other East European countries, that I have written this chapter.

Kidrić recalled:

Stalin treated us not as a socialist country but like any other nation which, as he and his associates felt, belonged to their sphere of influence—that is, under their hegemony, with all the economic exploitation that implied.

The purpose was to keep Yugoslavia as an agricultural and raw-materials-producing appendage, which is why they opposed our setting up basic industries that would help us become independent.

We were offended by their opposition to our economic plan and our industrialization program. As a matter of fact, we had hoped that they would invest in the major projects of our first Five-Year Plan.

After Tito's visit to Stalin in 1946, when agreement was achieved in principle on a treaty for economic cooperation between Yugoslavia and the Soviet Union (a treaty finally concluded in Moscow in August 1946), the Soviet side immediately submitted proposals for the establishment of joint stock companies. We accepted the idea in the hope that their investment in the companies would help us develop industry and systematically exploit the great natural wealth of the country.

Differences arose immediately. They called us megalomaniacs and said that our industrialization program was a
Utopian dream. But we agreed to the initial establishment
of two joint stock companies—one for civil aviation, JUSTA,
and one for shipping, JUSPAD—in the belief that the Russians would eventually give in and help us industrialize the
country through other mixed companies.

How difficult the initial negotiations for JUSTA and
JUSPAD were is demonstrated by a letter I received from
Vlatko Velebit, Deputy Foreign Minister in 1945 and Yugo-
slav ambassador to Rome in 1952:

Talk began in the summer of 1945 about the benefits of
establishing joint (Soviet-Yugoslav) companies for the purpose of developing our economy. At the beginning of 1946
I was informed that a Soviet delegation was coming to conclude an agreement with us to establish joint companies for
navigation along the Danube and for civil air transport. I
was assigned to conduct the negotiations with that delegation. In preparation, I asked our representatives in Hungary
and Rumania to send me copies of the agreements the Russians had already concluded with those countries. Luckily,
I received these before the Russians arrived, and had time
to study them. They simply astonished me. No attempt had
been made to conceal the obvious inequality, the brutal
hegemony of the Russians. I did not know what to think.
The agreements seemed politically stupid and legally absurd.
When I collected my wits, I tried to convince myself that
the Russian attitude was necessary because of the suspect
regimes of Nagy in Hungary and King Michael in Rumania.
Needless to say, the whole thing seemed utterly unsocialistic
to me, and I was more than confused by it. Not in my wildest
dreams did I imagine that the Russian delegation would try
to propose similar agreements with our country, a country
of the dictatorship of the proletariat.
    One fine day the Russian delegation, headed by General
Berezin (if I recall his name correctly), presented itself and
scheduled the begining of the talks. . . . I had expected that

the first meeting would be spent discussing the general principles on which joint stock companies should be founded. Instead, the minute he arrived General Berezin gave me a draft agreement brought ready-made from Moscow.

I asked for time to study the documents. As I read them in my office later, I was completely taken aback: they were faithful copies of the treaties the Russians had already concluded in Rumania and Hungary, the only difference being that some of the provisions were even worse than in the [first two]. Probably these were provisions the negotiators from Hungary and Rumania had succeeded in having ameliorated. I realized that some legal expert in the Soviet Ministry of Foreign Affairs had drawn up a standardized form for all countries in the Russian sphere of influence, and that this form was being applied regardless of whether a Tito or a King Michael was involved.

It seemed to me that we could not under any circumstances agree to treaties that were a textbook example of the *societas leonina* (where one side profits and the other side gets nothing).

I informed Stari, who instructed me to try to improve the terms. At the next meeting I told the Russians in a very roundabout way that the treaty as it stood was unacceptable and that it would be best to find another basis for it. I dared not use political arguments to bolster my thesis, but fell back on the rather weak arguments of international law in an endeavor to transfer this pre-eminently political problem to the juridical sphere. I don't think I succeeded very well, but what else could I do when I couldn't state openly that such treaties created unequal relations that were unacceptable?

My position was made even more difficult by the fact that I knew these treaties were the first in a series, with similar but much more important ones in the offing, and that the Economic Council expected them—the joint companies, that is—to help solve the question of economic cooperation.

Berezin knew even less than I about international law, so he was not able to refute my flimsy arguments, but resolutely refused to negotiate on any new basis for the establishment of joint stock companies. He made it clear that we would have to accept them as they were or break off negotiations—take it or leave it. I scheduled no more meetings with the delegation; three weeks later I learned that Berezin had left.

The whole affair was a painful one and depressed me. . . . I think the Russians complained about me to the Central Committee, although I was never informed of this. I only know that Berezin returned to Belgrade after a few months, and that our people agreed to the draft treaties. . . . I was not informed of anything and was left out of things completely (thank God).

The treaties were signed early in February 1947, and, as Kidrić told me, although the provisions were tough, we accepted them in the hope that similar proposals from us would be agreed to when submitted—that is, that we would get help in industrializing Yugoslavia. We especially desired installations for oil, aluminum, and steel.

The functioning of JUSTA and JUSPAD demonstrated that there was no question of the Soviet Union assisting the economic advancement of Yugoslavia, but rather of a pure loss for us. The Soviet Union wanted to acquire a monopoly over Yugoslavia, thereby depriving it of economic independence and sovereignty.

For instance JUSTA, the Soviet-Yugoslav Civil Air Transport Company, undertook to maintain all air service between Yugoslavia and foreign countries, leaving our domestic company, Jugoslovenski Aerotransport, without a single foreign route. JUSTA also maintained the most profitable domestic runs, leaving our own company to vegetate with the leftovers.

The joint company shared profits on the basis of invested capital, with no taxes, custom duties, or other levies to pay, so that the Russians made quite a sum. The assessment of assets was such that the Russians were able to extract high extra profits: they overestimated their share and underestimated the Yugoslav, our property being assessed at 1938 prices, when money was more stable and prices lower, and theirs at 1946–1947 prices, which were very high. Here the Soviet Union really did Yugoslavia a great deal of harm and made it im-

possible for her to get a return commensurate with her investment. With a far smaller outlay, the Russians were in a position to make more profit than the Yugoslavs, and more than
their share of capital was worth.

To take an example: Yugoslavia built an airport near Belgrade for JUSTA, assessed at 31,500,000 dinars—although its
real value was something like twenty times as much. Again:
in assessing the value of the airport, the Russians allowed the
Yugoslavs only the price for ordinary land and not for air-
strips—in other words, did not take into consideration the
labor invested on the land.

But that was not all. The director general of JUSTA, a
Soviet citizen, began to interpret the treaty to his own liking
and took upon himself functions that should have been carried
out by the Yugoslav authorities. In violation of the treaty, he
took over exclusive control for JUSTA of all installations at
the airport—all radio navigation and communications equipment—thereby gaining *full control over air transport in Yugoslavia,* though JUSTA had the right only to the commercial
exploitation of the airport. JUSTA even ceased informing the
domestic authorities of take-offs and landings of foreign planes,
leaving its director general a sovereign in his own right. Soviet
pilots went so far as to decide whom they would or would not
accept as passengers, regardless of whether the people in question had tickets or reservations. A public scandal broke out
in the autumn of 1947, and the matter had to be settled by
the Soviet and Yugoslav authorities. Naturally, it was not
mentioned in the press, but I noted in my diary:

Late in the summer of 1947, Svetozar Vukmanović-Tempo
[then head of the Political Department of the Yugoslav
Army General Staff] was returning from his vacation in
Montenegro to Belgrade via the airport in Titograd. All the
tickets for the plane had been sold, but when the passengers
started to embark, a quarrel broke out. The ticket-holders
could not board the plane because the Russian pilot had

let on a few people without tickets. The passengers protested, Tempo among them. The pilot, a Russian captain,
replied to Tempo's question as to how anyone could be
allowed on board without a ticket by declaring, "Because
I say they can!"

Tempo (who was wearing the uniform of a general of the
Yugoslav Army) tried to convince him he was not in the
right, whereupon the Russian said, "You're a reactionary
element, you're drunk."

Tempo felt the blood rush to his head and, as he told
me later, wanted to punch the Russian in the nose, but he
controlled himself. He called for the security men, told them
to forbid the plane to take off until the pilot's friends, who
had no tickets, were made to disembark. The security officer
asked Tempo if he should arrest the Russian, but Tempo
said no. The other passengers followed the conversation
carefully, as they all feared Tempo might give in. But after
an hour the pilot finally relented and the plane took off
for Belgrade.

Upon arriving in Belgrade, Tempo called the Soviet military attaché and described the incident to him. The latter
promised the pilot would be withdrawn, but he was not.

Tempo also informed Tito and Ranković. Tito was furious and told Tempo to insist that the pilot be withdrawn
immediately. Ranković said, "It's a good thing you didn't
hit him, but you could have listened to the security officer
and had him arrested. It is not a bad thing to take the
advice of the security men from time to time."

JUSPAD, the Soviet-Yugoslav Danubian Shipping Company, functioned on a similar basis. Through this company
the Soviet Union actually deprived Yugoslav shipping of its
previous importance along the Danube. (Of all the states
through which the Danube flows, Yugoslavia had had the
highest tonnage.)

According to Article 5 of the JUSPAD agreement the Soviet
Union, in return for its shares, undertook to deliver to JUS-
PAD the following:

(a) Equipment and materials for constructing a shipyard on Ada Ciganlija; resources for financing it to the sum of 125,000,000 dinars; and installations for a port on the Danube.

(b) Equipment and materials for constructing and repairing craft to the value of 67,500,000 dinars, within five years from the signing of the agreement.

(c) 7,500,000 dinars in ready cash for operation of the company.

Article 6 provided that Yugoslavia, in return for its shares, would deliver to the company:

(a) Vessels worth 164,750,000 dinars.

(b) The shipyard in Novi Sad and resources invested in the shipyard on Ada Ciganlija to the value of 271,750,000 dinars.

Thus did the Soviet Union get its hands on our best Danube ships without having invested a single craft itself.

A 1947 agreement between the Yugoslav State River Shipping Company and JUSPAD provided for utilization of the ships belonging to both, and for the two companies to tug each other's loaded and unloaded barges for seventy dinars per one thousand kilometer-ton, while JUSPAD made the same arrangement with the Soviet shipping outfit (the Soviet-Danubian State Shipping Company) for fifty dinars, or twenty dinars per one thousand kilometer-ton. (JUSPAD concealed this fact when concluding the agreement with the Yugoslav company.)

Throughout 1947 the Yugoslav company let JUSPAD tug its barges, while JUSPAD in turn depended on the *Soviet* company for tug services, even when JUSPAD barges had to wait weeks for a craft. As a result, the Yugoslav company had to pay JUSPAD the sum of 1,200,000 dinars.

By early 1948 it had become regular practice for JUSPAD barges carrying Yugoslav goods to the Soviet Union to have to wait as long as three months before being unloaded. The Russians claimed they did not have sufficient space, although vessels of the Soviet company managed to get unloaded in the meantime. That winter there was no ice or other navigational obstruction along the Danube and its tributaries, and the

Yugoslav company was operating with all available craft; but JUSPAD vessels put up for the winter and deprived the country of the export of 40,000 tons of goods and the import of 30,000.

Although the JUSPAD agreement was highly favorable to the Soviets, they did not fulfill their side of the bargain. For example, by the end of 1948 Yugoslavia had invested in goods and cash 87.20 per cent of its expected contribution, or 305 shares (craft, shipyards, and cash), while the Soviet Union had invested 9.83 per cent of its investment, or 39 shares! Again, under Article 5(b) of the JUSPAD agreement, the Soviet Union was to have invested 67,500,000 dinars in equipment and materials for building and repairing boats, but during the company's two years of existence it invested only 3,400,000 dinars. Because the required material was not invested, it was necessary to use supplementary Yugoslav resources of 15,000,000 dinars in foreign currency, which was a great loss for Yugoslavia in view of its difficulty in acquiring such currency.

The agreement also provided that the Soviet Union invest machinery and equipment for a new shipyard to promote Yugoslav shipbuilding. But the Russians failed to do so, and instead shipped trucks, cotton goods, glass, and so on. This caused double damage to Yugoslavia: she was importing goods she did not need and, more important, suffered a delay in the construction of an important branch of industry. The effects were felt by the Yugoslav economy for years.

At first glance the organizational structure of JUSPAD and JUSTA was democratic and based on parity between the two parties. With JUSPAD, each country's investment amounted to 200,000,000 dinars, divided into shares of 500,000 each. Each share meant one vote in the shareholders' assembly, which was supposed to be the principal governing body in the company.

The company board, elected by the assembly and consisting of four members from each side, was empowered to manage the company. It appointed a director general who always had to be a Soviet citizen! His deputy was a Yugoslav. According to Article 20 of the JUSPAD statute, the deputy was completely subordinate to the director general and could act only on his orders. The director general independently discharged all executive functions of the company's management board, which enabled him to pursue the kind of policy he wished without any supervision by the board or the shareholders' meeting.

The director general's independence and freedom from responsibility to any unit or agency of the company were constantly and artificially maintained through political pressure from the Soviet government and the Soviet embassy in Belgrade; he personified Soviet monopoly and the unfettered Soviet "bossing" of the Yugoslav economy. In JUSTA's two years of existence not a single annual meeting was held nor were accounts ever submitted for approval. JUSPAD had only one meeting, in 1947. There were no account sheets, which barred effective understanding of the directors' management policies. This meant that the directors general did not respect the laws of Yugoslavia, although it was theoretically binding upon them to do so. They considered themselves extra-territorial powers and worked—inevitably—for the benefit of the Soviet Union.

To take an example: in setting tariffs on the transport of goods from various countries, the director general of JUSPAD discriminated openly against Yugoslavia. He decreed that the tariff per net kilometer-ton for Soviet goods would be 0.19 dinar, for the other Danubian countries 0.28 dinar, and for Yugoslavia 0.40. This meant that Yugoslavia was paying 52 per cent more for the transport of its own goods on its own vessels ceded to JUSPAD! In 1948 Yugoslavia suffered a loss of 38,000,000 dinars on this alone. So although the purpose of these joint stock companies was to assist Yugoslav development, they actually were an obstacle. In 1948 40 per cent of JUSPAD's services were accounted for by Yugoslavia's economy and 60 per cent by the USSR and other countries, although the company's vessels were exclusively Yugoslav and intended for Yugoslavia's use.

The Yugoslavs employed in these companies were em-

bittered by the state of affairs and lodged many protests about
the way business was conducted. Soviet replies were always
brief: these protests were the work of bourgeois elements, reactionaries, and foreign spies. Right at the very first round of
negotiations on the formation of JUSTA and JUSPAD Vlatko
Velebit, as we have seen, let the Soviet negotiators know that
the drafts of the agreements were inequitable. The Soviets
lodged a complaint against Velebit with the Yugoslav Central
Committee, claiming that he was personally responsible for
the failure of the first negotiations. But they did not stop there:
at the Belgrade celebration of the Soviet national holiday on
November 7, 1946, they publicly accused the leaders of the
Yugoslav negotiating team of being foreign spies!

I received a letter about this on June 28, 1952, from Zvonko
Morić, Kidrič's assistant, who in 1946 was president of the
Yugoslav team negotiating the organization and operation of
joint Soviet-Yugoslav companies for oil, coal, iron and steel,
lead, bauxite, aluminum, banks, river shipping, and aviation.

I am sending you the documentation on the negotiations
for the establishment of a Soviet-Yugoslav aviation company,
conducted by Velebit and General Berezin in 1946.

As you know, they parted ways at these talks. I was given
the necessary material to continue the talks with Berezin.
The material is rather interesting, especially as even then
Velebit complained that Berezin was blaming *him personally*
for the agreement's not being signed.

Yet another detail about my talks with [the Soviet nego-
tiator] Yatrov. A Soviet trade representative in Yugoslavia,
Lebedyev, was also a member of Yatrov's delegation. The
negotiations began at the end of August and by early November it was clear to me that there were no results. On
November 7 there was a reception in the Russian Center
attended by all our leaders. One circle consisted, as I remember, of Major General Pavel Jakšić, Salaj, Vraneš, myself, General Berezin, Lebedyev, and Hebrang. Someone
asked why the talks about the company were going badly,
to which Lebedyev replied:

"Because they are conducted by an English spy."

I wanted to strike him, but seeing that Marshal Tito was in the room, I desisted, protested, and immediately told Kidrić about the matter. Boris said later that he told Tito of it. A few days afterward Boris said that Lebedyev had tried to get out of it by saying he had been drunk.

The Fight for Yugoslavia's Raw Materials ★

Negotiations to set up joint Soviet-Yugoslav production companies were long, painful, and abortive. As work started on the committees and subcommittees, certain questions of principle arose, and both parties agreed that the following rules should be followed.

1. The companies would not be monopolistic.

2. Yugoslavia might invest in the companies such enterprises, mines, etc., as had the potential for development but lacked some or all of the means of production. Furthermore, the companies should not be small, but large enough to make possible the advancement of backward sectors of the Yugoslav economy.

3. In assessing the investment, existing Yugoslav investments were to be evaluated at their worth in dollars on the world market, after subtraction of the depreciation coefficient. Soviet investments and new Yugoslav investments were to be assessed on the basis of their dollar value on the 1938 world market, plus the coefficient on modernization.

The Yugoslav delegation then proposed that the Yugoslav side should set a five-year production target for all companies; on that basis, an appropriate (50 per cent) investment in installations was requested of the Soviet Union.

But the moment discussion began about Yugoslav investments, the Soviet Union displayed a tendency to undermine the principles established in the course of negotiations. Yatrov, the Soviet negotiator, made it obvious that his instructions were to set up joint companies designed to exploit Yugoslavia. It became clear that the Soviet purpose was not development of backward economic sectors in the new Yugoslavia—and, on that basis, equitable distribution of return on the invested capital—but the immediate extraction of profits. This approach would enable Russia to utilize Yugoslavia's natural resources and confine her primarily to the role of an exporter of raw materials. In other words, Yugoslavia would not develop her own industries, without which there could be no basis for building a modern society in the country.

During negotiations Yatrov said openly, "What do you want with heavy industry? We have everything you need right there in the Urals."

But the Yugoslav delegates stood firm in their insistence that Yugoslavia's natural resources should be utilized properly, that it was economically feasible to do so, and that we were not aiming at autarchy—a condition both impossible and dangerous in the modern world. The new Yugoslavia supported the closest possible economic cooperation with the Soviet Union and other East European countries, but on condition that her own economy develop, since this was essential to the interests of the Yugoslav people.

The Soviet negotiators also had another aim: they wanted the joint companies to have a monopoly on the Yugoslav market through which the Soviet government could gain control over the basic sectors of the economy. Their intentions became patently obvious during the discussion on a joint company for oil exploitation.

At first the Soviet representative asserted that such companies were unnecessary since in his opinion, on the basis of the established reserves, no more than 450,000 tons' annual output could be achieved in a five-year period. Instead he suggested a smaller number of drills. But the Yugoslav experts submitted proof of quantities of oil large enough to make profitable exploitation possible; in parliament Boris Kidrić described the positive results of prospecting in Yugoslav oil fields. After that the Soviet representative agreed to discuss the formation of a joint company, but laid down impossible conditions.

According to the Soviet proposal, the Yugoslav investment was to be: first, the Gojlo, Janja Lipa, and Donja Lendava fields; second, the right to prospect and exploit these fields as well as new fields where oil was discovered; third, geological maps of the areas where oil prospecting was in progress; and fourth, the Rijeka refinery.

The Soviet delegates thought that only the Gojlo field should be considered as functioning, since production there was already under way, whereas the others should be considered as new fields valued only at the price of the land itself, although even then the worth of the wells in Donja Lendava and Janja Lipa was 42,000,000 dinars, and they had already started producing oil and gas. No value was to be attributed to Yugoslavia's oil-bearing fields because, they claimed, invoking Marx, these were natural riches with no social value! (The Yugoslav negotiators produced copies of Soviet-Iranian and Soviet-Hungarian agreements in which the Soviet government had recognized the value of oil-bearing fields to the amount of 50 per cent of the fixed capital of Iran's investment in the joint company, and 15 per cent of Hungary's.) Moreover, if oil was to be exported by the joint companies, Soviet needs had to be filled first—and under the most favorable conditions, without any taxes or export duties for the first five years. After that, the Yugoslav government had the right to charge a tax on profits, but no other levies or duties. Whatever production remained, Yugoslavia could utilize for its export needs.

On top of all this, the Soviet proposal placed the entire retail network for selling gas and other oil derivatives in the hands of the joint company.

There were other disagreements as well. The Russians claimed that production per well was an average five tons a day—a low figure that could hardly justify the investments made. (At the same time, the Soviet journal *Nyeftanoe Hozyaystvo* published statistics for 1946 according to which average production in the U.S.S.R. was 2.6 tons per well.) The Soviet representative further asserted that the Yugoslav's physical and geological maps were of no value. During the war, work in the

Lendava field had been done by Hungarians under German supervision, and Russian occupation authorities had captured the Hungarian part of the Lendava field and were running it. In June 1945 we asked for the geological data on our section of the field, so that work could proceed; although we proved to them that they had come into possession of the data in Vienna and Budapest, the Russians did not give it to us. The request was repeated in Moscow in 1946 and 1947, but to no avail, although the maps were our property.

It was perfectly obvious that the Soviet delegates were trying to reduce the value of our investment and make a big profit with a small investment of their own. The Soviet proposals, made to a socialist country, in fact contained much harder terms than those submitted to a semifeudal country like Iran.

Soviet representatives revealed the same intention to exploit and monopolize during negotiations for a joint Soviet-Yugoslav coal company.

As their contribution to the company, the Yugoslavs suggested the central Bosnian coal fields of Zenica, Kakanj, and Breza, important for heavy industries in Bosnia and Herzegovina; the mines of Siverić, Livno, and Mostar, to be used for supplying ships; and the Kosovo field, for establishing power stations and promoting the general development of backward areas. All these coal fields, with their established reserves, were to guarantee the pace of development planned for a five-year period.

The Russians, however, did not recognize the established reserves as part of the Yugoslav investment and wished to exclude the Breza, Siverić, Livno, Mostar, and Kosovo mines as well, although they did agree to include the already smoothly functioning mines of Zenica and Kakanj. They also asked for inclusion of the Tito-Banovići mines, which had just begun operating (with great effort and practically no funds), and the mines of Zagorje and Velenje, with their open coal reserves.

It is apparent from the foregoing that the Russians were

not interested in developing Yugoslav coal production but in turning a quick profit from the country's best mines—Banovići, Zagorje, and Velenje—without making any great investment. The Yugoslav delegation refused to comply with these conditions.

For the proposed joint-stock lead and zinc company, Yugoslavia offered the Mežice lead and zinc deposits and plant; the Zletovo mine; the Kopaonik mine (which would have to be reconstructed); and the Lece lead, zinc, and gold mines. The Yugoslavs also believed that the Ajvalija and Novo Brdo lead and zinc deposits, prospected before the war, should be opened, and that annual zinc electrolysis production should rise to 12,000 tons and annual lead output to 30,000 tons.

The Russians said these mines were too poor and asked for the inclusion of the Trepća mine and smelter, which had been expanded and was producing profitably. Again the Soviet aim was clear: quick and immediate exploitation with a small investment.

In the case of aluminum the Yugoslavs proposed the following bauxite mines: Krupa and the Istrian mines and plants, then under construction; Strnišće, still to be completed; and the small alumina factory at Ljubljana. Our goal was 50,000 tons of alumina and 12,000 tons of aluminum a year, and the construction of a new smelter for electrolysis at Mostar with a capacity of 30,000 tons annually. These goals were justified by the size of Yugoslavia's bauxite reserves and even allowed for a certain amount left over for export. This meant that the aluminum joint-stock company could immediately start producing and earning.

The Russian delegates used delaying tactics, saying that the goals were too high, and wanted to include in the company the smelter at Lozovac, which the Yugoslav delegates refused to do. The same conclusion may be drawn: the Russians wanted the greatest possible profit, while leaving the burden of new investments to the Yugoslavs.

Negotiations over the iron-and-steel company were long and trying. The Yugoslav delegation had prepared a recommenda-

tion for a company including Zenica, the Vareš mine, the
Čevljanovići and Ver manganese mines, as well as a plant in
Šibenik producing ferrous alloys and electrodes.

The proposal also provided for expansion of the Vareš capacity of 1,000,000 tons of ore, and for enlargement of the manganese mines to satisfy the requirements of Yugoslavia's industries. Special efficiency-improvement reports were drawn up
for the Zenica iron works; for expansion of Šibenik; and for
construction of a new steel plant to produce 500,000 tons,
including a coking plant which would utilize domestic coal
(lab experiments in 1946 had proved this feasible).

Obviously, these plans were not overly ambitious. And upon
them hinged the entire future course of Yugoslavia's industrialization and modernization. But the Soviet representatives
simply knitted their brows disapprovingly, spread rumors about
our being megalomaniacs, and tried to grab as much as they
could. The Jesenice iron works had caught their eye and they
insisted that it be included in the company. The Yugoslavs
refused. Their mouths watered even more at the thought of
the iron mine of Ljubije in northern Bosnia. This mine produced high-quality ore for export, bringing Yugoslavia foreign
currency. If Ljubije were included in the joint Soviet-Yugoslav
company, the Russians would soon be earning foreign exchange at Yugoslavia's expense. This deposit of the best possible ore would then be exploited as the Soviet experts wished,
regardless of the fact that it was one of the biggest strategic
reserves in the Yugoslav economy.

The Soviet delegates turned down all our offers, one by
one. They tried to prove that it would be very difficult to
raise ore production in Vareš, that there was no ore there, etc.
(although reserves had been estimated at 180,000,000 tons in
1946 and plans were under way to construct a mine with an
annual capacity of 1,750,000 tons a year); that Zenica should
simply be expanded and that it would be too expensive to
build a new plant there; that it would be impossible to make
coke out of Yugoslav coal and therefore the coking plant
project made no sense.

The reader may wonder why I dwell at such length on the long and unsuccessful negotiations between the new Yugoslavia and the Soviet Union for the establishment of joint companies. It is necessary because these negotiations offer the best evidence of the essential difference between the announced principles of Soviet policy and the realities of its great-power interests: on the one hand, fine words about internationalism and selfless assistance on the basis of socialist solidarity; on the other hand, persistent attempts to impose unequal conditions and to exploit the young Yugoslav republic.

The Soviet proposals for the joint-stock companies for oil, nonferrous metals, coal, iron, steel, etc., clearly reflected two demands characteristic only of relations between capitalist countries and their colonies—and during the very first stage of capital export, at that. The first was the demand for a Soviet monopoly in Yugoslavia, in violation of socialist principles; the second, the right to "capitulations"—that is, a system in which the joint companies would be exempt from local jurisdiction.

In the Soviets' draft agreement for the joint oil company, the demand for a monopoly was revealed in Article 8, which stated that "the Government of the Federal People's Republic of Yugoslavia grants the company the right to prospect for and extract oil deposits throughout the territory of Yugoslavia." Another instance was Article 10, stipulating that it was a special privilege of the company to exercise all rights granted to companies with purely Yugoslav capital. However, the company would not be obliged, as Yugoslav companies were, to conform to existing statutes. In the case of each single obligation, the two governments were to negotiate a solution —a stipulation that violated the sovereignty of the new Yugoslavia.

In their desire to exempt the companies from Yugoslav laws and government measures, the Russians were vigorous in rejecting any obligations for the companies to conform to the country's economic plans. This virtually meant that the Yugoslav government could not draw up its annual economic plans without the approval of the Soviet representatives in the joint-stock companies; in the final analysis, it could not independently plan its economic development.

The Soviet delegates even insisted that each company pay no social insurance for the workers, as Yugoslav law required but rather "as much as it could according to its own calculations," meaning less than what our provisions stipulated. They wanted to settle this question, too, on the basis of some kind of "world average" and not in line with Yugoslavia's socialist laws, which guaranteed complete social security and health insurance for workers. Obviously, if that condition had been accepted, we would have had to make up the difference ourselves.

The climax was reached in the negotiations to set up a joint Soviet-Yugoslav bank. This bank, which would not really have been a joint-stock operation but purely Soviet, was an attempt to get to the very heart of the Yugoslav economy, to gain control over Yugoslavia's central finance and credit institutions. In view of nationalization and integrated financing, this would have let the Soviet Union completely dominate Yugoslavia's economy.

According to Soviet proposals, the Soviet-Yugoslav bank was to transact the following business:

1. Credit, bookkeeping, and accounting services for all Soviet-Yugoslav joint-stock companies;

2. All clearing transactions in Soviet-Yugoslav trade;

3. Other business usually transacted by domestic banks.

The bank's resources were to be:

1. Capital in shares of 200,000,000 dinars;

2. Resources of the joint-stock companies, which would be invested in the bank;

3. Credit from the National Bank of Yugoslavia.

Our negotiators were quick to perceive the consequences to Yugoslavia's economy of such banking arrangements. The joint-stock companies would cover the most important sectors of the economy, and the common bank, through credit and financing, would control it. This would encroach upon Yugo-slavia's sovereignty in finance and foreign exchange, as it is usually the prerogative of the sovereign government to con-cern itself with the international clearing transactions that in this case would be handled by a joint bank dominated by the Russians. Slowly the Yugoslav economy would come to depend on this bank; since it was expected that Yugoslavia's trade balance with Russia would be adverse and of a high volume for some time, the bank would have substantial clearing funds, increasing its working capital and strengthening the Russian position. Besides, this would increase its credit business for the whole of the debit balance; its operations would encroach upon the independence of Yugoslavia's credit policy and bank of issue.

Through its third authorization, the bank could carry out any kind of banking transactions whatsoever in Yugoslavia with any client it pleased, since no restrictions on such opera-tions were provided for in the draft. It would thereby acquire even greater resources, enabling it to interfere in all kinds of economic operations. With the same rights as Yugoslav banks but with special financial power, it could become the strong-est competitor in the country in every kind of banking trans-action. It would have no difficulty in eventually controlling Yugoslav banking, and indeed would be aided by its organiza-tional structure and the privileged position of the director general, a Soviet citizen.

Naturally Yugoslavia rejected this draft agreement for the bank. In Moscow this was viewed as a hostile act. There were more and more signs of a gathering storm.

Painful Perception of the Truth ★

Today's young reader may well register surprise and ask why a stronger reaction was not forthcoming on the part of Yugoslavia to the Soviet Union's discriminatory demands in 1946 and 1947.

There were a number of reasons. First of all, there was the general international situation. Relations between Yugoslavia and the major Western states—the United States and Great Britain—were extremely tense. Those with Washington were obstructed by a number of factors: the conflict over Trieste in 1945; our shooting down of American planes that had flown over our territory without permission despite numerous protest notes from our authorities; the American delegation's lack of understanding of our demands at the Paris Peace Conference in 1946; the outright assistance rendered to Yugoslavia's political émigrés. Nor were relations with London of the best.

Other international problems also remained unsettled. The Slovenes' age-old dream of being united in one state was far from being fulfilled, and the frontier disputes with Italy and Austria persisted. The situation of the Macedonians was even more difficult: they were split up into three states, in some of which they were not even recognized as Macedonians!

Under the circumstances, we could not expect the West to help us solve our industrialization problems, supply our army with modern weapons, or build up our arms industry. Consequently, the Soviet Union and other East European states were the only hope we had of defending ourselves against the West's pressure—also, we felt, the only source of investment aid for developing the economy.

Moreover, we were still living in the atmosphere of a partisan idyll. For the first time in the history of the peoples of Yugoslavia, relationships of equality and fraternal cooperation existed. And we felt that the Soviet Union was the main bulwark of justice and equality among nations. This was a special psychological state—more than mere faith, closely approaching exaltation. The great majority of old partisans refused to allow that faith to be questioned. I myself passed through various phases in this regard.

I have a cousin Pavle, son of the late Milan Kićevac, professor at the University of Belgrade. As a ten-year-old boy in 1940, Pavle saw Moša Pijade coming to his father's apartment to write Party reports; he remembers Edvard Kardelj sitting out the first bombardment of Belgrade with his family on April 6, 1941. In a word, from his early youth Pavle had learned to love and respect revolutionaries and partisans.

In 1946 a Soviet soccer team—I think it was the army team —came to Yugoslavia for the first time, and I took Pavle to the game. Pavle rooted for our team and I was for the Soviets! After the game Pavle told his sisters, "Boy, you should see the dirty game the Russians played! They kicked our players in the stomach, and when the referee couldn't see them, they stole a couple of yards. They really are bandits. Good sportsmen wouldn't behave like that." I upbraided Pavle roundly. He was telling the truth, but it hurt. The Russians' behavior had been an exception, I thought, but it hit hard at the idyllic feelings which had kept me going for so many years in the war and revolution. I raged at the poor child.

When you live in this kind of mental climate, it is difficult to pass rational judgment. Stalin himself, who was a good psychologist, was aware of that mentality not only among the Yugoslav revolutionaries but among revolutionaries the world over, who looked upon the Soviet Union starry-eyed. He had a special name for the type of person who revealed it—"honest fools," as he told one of our partisan delegations visiting his country home.

Stalin also played a very subtle game, and this was a big factor in sustaining our illusion that equitable economic cooperation with the Soviet Union was possible. Although many historical facts now lead to the conclusion that Stalin initiated all these projects for joint-stock companies, not only for Yugoslavia but for other East European countries as well, in the first few years after the war the partisans believed that in Moscow "the water ran pure at the source"—that is, that Stalin was the personification of honesty and that it was the unwieldy Soviet bureaucracy which had submitted the glaringly unsocialistic proposals.

In the spring of 1946, during Tito's visit to Moscow, Stalin evinced great interest in the details of Soviet-Yugoslav economic relations and the negotiations for joint-stock companies.

"Our people tell us that your comrades working in economic affairs feel that you do not agree with the organizing of the joint-stock companies."

Tito replied, "No, that is not my opinion, nor is it the opinion of other Yugoslav leaders. We feel that such companies could be established—naturally such companies as would promote our country's industrialization."

Molotov confirmed what Stalin had said about the need for joint companies in fields "where they would most benefit both you and us[!]"

Then, a year later, when it became clear that the negotiations were not proceeding successfully, Stalin remarked during a meeting with Edvard Kardelj that *joint-stock companies were suitable for satellite countries.* Yugoslavia, on the other hand, should be granted investment credit: "How would it be if we did not form joint-stock companies at all, but simply helped you, gave you an aluminum factory, helped you in drilling and refining oil? Clearly, joint companies are not a suitable form of cooperation with a friendly allied country like Yugoslavia. There would always be disagreements, differences; the very independence of the country would suffer and friendly relations be spoiled."

We were elated by this attitude. Stalin lulled us into hopes, and convinced us that he was fair and the Soviet bureaucracy alone responsible for our difficulties. He already had the joint companies that gave him a monopoly over civil aviation and river transport; he dropped the others in the face of Yugoslav intransigence, and generously allocated investment credit of $135,000,000. Of that sum, equipment worth $800,000 was delivered. After the conflict came out into the open, the investment agreement was canceled.

Stalin played his game well. He kept on deceiving us. When he realized that the plan to conquer Yugoslavia by way of the joint-stock companies had fallen through, he lost no time in drawing up another much more dangerous plan—open attack on Yugoslavia. In the meantime he was full of fine words, in order to gain time. A sacrilegious thought, may God forgive me, comes to mind: looking at Stalin's methods in perspective, I cannot but conclude that he was not very original. Quite some time back, when American Marines were conquering some Central American state or other for the benefit of American companies, Teddy Roosevelt had said: "Speak softly and carry a big stick!"

4.
The Opening Gambit

Stalin's Model for Yugoslavia ★

After the new Yugoslav state was established in 1945, in the face of all the obstacles put in its way by enemies (and friends as well), the Soviet Union made every effort to gain control of it by Trojan-horse methods.

This was first seen in the endeavors to make it fit the Soviet model of the Stalinist period as closely as possible. Secondly, the Russians made every attempt to have "their own" people in key state and Party positions, either by winning them over politically or by inveigling them through the Soviet intelligence service in Yugoslavia.

The Soviet Army brought ready-made governments with it to some of the East European countries where there had been no strong resistance movements or revolutionary changes during the war. They had their work all programmed—the same model being used for all countries—and they had certain set methods of going about it.

In Yugoslavia, however, the revolution had brought into being a special kind of government based on the broad initiative of the people; upon this fundamental condition the success of the revolution had hinged. That initiative had generated certain specifics: the equality of Yugoslavia's various nationalities within a federal framework; the mutual effort of these nationalities to achieve national programs; socialization of the means of production; equality of women; and full participation by youth in the life of the nation. (In most partisan units, for instance, men and women under eighteen years of age had formed 80 per cent of the fighting force.) The Yugoslav revolution was in every sense of the word a revolution of the young; it shrank from no sacrifice and was able to achieve what had seemed impossible before.

The partisans' first direct contacts with representatives of the Soviet system generated strange and mixed feelings—on the one hand gladness at having established contact, and on the other hand astonishment at the Russians' behavior, which seemed odd, if not impossible, for socialists.

In the battle of Belgrade in October 1944 I could not but admire the courage of Soviet soldiers. At the same time, one incident shocked me. A tank was entering a village at the foot of Avala Hill. A Russian soldier jumped out and asked a peasant for a keg of brandy in exchange for a keg of gasoline. The peasant gave it to him and the soldier handed over the gasoline. One of our men, seeing this, jumped on the tank and said to the soldier: "Are you a soldier of the great liberating Red Army? How can you behave like that? You're not worthy of the Red flag!"

The Russian eyed him coolly before shutting the hatch of his tank. "You talk like our political commissars in 1941. And if they had been worth anything, Stalin wouldn't have disbanded them."

The first Soviet military delegation which arrived at our Supreme Headquarters in February 1944 brought similar disillusion. We had expected them to discuss strategy and tactics, but all they did was ask whether we had military police and tell us to get rid of "egalitarianism" in the partisan army, maintain the strictest possible discipline, and centralize everything. Anything that was not on the Soviet model seemed to annoy them.

In 1945, after the establishment of normal diplomatic relations and the arrival of Soviet advisers in Belgrade, this insistence on imitation of Soviet models in everything became even more apparent.

I do not mean to assert that Stalin was solely to blame for all the centralistic and undemocratic deviations that cropped up in Yugoslavia after the liberation. Certain unsound tendencies had appeared even during the most difficult war days, at the beginning of the profound process in which the masses started to take the initiative. Our new society was not immune from new contradictions. One need only leaf through the *Documents from the People's Liberation War* to see the extent of undemocratic procedure, bureaucratic despotism, egoism, etc., as criticized in Supreme Headquarters instructions and in letters and reports from members of the Central Committee. And when the end of the war drew near, when the partisans were joined by hundreds of thousands of peasants and apolitical town dwellers with all their prejudices, matters became even more complex. But the initiative of the masses—the prerequisite of the revolution and of its progress—was the best brake on these manifestations.

Be that as it may, the Soviet experts who arrived in this country in late 1944 and 1945 made their influence felt, and many of them in the wrong way. They insisted on bossing the people. They were especially annoyed at the evident equality among the peoples of Yugoslavia—something which radically differentiated Yugoslavia from the Soviet Union—and all of them, from top to bottom, attempted to provoke distrust and dissension by asserting that the Serbs, as the largest nationality in Yugoslavia, should play the same leading role as the Russians in the Soviet Union. There are numerous documents in our archives to prove this. Typical is a message brought to some of our leaders by the Soviet ambassador, Sadchikov, to the effect that "there is no need to set up a separate communist party for Serbia as the Serbs are in any case numerically superior in the Communist Party of Yugoslavia." If the Yugo-

slav example of equality among nationalities were firmly established, the Soviet bureaucracy feared, it would be a con-
tagious example for both the U.S.S.R. and other multinational
East European countries.

Thoughts along these lines also bothered Stalin. At a dinner
in the Kremlin on May 27, 1946, attended by Tito, Ranković,
Kidrić, Koča Popović, Nešković, and Vladimir Popović, the
party got rather gay after midnight. Stalin, skillfully turning
the conversation to the subject of nationalities, seemed to bear
down especially hard on Kidrić: "Hey, you Slovene you, I am
a pure Serb!"

Kidrić raised his glass and replied, "I am a pure Slovene!"

"Well, you Slovene," Stalin continued, "how many Slovene
bourgeois did you kill?"

"Only as many as was absolutely necessary. Not one more,
not one less!"

What the drunken master thinks, the sober servant does.
Soviet Ambassador Lavrentiev, speaking once with some of our
Serbian comrades, spun out a tale about what a scandal it was
that the Cyrillic alphabet, common to Russia and Serbia, had
not been introduced throughout Yugoslavia.

There is no doubt that Soviet influence on Yugoslavia was
strong between 1945 and 1948, and that traces of it were
present in the first Yugoslav constitution—especially in its form,
basic categories, the relationship between the executive government and the legislature, and the system it established for
elections. Without question, Soviet influence also helped to
bring out latent tendencies toward centralism and similar
bureaucratic inclinations that had existed among the partisans.
However, the breath of revolution continued to be felt both
in the substance of the Yugoslav constitution and to an even
greater extent in Yugoslavia's political life, in the unwritten
law that there could be no ruling of the masses against their
will.

Therein lay a major cause of the conflict between the Soviet
Union and the new Yugoslavia.

The Economic Blockade Begins ★

In early February 1948 Stalin felt that the time was ripe to liquidate Yugoslavia as an independent state and through its subjugation to bring the whole of Eastern Europe to heel. This was the first round of "silent strangulation," when Stalin presented Yugoslav representatives Kardelj, Djilas, and Bakarić with an ultimatum to the effect that a federation between Yugoslavia and Bulgaria must be formed immediately. Both Tito and Dimitrov had wanted rapprochement between the two countries even during the war, and were further inclined toward the creation of a south Slav federation, but our representatives in Moscow at the time felt that something else was concealed behind this sudden demand of Stalin's. They therefore turned it down, using the excuse that these questions would be settled by the Central Committee of the Yugoslav Communist Party. At a session of March 1, 1948, the Central Committee approved the position taken by the Yugoslav delegates and rejected the demand for federation with Bulgaria. Thus did Stalin's first offensive end in failure.

Somewhat later an authoritative source told me what was actually behind the conversation held that February evening in the Kremlin: Stalin had been toying with the idea of bringing all the East European countries, including Yugoslavia, within Soviet borders. This was to be done in two stages: first, Poland and Czechoslovakia were to form one federation, Rumania and Hungary another, and Bulgaria and Yugoslavia still a third; secondly, these new states would merge with the Soviet Union. Only when the Soviet archives are made accessible will we learn the motives behind Stalin's intentions—the international and internal factors that influenced him.

We may safely say that Yugoslavia's determined stand in February 1948 put a damper on these plans. But Stalin quickly set about plotting other measures to get the Yugoslav rebels in line. He decided on two moves which he was certain would achieve his goal. One was a favorite method with big states when they want to tame the disobedient: economic blockade.

After the war trade rapidly developed between the Soviet Union and Yugoslavia.* The Russians insisted on trading at what were called world prices. A number of our people felt it was not right for trade between socialist countries to be based on world prices, since an underdeveloped country like Yugoslavia found itself in an unequal position: because of its low labor productivity, it would have to yield extra profits to the more developed trading partner—in this case, Russia.

We also raised objections to the type of goods exchanged. The Russians insisted that we export to them commodities that we would have had no difficulty selling elsewhere on the world market—nonferrous metals, various ores, hemp, and hops. (Our exports to the Soviet Union in 1948 were 40 to 50 per cent metals.)

But in our boundless faith in the Soviet Union we forgot the wise old saying that you should not put all your eggs in one basket. In 1947 we decided to expand trade with the Soviet Union even further, and in December Bogdan Crnobrnja, Assistant Minister of Foreign Trade, was sent to Moscow for this purpose.

He waited until January 20, 1948, when he, Djilas, and Vladimir Popović, Yugoslav ambassador in Moscow, were received by Anastas Mikoyan, then Minister of Foreign Trade. Djilas declared that the Yugoslavs desired to expand trade with the Soviet Union, and Mikoyan stated that the Soviet government would agree to start negotiations.

On February 10, however, Stalin delivered his ultimatum about federation with Bulgaria, which was turned down. On February 22 Crnobrnja was informed in the Soviet Foreign Trade Ministry that they did not wish to talk about a new

* The following data are taken from an aide-mémoire provided me by Assistant Minister of Foreign Trade Bogdan Crnobrnja concerning the first Soviet measures of economic blockade early in 1948.

protocol and that Yugoslavia could not count on any trade expansion in metals, oil, or cotton. On February 26 this information was given to him officially in the name of the Soviet government.

He could do nothing but come home. The big game had begun. And in the two months during which the Soviet government had drawn out the negotiations, we had done nothing, absolutely nothing, to purchase the most important raw materials elsewhere, in the continued expectation that we would get them from the Soviet Union. Now, a terrible crisis set in. The sowing season was approaching, we had enough gasoline reserves for only ten days or so, and the textile factories had cotton reserves for as long.

Immediately after the liberation we had taken on a number of Soviet civilian and military specialists. Disagreements arose immediately between them and our people. The Soviet experts wanted simply to transfer Soviet practices blindly to our country, ignoring specific Yugoslav features. In 1945, for instance, one Soviet specialist told the public prosecutor of Yugoslavia that secret courts should be introduced to handle the cases of Communist Party members. When told that it would be impossible to institute such courts in Yugoslavia, that the people would highly disapprove and Party members revolt, the Soviet expert invoked Stalin! Boris Kidrič had similar experiences. He told his associates to ask the Soviet experts for advice, to listen carefully and take down all they said, and then to do as common sense dictated. And in the realms of science and culture, the Soviet experts often acted as though Yugoslavia were a completely underdeveloped country. Andrei Zhdanov once asked whether there was any opera in Yugoslavia!

The military experts could have helped us a great deal, but they too simply tried to apply Soviet models. Our people told them that while it was true the Soviet Union had had a wealth of military experience, this was no reason for underestimating what we ourselves had learned in World War II. If we were to ignore our own experience and blindly copy the Red Army, only harm could result.

As early as 1946 Tito had told the Soviet government that the number of Soviet military specialists in Yugoslavia would have to be reduced for financial reasons. (Their salaries were four times as high as our army commanders' and three times those of our federal ministers.) But Stalin bided his time. It was not until after March 1, 1948, when informed that our Central Committee had rejected his ultimatum on federation with Bulgaria, that he ordered Bulganin to inform the Yugoslav government (on March 18) that all Soviet military experts were being withdrawn. One day later he ordered all civilian specialists withdrawn as well.

In 1964, during a talk with British Labourite Koni Zilliacus, I learned that the Soviet government had launched its conflict with China by striking first at economic ties: all Soviet experts were withdrawn and Soviet investment in Chinese industrial projects stopped. It made me think of 1948 and those crucial days when Yugoslavia was left without gasoline, without cotton —all alone with enemies on all sides.

The Conflict Comes Out in the Open ★

During that fateful spring the parties to the conflict were in many ways in an unequal position, and certainly their mental climate differed.

Today that is as clear as daylight, but in those tumultuous times it was not. The clash between two socialist countries created a great deal of confusion among Yugoslavs, particularly communists. They wondered if it were possible, if the whole thing were not just some sort of misunderstanding or complicated intrigue. The prevailing mood was extremist, ranging from the most sinister forecasts to the maddest hopes that the controversy would somehow be ironed out.

And there in the Kremlin was Stalin, who knew exactly

what he wanted, making one move after another, through his clumsy machinery of state, to bring a small country to its knees.

In mid-March he struck another blow. He decided to bring the dispute into the open—to inform Yugoslav Party members of his accusations against their leaders and to disseminate those accusations abroad among other communist parties, so as to get them to exert pressure on Yugoslavia to expiate her sins.

Stalin delivered his first letter to us on March 27. He played strange games in selecting the dates for ultimatums to Yugoslavia. Throughout the conflict he made a terrible mistake in underestimating us—in this instance, in believing we were superstitious. For his first letter he chose March 27, the date of the 1941 revolt against the pro-Hitler government of Cvetković and Maček. Was he hoping that another March 27 would bring a revolt against Tito's government, which in his letters he even accused of collaboration with the occupation forces? (Similarly, the Cominform resolution proclaiming *urbi et orbi* that Yugoslavia was a traitorous country was published on June 28, the aniversary of the battle of Kosovo, during which, many hundreds of years ago, the "Serbian empire had collapsed." The second Cominform resolution was published on November 29, the national holiday of the new Yugoslavia and anniversary of the Second Session of the Anti-Fascist Council.)

In this letter of March 27 Stalin first replied rudely to concrete questions concerning the specialists and their withdrawal, and then went on to more important matters:

We know that anti-Soviet statements are circulating among the leading comrades in Yugoslavia, as for instance that "the Soviet Communist Party (Bolsheviks) is degenerating," that "great-power chauvinism prevails in the U.S.S.R.," that "the U.S.S.R. wants to conquer Yugoslavia economically," that "the Cominform is a means for the conquest of other parties by the Soviet Communist Party," and so on in this vein. These anti-Soviet statements are usually concealed in left-wing phraseology to the effect that "socialism in the U.S.S.R. has stopped being revolutionary," that "only Yugoslavia is the true standard-bearer of revolutionary socialism." Naturally, it is absurd to listen to talk like this about the Soviet Communist Party from suspect Marxists of the type of Djilas, Vukmanović, Kidrić, Ranković and others.

The case of Trotsky was threateningly recalled: "We think that the political career of Trotsky is sufficiently instructive." Passing from the defensive to the offensive, Stalin then claimed that the Yugoslav Communist Party had not been legalized and was still semilegal, and that

> there is no internal party democracy in the Yugoslav Communist Party. The majority of members of the Central Committee of the Party were not elected but co-opted. There is no criticism or self-criticism in the Party, or virtually none. It is typical that the Party cadres secretary is also the Minister of State Security: in other words, Party cadres are under observation by the Minister of State Security.
>
> The spirit of the policy of class struggle is not felt in the Yugoslav Communist Party. Capitalist elements are growing in the rural districts, similarly in the cities, but the Party leadership is not taking any measures to restrict them. The Yugoslav Communist Party is lulling itself with the rotten opportunistic theory, borrowed from Bernstein, Folmar, and Bukharin, that capitalist elements will peacefully merge with socialism.

Stalin was greatly annoyed, it appeared, by the breadth of the Yugoslav revolution, and he struck out hard at the People's Front:

> According to the theory of Marxism-Leninism, the Party is considered the basic leading force in the country; it has its separate program and does not diffuse itself among the non-Party masses. In contrast to this, in Yugoslavia the People's Front is considered the basic leading force, and attempts are made to dissolve the Party in the People's Front.

At the end of the letter, Stalin used a tried-and-true method he had applied during the trials of old Bolsheviks in the U.S.S.R.: slandering them as imperialist agents. He began with Vlatko Velebit, the first to arouse his ire for having pointed out as early as 1946 the exploitative character of the Soviet proposals for the joint-stock companies. Now he was referred to as an "English spy." Velebit's attitude in 1946 had struck home.

I have described in *Tito* how Soviet Ambassador Lavrentyev delivered the first letter.* The following account is excerpted from a talk I had with Tito on June 15, 1952, on Brioni Island:

They delivered the first letter to me in Zagreb, in Tuškanac —Lavrentyev accompanied by a counselor of the embassy, an NKVD man who later became chargé d'affaires. They entered, and I could see from their expressions that something important was up. When they handed me the letter we remained standing, for I did not offer them a seat. I myself also stood while I read the letter, one hand leaning on the table. After reading the first few lines, I felt as though I'd been struck by lightning. Lavrentyev and the other fellow stared hard at me to see how I would react. I didn't bat an eyelash, and kept my composure as best I could. They kept on staring me straight in the eye. When I had read it through, Lavrentyev could bear the suspense no longer.

"When shall we get an answer?"

"We shall consider the letter."

I waved my hand to signal that the meeting was over. They left. I immediately sat down to telephone Kardelj, Djilas, Ranković, and Kidrić. After that I started outlining a reply and had it finished in two hours.

I am particularly sorry that the last part [of my reply] was not approved at the session of the Central Committee [held on April 12, 1948]. I had made it clear that the Russians want to get us on thin ice ideologically so as to justify their pressure on us. I stated very clearly what was at issue:

* *Tito* (New York, 1953), p. 332.

that we should not allow ourselves to be drawn into a discussion of theoretical questions, but should rather cross swords on the matter of relations between states. The Russians wanted to deal only with the Yugoslav Communist Party and not with the entire nation.

At the plenum of the Central Committee many of our comrades were uninformed and had been under pressure from the Russians.

Just before the first letter, the Russians [had been] continually trying to feel my pulse, to see what our reaction would be. Yudin came to see me a week before the first letter to ask for an article for his newspaper. But what he really wanted was to draw me out to see how I was going to put certain matters. Lavrentyev had also come to see me and even threatened, "We have the bigger apparatus."

Stalin believed that the accusations in the letter of March 27 and other letters sent later to the Yugoslav Central Committee would suffice to convince the majority of Party members here and to bring down the regime. Although the letters were stamped SECRET, Soviet representatives disseminated their contents throughout Yugoslavia. What were the "sound forces" Stalin relied on in Yugoslavia for support? He had a number of cards up his sleeve.

First of all, he tried to disrupt the unity of the Central Committee itself. Djilas had caught his eye back in 1944, when they had met in Moscow, and again after Djilas had published his very favorable article on Stalin following his return. But that move bore no fruit. Then, in the March 27 letter, he singled out four "suspect Marxists"—Djilas, Ranković, Kidrić, and Vukmanović—as distinct from Tito and Kardelj. But that was no good either. In a letter of May 4 an attempt was made to drive a wedge between Tito and Kardelj. (On an earlier occasion, during Tito's visit to Moscow in 1946, Beria, pretending to be drunk, had confidentially whispered in Tito's ear that he should believe no one around him.)

Secondly, Stalin counted on the Yugoslav communists' being "honest fools," as he called revolutionaries who looked starry-eyed upon the Soviet Union. But with his attacks on the leaders, Stalin aroused grave dilemmas among many Yugoslav communists. No one has ever tried to describe these inner struggles. There are in them elements of Greek tragedy—a conflict between two concepts of duty: one to Moscow, capital of the first successful socialist revolution, and the other to one's own socialist revolution.

And lastly he reckoned on human weakness. There were communists in Yugoslavia who were dissatisfied for one reason or another. The Soviet intelligence service watched them carefully and approached them when the time was ripe.

Others were approached by other means. For instance, there were many Russian émigrés who had taken refuge in Yugoslavia after the collapse of Wrangel's anti-Bolshevik offensive in 1920. Most of them had been hospitably received, and with their culture and good education had contributed to the country's progress. True, a small section of them could not renounce their anti-communism and had sided with Hitler during the war; they even had their own military detachments which fought against the partisans. An Orthodox priest, Vlada Zečević, told me once that in the terrible winter offensive of 1941–1942, when all the partisan detachments in western Serbia were routed, the most persevering fighters on the enemy side had been precisely those "White Russians": "They were all old men, practically on crutches as they came at us, but they fought to the last bullet!"

When Soviet representatives arrived in 1945 in our country, they started enticing these Russian émigrés into their service. They got some of them by blackmail, dredging up past sins and threatening to turn them in to the Yugoslav authorities; others they won over with patriotic slogans—they were Russians and it was their duty to obey the Soviet state regardless of where they lived.

Generally speaking, Soviet intelligence during the first postwar years operated according to standard models and, it might be added, not very intelligently. Apparently, some of its officers sent information not on the basis of what they had seen and heard but what they thought their superiors would like to hear. No good can come of such methods, and Stalin's erroneous reading of the situation in Yugoslavia was in large part due to such errors. The methods themselves were simply grotesque. I noted, for example, the following episode.

In the autumn of 1943 a group of men from the Soviet Union parachuted to our Supreme Headquarters, then in Jajce. Among them was Sterija Atanasov-Viktor, of Bulgarian descent, who had been sent on a mission to Bulgaria via liberated Yugoslav territory. He thus arrived in the Sandjak with the headquarters of a partisan division early in 1944. The men spent the night in a tiny, remote village at the home of an old Moslem peasant. Early in the morning members of the staff heard an argument going on between the Bulgarian and the peasant in the barn below their sleeping quarters. The Bulgarian, keeping his voice low, spoke sharply to the old man: "Sign it, sign it." Later the old man complained to our officers, "That officer wanted me to sign some sort of voucher, but I didn't want to. I was afraid it was an IOU." The Bulgarian, a Soviet intelligence officer, had in fact been trying to get the old Moslem in this virtually inaccessible Sandjak hamlet to sign an obligation to work for the NKVD. Such methods were used throughout Yugoslavia; in Slovenia especially, people were on the alert for this sort of thing.

After the liberation, attempts to persuade people to serve in the Soviet intelligence network were stepped up. Soviet operators swarmed after persons working in places they considered important: the Army, the security forces, the economic ministries, the Central Committee (they tried to snare the principal code clerk at the latter.) By the spring of 1948 these hunters of "dead souls" were trying to press all of us into their service, so as to split our ranks and gain control more easily.

One day Kirsanov, a representative of the Soviet Information Bureau—a tiny man in a Moscow suit (short in the jacket and wide in the trousers)—came to my office in the Agitprop department of the Central Committee. Under his arm he carried a sheaf of articles written in Moscow for Yugoslav newspapers;

they were about various Soviet subjects: collective farms, the anniversaries of various Russian writers, etc. Kirsanov took out a list of these articles, which numbered over two hundred.

"Please publish these in the Yugoslav newspapers. Some papers are unwilling to publish Soviet articles. For instance . . ." He took out another piece of paper with exact statistics about who had published how many of these articles. He set them on the table in front of me and stared, waiting for a reply.

"That is all very fine and well," I said, "but if we published these articles we'd have room for nothing else! And we are, after all, the Yugoslav press. By writing about socialism in Yugoslavia we are also writing about the Soviet Union."

Kirsanov realized he could gain nothing by continuing. He never came again.

The reply of the Central Committee to the letter from Moscow came on April 13, after its historic meeting on April 12–13. The Committee rejected all the Soviet accusations, and of the Committee members only Sreten Žujović, the Minister of Finance, tried to defend the Soviet letter. At the same meeting a three-man committee was set up to investigate the behavior of Žujović and Andrija Hebrang, Chairman of the State Planning Commission, who had also come out in support of Stalin. There was evidence that Žujović had given Ambassador Lavrentyev notes from the Central Committee meeting of March 1, at which Kardelj, Djilas, and Bakarić had reported on their meeting with Stalin in Moscow on February 10 and his ultimatum about Bulgaria.

The reply to Moscow of April 13, signed by Tito and Kardelj in the name of the Central Committee, dealt with the Soviet accusations point by point. Stalin's challenge had been taken up.

Three full weeks passed before Stalin answered. In the meantime Yudin's newspaper *For Lasting Peace, For People's Democracy*—the official organ of the Cominform—in its April 15 issue published its first criticism of the Yugoslav Party. Names were not given, but it was clear to everyone what they were talking about.

On our borders there was no peace. American planes were again flying provocatively over our territory.

On April 24 the Soviet government informed us that it was canceling the agreement for mutual consultation on foreign-policy matters signed by Kardelj in Moscow in February. Our Moscow representatives tried to contact Soviet statesmen and officials with whom they had previously worked, but the Russians were not in the least interested in Yugoslav arguments; as on command, they refused to talk to Yugoslavs.

All we learned was that the Central Committee of the Soviet Communist Party was checking everywhere to see whether the contents of our April 13 letter were true. All Soviet experts and citizens in Yugoslavia submitted information on the points raised—the role of the Front, the role of the Party, the situation in the rural districts, and so on. Every day we wondered what the next would bring, and there were usually surprises. Soviet underground propaganda was obviously at work. A Soviet official who came into contact with us spread the opinion that the Soviet letter of March 27 was the result of one-sided information.

Then some of our comrades got the idea that we *should* accept some of the Soviet criticism. The bill for that kind of thinking was paid by various hotels, groceries, small shops, taverns, and coffeehouses—all of which were nationalized overnight! One of my good partisan friends, a high-ranking official, gave a speech in Šumadija—in the heart of Serbia, his native land—in which he threatened the peasants, "You kulaks, you have caused this conflict with Stalin."

"Don't cut off the branch we're sitting on," I remonstrated. "Who was it in Šumadija who fed us, sent us fighting men, and kept you hidden for two years while you were underground?"

But he would have none of this. Instead he read me passages from *The History of the Soviet Communist Party* about the kulaks and the need for stepped-up collectivization.

On the eve of May 1 news came from Moscow that bode no good. The Foreign Languages Publishing House had been preparing a collection of articles and addresses by Tito; though orders had been issued to publish it quickly, a month had passed and nothing had been done. Other publishing houses stopped translating books by Yugoslav authors and books by Soviet authors about Yugoslavia. The press reduced information about Yugoslavia to the briefest possible news items. The radio commission, which supplies news to all radio stations in the Soviet Union, stopped issuing any reports at all on Yugoslavia. The Moscow *Bolshevik* had prepared an article about the third anniversary of the Soviet-Yugoslav treaty, and the piece had already been approved for publication; but at the last moment orders came to withhold it. The writer Filip Nasyetnik, after returning to the Soviet Union from his second visit to Yugoslavia, observed: "In 1945 the Yugoslavs had much greater esteem and affection for the Soviet Union. Now they are acting independent, boasting that they too are building socialism and therefore consider themselves to be on an equal footing with the Soviet Union."

The Soviet answer arrived in Belgrade on May 4—a bolt from the blue. No one had expected Stalin to go so far in his accusations. The thing that astonished and embittered Yugoslavs most was an unbridled attack on our people's liberation struggle:

> We feel that the exaggerated conceit of the Yugoslav leaders lies at the bottom of the unwillingness of the Politburo of the Central Committee to admit its mistakes honorably and correct them conscientiously. Their achievements have gone to their heads; they have been carried away and think that the sea comes only to their knees. Not only have they become conceited, but they have gone so far as to preach conceit to others, not perceiving that this conceit can bring about their own downfall.
> "All the revolutionary parties that have failed so far, failed because they were carried away and were unable to perceive

wherein lay their strength; they feared to speak of their weaknesses. We shall not fail as we do not fear speaking about our weaknesses, and we shall learn how to overcome them."

We must unfortunately observe that the Yugoslav leaders, who do not suffer from modesty and continue to be carried away by their achievements (which after all are not so great), have forgotten this teaching of Lenin's.

In their letter comrades Tito and Kardelj refer to the merits and achievements of the Yugoslav Communist Party, saying that the Central Committee of the CPSU previously recognized those merits and achievements and now supposedly ignore them. That is, of course, untrue. No one can deny the merits and achievements of the Yugoslav Communist Party. That is indisputable. But it must be said that the merits and achievements of, say, the Communist Parties of Poland, Czechoslovakia, Hungary, Rumania, Bulgaria, and Albania are not less than those of the Yugoslav Communist Party. Nevertheless, the leaders of those parties behave modestly and do not go about shouting of their achievements—in contrast to the Yugoslav leaders, who have pierced everyone's eardrums with their exaggerated bragging.

It must also be observed that the French and Italian Communist Parties deserve even greater credit than the Yugoslav Communist Party as far as revolution is concerned. The fact that, for the moment, the French and Italian Communist Parties have less success than the Yugoslav Communist Party cannot be attributed to any particular qualities of the Yugoslav Communist Party but by and large to the fact that after German paratroopers broke up Yugoslav partisan headquarters, at a time when the people's liberation movement in Yugoslavia was in the throes of a severe crisis, the Soviet Army came to the aid of the Yugoslav people, routed the German occupying forces, liberated Belgrade, and created the conditions necessary for the Communist Party to take power. Unfortunately, the Soviet Army did not and could not extend such assistance to the French and Italian Communist Parties. If comrades Tito and Kardelj would take this circumstance into consideration as an indisputable fact, they would be less noisy about their merits and would behave with more deference and modesty.

The Yugoslav Central Committee had decided that all the letters in the Soviet-Yugoslav exchange would be read to Party members. One morning in May, Krsto Popivoda read the letters to a group I was in. He was excited, and his excitement was transmitted to us. I was probably most affected by the passage in the letter in which Stalin and Molotov spoke disparagingly of the people's liberation war, claiming that the liberation movement in Yugoslavia was in crisis after the airborne attack on Drvar. We knew well that quite the opposite was true: the people's liberation movement was then at its peak; the German offensive in western Bosnia was rapidly smashed and the partisans won important new victories. On June 4, 1944, *Pravda* itself had written:

In Italy, Allied military operations are proceeding successfully, for which special credit goes to the heroic struggle of the People's Liberation Army of Yugoslavia against Hitler's invaders and their foul collaborators. With each day, the end of the war now being waged on all sections of the front in Yugoslavia draws nearer. . . . The Germans are rushing into new adventures to achieve some success. It is well known that the Germans failed in their attempt to capture Marshal Tito's headquarters; the German attack was broken by the resistance put up by Marshal Tito's heroic army. . . . The Front in Yugoslavia is keeping considerable German forces pinned down, preventing them from going to Kesselring's aid. This is the special significance of the persistent efforts being made by German fascist invaders to achieve some sort of victory in Yugoslavia. . . .

The units of the People's Liberation Army have become celebrated for their courage and audacity, but they lack weapons. It is indispensable to send Tito arms and give him the opportunity not only to prevail over the enemy but to destroy him, on behalf of the liberation of the Yugoslav people and the general Allied cause.

Why, Stalin is using unverified facts, I thought, as I listened to his letter. From then on, everything was clear. The lies were so glaring and so insulting that I realized the leaders of the Soviet Union were not what we had thought they were. They used lies, although in the international workers' movement and generally in relations among nations such methods could never bring victory. I began to recall various details of Soviet-Yugoslavian relations which I had not previously considered important. (I had attributed them to Russia's terrible backwardness; after all, I thought to myself, she cannot overcome centuries of it overnight.)

Immediately another question came to mind. What would be the fate of socialism now that the beacon in the lighthouse had gone out? In the interests of unity in the workers' movement, would it be better to bow our heads, to swallow this injustice? But what was the good of a "socialism" where injustice prevailed? No, no, a hundred times no!

A friend sitting near me began to sob. Then another question occurred to me: what about Sreten Žujović? I was sick at heart, for I loved him very much. We had been together for a considerable part of the war, and he was one of the most upstanding men I had known in the revolution, with a rare personal modesty. He had been wounded in the First Offensive and later, when we had no food, he would dole out to all of us the tiny bread ration he received as a seriously wounded patient. He had been best man at my wedding.

How could he have fallen for the Russians' line? Was it the result of his long training in the Soviet Union? I tried to find justification for him, to understand him, but when I remembered all the injustices done Yugoslavia in the letter—regarding the war, the Party's having dissolved itself, our allowing capitalist elements to do as they wished, the kulaks' having their own way, Vlatko Velebit's being a spy (that same good Vlatko who had kept the secret of the Comintern's radio station in Zagreb before the war)—my feeling for the truth prevailed.

That evening I went home earlier than usual and, as was

my custom, looked over my diary to find out what we had been doing on the same day of the month during the war years. I found the entries for May 1943, when the Fifth Offensive was launched. How could one reconcile our truth with the lies in that letter? Tears of sorrow fell on the pages of my diary, but sorrow soon gave way to rage.

Shortly after, I had to see Tito on official business. He had suffered his first gall-bladder attack and did not look well. He told me, "This is an injustice and we cannot give in! They are telling enormous lies, and any progressive movement that tries to use lies ceases to be progressive. The Russians are wrong if they think they can break us by such methods. . . . If we agreed to admit we were guilty of everything the Russians accuse us of, they would surely praise us for our discipline and might even decorate us. But no—*the truth comes first.*"

The Conflict Is Internationalized ★

At a meeting of the Central Committee on May 25, it was decided to convene the congress of the Communist Party of Yugoslavia. This meant accepting Stalin's challenge. In my diary I jotted down Tito's opinion:

"The convening of the congress was really a bold step.

"It was perhaps the most fateful period in our history. Urgent action was required under the circumstances. The least hesitation would bring disaster.

"The revolution would be able to survive and engender something new only if the masses intensified their self-initiative, only if all the facts were laid before them and they were given a chance to decide for themselves.

"Truth was on the side of the weaker, and that truth was the strongest and the only ally we had."

During that time, in the spring of 1948, I read some new documents about Adam Chartorisky, a Polish nobleman exiled in Paris in the middle of the last century who advised some

Serbians as to how they should pursue the struggle for the liberation of their people. He warned that they should not err in thinking that what was involved was only the struggle of little Serbia against the powerful Turkish and Austro-Hungarian monarchies; no, it was a matter of principle—the defense of a small nation, and a general problem concerning all Europe. When Chartorisky lived, the principle of the sovereign equality of states and the right of each to freedom and self-determination were merely the dreams of poets and farsighted revolutionaries. But in 1948 the Utopian ideas of a melancholy Polish exile in Paris became a cause for which the broad masses of the people struggled—a cause involving not only Europe but other continents as well.

The conflict between the U.S.S.R. and Yugoslavia acquired international dimensions in the spring of 1948: first, in relations between states, particularly small and large ones; second, in relations between states striving to build socialism; and third, in the international working-class movement on all continents.

Stalin tried to skirt all this in his attempt to present the clash as primarily ideological and Yugoslavia as deviationist.

In the spring of 1943, purely for reasons of foreign policy, Stalin had dissolved the Comintern; the end of the war was still far off and he thought that the masses in various countries would rally to the struggle against Germany more fervently if communist parties were allowed greater independence. In addition, the dissolution of the Comintern brought him certain benefits in Washington and London.

But in 1947, when he was feeling stronger, he had established the Cominform. The Yugoslavs also showed a great deal of initiative in setting up this body, but Stalin had his own reasons for supporting it, and the Yugoslavs had others. Stalin wanted to use the Cominform to rein in all the world's communist parties and thus return to Comintern days; in Belgrade it was felt that the international working-class movement really *should* have a consultative body for exchanging views and a clearing house for the wealth of experience amassed during and after the war. At the founding of the Cominform, the Yugoslav concept was adopted only *pro forma*. The resolution on the principles governing the new organization referred to the *need for exchange of experience and voluntary coordination,* and this principle was underscored again in the second paragraph, which stated that "the Cominform is charged with the task of *exchanging experience* and, in case of need, coordinating activities by communist parties *on the basis of mutual agreement.*"

But from the first day of its existence, the Cominform was a blind instrument for the pursuit of Stalin's hegemonistic policy. First, at the constituent assembly, he induced the Yugoslav representatives to make a searing criticism of the two biggest communist parties in Europe, those of France and Italy. There was much truth in that criticism, but the Soviet purpose was obviously "divide and rule."

Cominform headquarters were in Belgrade and its newspaper was published there; down to the very last detail, however, Moscow ran the show. I have kept a report from 1948 on how the paper was managed:

The entire business [of runing the newspaper] was in the hands of Soviet citizens—Yudin, his two assistants, and the head of the editorial board, Pashkov. Representatives from other parties simply carried out orders. . . . Working with Yudin were a number of Russian journalists who attended editorial meetings for no reason whatsoever. . . .

At editorial board meetings it was decided what would be covered in various issues of the paper, but the articles were greatly changed without the knowledge or approval of the writers or editors.

The case of Rakosi's speech was an interesting one. The secretary of the editorial board, Shumilov, informed the Hungarian representative, Zolton Biro, that corrections would be made in the speech: "Tell Biro that if he does not come to the office, I will correct Rakosi's speech as I see fit."

Authors frequently complained that things they had never

written or even said had been inserted in their articles. Among those who made these complaints was the representative of the French Party, Anges. And there was a big argument with the Polish representative Finkelstein. Finkelstein protested against changes made in an article by one of the Polish leaders, and the Russians retaliated by making things uncomfortable for him—not giving him a radio, not allowing him to use a car, and so on.

When the first hundred copies of each issue had been printed, the printing was stopped, the plates removed, and the offices locked. Publication was postponed for several days while copies were sent to Moscow for Stalin's and Molotov's approval. Only after they had given their consent could the printing continue. . . .

It once happened that approval had arrived from Moscow and the paper been printed, when another message came to stop publication. All copies—French, English, and Russian— were then returned to the editorial office and burned in the boiler room of the Cominform building in the presence of the Russians; it took all day and all night. A search was made to make sure that no employees had taken a copy.

I went on to note that the Soviet representatives in the editorial offices reserved the best rooms and furniture for themselves, at the expense of the other "fraternal parties":

A real race developed to get the best furniture. Everyone tried to get as much as he could for himself, with no consideration for proportion or esthetics, etc. Tables, rugs, and telephones disappeared, and the rooms of representatives from the other "fraternal parties" were left bare. Quarrels broke out between the Russians dragging furniture to and from each other's rooms.

It was obvious from the outset that even the most insignificant Russian employee considered himself superior to the representatives of other parties.

The following may serve to illustrate the attitude of Russians toward everything "non-Russian." On two different occasions—a Belgrade première and the guest appearance of the prima donna of the Budapest Opera—the Russians left the theater one by one and the next day vied to see who had been the first to go. They were afraid to say that they liked the performances, as nothing from beyond the borders of the U.S.S.R. could be praised. Whenever anyone dared say something good about a Yugoslav production, the others reacted sharply by asserting that it had been far below the level of the Russian theater; the final accusation would be that the eulogist was a "cosmopolitan."

Zhdanov: The Dispute Will Be Settled Quickly ★

Stalin's views on the basic organizational principles of the Cominform were expressed in his first letter of March 27 to the Central Committee. Stalin sent that letter not only to the addressee but to all members of the Cominform, asking the leaderships of the eight parties to take a stand on the conflict between Russia and Yugoslavia on the basis of this letter alone, and instructing each to send its answer directly to the Central Committee of the CPSU.

That was Stalin's concept of democracy in an organization of the international working-class movement! In the old days, when parts of what is now Yugoslavia were under Turkish rule, the people used to say, "The kadiya* accuses you, and the kadiya judges you!"

The Kremlin was certain that this new pressure would make the Yugoslav heretics yield. The Soviet Union's principal ideologue, Zhdanov, showed superb confidence in May 1948, when asked by Soviet research workers if they should continue studying aspects of Yugoslavia; he smiled and replied, "I think the dispute will be over soon."

The first person to respond to Stalin's call to battle against Yugoslavia was the Hungarian leader Matias Rakosi. As early

---

* Turkicized word for "judge."

as April 8, speaking in the name of the Politburo of the Hungarian Party, he agreed with all of Stalin's accusations against the Central Committee of the CPY. Zhdanov sent his letter on to Tito, and it was delivered personally by Yudin on April 15, the idea being to present it as only the first in a series (which it was).

The reply from the Yugoslav Central Committee to Rakosi was prompt and cutting. Tito was particularly offended by Rakosi's hypocrisy: in practically every previous meeting with Yugoslavs, Rakosi had complained bitterly that the Red Army was plundering Hungary and that the Russians were subordinating the Hungarians, yet now he presumed to lecture the Yugoslavs on respect for Russia. A letter was also sent to the CPSU objecting to how it had used the Cominform as an instrument of Soviet policy.

One day a young Chinese arrived in Belgrade from Prague. Veljko Vlahović and I received him. He asked what the dispute was all about and what our position was. We gave him our replies and carefully explained our view on the essence of the controversy. He listened attentively, filled practically a whole notebook with Chinese characters, nodded, and left. Veljko and I were pleased at the thought that some good might come of it if the Chinese Party acted as mediator.

In the meantime Stalin was playing with us, indulging in a war of nerves. For weeks there had been no news about Yugoslavia over Radio Moscow, not even Yugoslav songs: then suddenly, one day, Soviet radio stations broadcast Yugoslav music from morning till night. This seemed like a ray of hope, and we started coming to all sorts of conclusions.

Then sometime early in May another letter arrived from Rakosi announcing that a congress of the Hungarian Communist Party would be held on June 12 and requesting us to send a delegation "so as to preserve the international unity of the working class."

Our first reaction was positive. For a moment we forgot everything that Rakosi had done and appointed a delegation headed by Moša Pijade and Jakov Blažević.

But the campaign against Yugoslavia ground on. During a lecture for Budapest students, a member of the Hungarian Central Committee remarked that the Yugoslav Party was "reformist," that Tito himself was a reformist. Members of the audience protested, and the lecturer threatened to take measures against them. After a number of like incidents, the CPY changed its mind and decided not to send a delegation to the Party congress in Hungary. As the letter to the Hungarians concluded:

These facts do not confirm in any way the unjustified stand and attitude of your Central Committee toward the Communist Party of Yugoslavia and its Central Committee. The Central Committee has no guarantee that in such an atmosphere our delegation would not be subjected to insults and undeserved disparagement.

For these reasons the Central Committee has been forced to rescind its earlier decision to send a delegation to your congress, since the attack on the Communist Party of Yugoslavia and on the leaders of the new Yugoslavia is simultaneously an attack on our country and our peoples, who sacrificed so much during the war to destroy fascism, who are building socialism, and who are making a great contribution to the consolidation of peace and the victory of democratic forces in the world.

At the same time the Yugoslav Central Committee took the measures necessary to preserve the country's freedom and to protect itself from possible repetitions of the Hebrang and Žujović cases. The decision was taken unanimously to expel these two from the Central Committee and the Party. It was also resolved to put the whole matter to the members of the party and to explain the allegiances of Hebrang and Žujović. The public prosecutor also established that crimes against the security of the state were involved, and the two men were taken into custody.

Stalin was furious. Authorizing one of his envoys to threaten the Yugoslav Central Committee of the CPY and to issue an ultimatum, he insisted that Soviet representatives take part in the investigation of the Žujović and Hebrang cases. The Yugoslavs replied:

> The Central Committee has never made preparations to kill anyone, and that includes Hebrang and Žujović. They are being investigated by regular authorities.
>
> The Central Committee considers it improper for the Central Committee of the CPSU to pose the question in this manner and emphatically rejects the very thought of our party leaders being described as "criminal murderers."
>
> Consequently, the Central Committee feels that participation by the representatives of the Central Committee of the CPSU in the investigation of Hebrang and Žujović cannot even be considered.

Moša Pijade remarked: "The Russians apparently forget that Austria-Hungary made a similar demand in its ultimatum to Serbia in July 1914, that is, that Austro-Hungarian agencies participate in the investigation of Serbian citizens accused of taking part in the assassination of Franz Ferdinand at Sarajevo. Serbia had to reject that demand, for it meant fundamental violation of the sovereign rights of a country."

Some time after our reply, information reached Belgrade that Russian intelligence agents were preparing to abduct Žujović and Hebrang from prison.

Thus the conflict deepened, and Stalin persisted in bringing matters to a head. The date of the scheduled Fifth Congress of the CPY was made public—July 21. Decisions were made as to who would submit reports, and work was begun on drafting the statute.

Why Didn't Tito Go to Bucharest? ★

Why did Stalin, and Stalinism as a system, not only demand death for heretics but also insist on forcing the rebel to undergo self-criticism or (better still) to kill his own conscience?

This problem, which had been haunting me, came to mind again on May 19, 1948, when a youthful-looking fellow by the name of Meshetov, from the Central Committee of the CPSU, came to Belgrade bearing a letter signed by Suslov demanding that a delegation of the Yugoslav Central Committee attend the next Cominform meeting. They wanted Tito personally to attend. Yudin spread rumors that the meeting would be held in the Ukraine and that Stalin would be coming.

Discussions began in the Central Committee the next day as to whether a delegation should go. The majority was opposed. It was clear that there was to be no discussion of the Yugoslav situation; what was wanted was capitulation—confession of guilt. Here and there a contrary opinion could be heard to the effect that "the gravity of the unfounded charges, even the most horrible and most monstrous accusations against us, could not justify our absenting ourselves," that "a plan was in the making which we would not perhaps perceive clearly from our vantage point." But these opinions could not prevail. Some of the older comrades recalled that the youthful-looking Meshetov had participated in the liquidation of Yugoslav communists in Moscow in 1937–1938: this probably did not bode good for us at the Cominform meeting. The Central Committee unanimously decided not to go.

Back then, in the spring of 1948, I could not answer the question why Stalin demanded that the heretics kill their own consciences before being physically liquidated. In 1949, during the trials in Hungary and other East European countries, it was clear that they all followed the same pattern: like the old Bolsheviks at the Russian trials in 1936–1938, the accused admitted their "errors," criticized themselves, and confessed to being foreign spies. After having thus disgraced themselves, they got death sentences for their pains. Was it in the theological seminary that Stalin had learned that heretics must be forced to disavow formally and publicly their sacrilegious thoughts before giving up their souls, or was this some sinister remnant of Byzantine civilization, where the Emperor had been the repository of secular power and the sole true interpreter and defender of the faith?

It was a fact that Stalin did his utmost to make Tito and other Yugoslav leaders come to the Cominform meeting. When he got a clear and unequivocal refusal from the Yugoslav Central Committee, the Russians sent another letter (on May 22) in which, allegedly at the request of the "Czechoslovak and Hungarian comrades," they postponed the Cominform meeting for a month, to late June—a move to gain time. In the meantime Gomulka appealed to the Yugoslavs to attend, and proposed that he and Berman, one of the leaders of the Polish Party, come to Belgrade to talk things over.

What happened meanwhile in the editorial offices of *For Lasting Peace, For People's Democracy* convinced those still undecided of the futility of attending the Cominform meeting. On June 7 the Yugoslav Central Committee inquired of Yudin why his Cominform paper systematically refused to publish news or articles about the development of socialism in Yugoslavia. It demanded that Yudin publish in the next issue a report on the tremendous response of the Yugoslav people to the convening of the Party's Fifth Congress, and an article on the significance of that congress, written in the spirit of a *Borba* editorial of June 5.

Yudin called together the members of the editorial board, read them our letter, and commented briefly: the Central Committee, he said, should be grateful to the Cominform for having restricted itself to indirect criticism. The Yugoslav argument that the paper was using the letters of Stalin and Molotov for attacks on our Party he described as an "impermissible demand for the editorial board to renounce Stalin." The Yugoslav letter, in short, was the epitome of noncommunist and non-Marxist behavior.

Like a well-trained chorus, all the non-Yugoslav editors agreed. The only exception was the Italian representative, who even stressed how grateful the Italian Party was to the Yugoslav Party and how both had solved many grave problems in agreement. But at the end he sided with Yudin, who took the floor once again and concluded by saying loudly, "We are here to pledge our loyalty to Stalin!"

A few days later Yudin and all the editors left Belgrade. Their departure was described in a confidential report received by the Yugoslav Central Committee: "The Russian employees literally bought up everything they could in the special diplomats' shops, . . . everything they could lay their hands on. They even packed up things that did not belong to the editorial offices (rugs, telephones, etc.). They stole from each other—wrist watches, wall clocks, and so on."

Tito's best friends among European communist leaders were first Dimitrov and then Wilhelm Pieck. In 1938, when the Yugoslav Party was about to be banned by Moscow, Dimitrov and Pieck advised against it, and Pieck had protected Tito from direct persecution in the Russian capital. After 1945 Tito kept up a close relationship with Pieck. Early in 1948 he sent him four volumes of his collected works, bound in red leather and inscribed, in Russian, "to a great scholar on Marx, Lenin, and Stalin, W. Pieck—Tito." The books were presented to Pieck at a ceremony in the Yugoslav military mission in East Berlin also attended by other East German communists, including Walter Ulbricht.

But then came Stalin's letters. One day Pieck sent an urgent message through our military mission that he wanted to meet with Tito immediately. (He personally told the Yugoslav representative in East Berlin that in the Comintern before World War II he had been in charge of the Balkans and that it was at his suggestion that Tito had been sent to Yugoslavia in 1937 as secretary-general of the CPY.) Sofia, he thought, would be the best place for the meeting; Dimitrov would have nothing against it, as he too was a good friend of Tito's.

Tito replied the same day, saying the pressure of business prevented him from leaving Belgrade. But Pieck continued to press for the meeting. Another message came to Belgrade: Pieck realized Tito was busy, but it was imperative for them to meet, at least on the Bulgarian-Yugoslav boundary. Pieck would come to Belgrade personally, but his own situation was complicated by his Party's coalition with the social democrats: he might be accused of going to Belgrade in response to directives, Belgrade being the headquarters of the Cominform. The Yugoslav reply explained that Tito was not refusing to meet Pieck, but stressed that Pieck should come to Belgrade. Pieck stuck to his guns, saying he could not for the reasons given. And so Pieck's initiative fell through. Whether it *was* his initiative will be learned when the relevant documents from Berlin and Moscow are published.

Stalin had still not given up hope that the Yugoslavs would come to the Cominform meeting. On June 19 a telegram arrived as follows:

> To the Central Committee of the CPY:
> The Communist Information Bureau, convened to discuss the situation in the Communist Party of Yugoslavia, invites representatives of the Central Committee to participate in the work of the Cominform.
> In case of your concurrence, the Cominform will expect your representatives not later than June 21 in Bucharest where they should report to Comrade Gheorghiu-Dej at the Central Committee of the Rumanian Workers' Party for instructions on how to reach the place where the Cominform will sit in session.
> We expect an urgent reply through Filipov—Moscow.
> The Cominform

Moscow left open a special radio connection for twenty-three hours for the reply to this telegram. The connection was extended to eleven a.m. on June 20, when the Yugoslav answer was relayed. Once again the Yugoslavs set forth the reasons why they would not take part in the Bucharest meeting, stressing that discussion on a basis of equality would be impossible, and that the entire meeting was at variance with the spirit of the agreement and the principle of voluntariness on which the Cominform was based.

Two days later Moša Pijade and I went to see Tito. Pijade referred to the tragic fate of the Politburo of the Central Committee of the Ukrainian Communist Party, headed by Kosijer, which had been invited to a "comradely consultation" in Moscow in 1937. They all ended up with bullets in their heads. Tito asked me what I thought about going to Bucharest. I replied:

"The Bishop-Governor Juraj Drašković has prepared the stake and the iron crown, but this time Matija Gubec* will not appear."

Public Anathema ★

On June 28, 1948, a resolution was passed at the Cominform meeting in Bucharest publicly anathematizing Yugoslavia and the Central Committee of the Yugoslav Communist Party. Although those present were supposed to be the judges and not the accused, six of the fourteen representatives from East European countries under the military occupation or control of the Soviet Union ended up either executed or out of power during Stalin's lifetime: the Bulgarian Kostov; the Czechoslovaks Slansky, Geminder, and Bareš; the Rumanians Vasili Luka and Ana Pauker.

During the discussion of the resolution against Yugoslavia Zhdanov used the favorite Stalinist charge: "We have at our disposal information to the effect that Tito is an imperialist spy!" It is reliably known that Gheorghiu-Dej asked a few inconvenient questions, but the Russian machine ground on and the resolution was passed.

On that particular June 28 I was attending a session of the Physical Culture Federation of Yugoslavia. Several thousand young athletes and sailors were on their way to Prague, where

---

* Matija Gubec was the leader of a fifteenth-century peasant uprising against the feudal lords in Croatia and Slovenia. After a decisive battle at Stubica, near Tito's village, Gubec was captured and executed.

a big Sokol rally was being held; also, we were making up a soccer team for the Olympic Games in London. Centralism was then in full flower in Yugoslavia, even in soccer, and I, as president of the Federation, was to have the final say as to who would play left half on the state team.

Our discussion as to who played better left or right was interrupted by a telephone call from the Central Committee. It was Djilas: "Since three o'clock Radio Prague has been giving the text of the Cominform resolution against us. Go to Tanjug [the Yugoslav news agency] and then please come to me with the whole text." I had received an urgent message from the Central Committee that sabotage was afoot in Tanjug and that this was why it was not releasing the text of the resolution. I did not have to be told twice; I rushed immediately to Tanjug and carried out a veritable coup there. I thought to myself, "This is just like 1941 and there is no time for reflection. Who will get the upper hand is a matter of seconds."

The text of the resolution was being transmitted by United Press and it was true that reception was difficult. I arranged for messengers to deliver it piece by piece straight from the ticker tape to the Central Committee without waiting for it to be translated and retyped. My secretary, a communist from Istria named Slavica Fran, was somewhere at a trade-union meeting. I pulled her out of it, summoned Djilas' secretary Dragica Vajn-berger, and told them to retype the text carefully and try to fill in the missing words. I also told them not to tell a soul what they were doing. Later on I had a good laugh at myself for being so stupid: the resolution had been sent out to the whole world, and there I was acting secretive about it! Djilas arrived. After Slavica had typed up the first page, she calmly said, "Why, this is an ordinary American trick."

Djilas waved his hand. "Unfortunately, no, it's true. But don't tell anyone what you're typing."

The retyping took a long time. As soon as each page was finished, copies of it were sent to members of the Politburo.

The anathema was complete: Stalin had forced the representatives of the six East European countries (among whom

were a number of vice-premiers and foreign ministers) to sign
an appeal to the citizens of Yugoslavia *to force their government*
to obey the Soviet Union; if the Yugoslav government refused,
the people were to replace it and set up a new one that would
obey the dictates of the Soviet Union:

> The Cominform asserts that, in consequence of all this, the
> Central Committee of the Communist Party of Yugoslavia
> is expelling itself and the Communist Party of Yugoslavia
> from the family of fraternal communist parties, from the
> united communist front, and, therefore, from the ranks of the
> Cominform. . . .
> The Yugoslav communists probably do not realize, or pre-
> tend not to realize, that such nationalistic conceptions can
> only lead to the degeneration of Yugoslavia into an ordinary
> bourgeois republic, to loss of Yugoslavia's independence, and
> to the transformation of Yugoslavia into a colony of the im-
> perialist countries.
> The Cominform does not doubt that there are within the
> Communist Party of Yugoslavia sufficient sound elements,
> loyal to Marxism-Leninism, loyal to the internationalist
> traditions of the CPY, loyal to the socialist front.
> It is the task of these sound Party members to force their
> present leaders to admit their mistakes openly and honestly
> and to correct them, to abandon nationalism, to return to
> internationalism, and with all their might to consolidate the
> united socialist front against imperialism, or—if the present
> leaders of the Party prove incapable of this—to replace them
> and to form a new internationalist leadership.
> The Cominform does not doubt that the Communist Party
> of Yugoslavia will be able to achieve this honorable task.

On June 29 the Yugoslav Central Committee met in plenary
session. Working all night, Djilas had prepared a draft reply,
and his text was adopted as the basis for the answer. (I have
kept a copy of this historic document. The corrections made by
the plenum were mostly formulated by Kardelj, some by
Djilas.) Each one of the Cominform's basic charges was dealt
with. They were based on inaccurate and unfounded claims, it

was stated; they represented an attempt to destroy the prestige of the Communist Party of Yugoslavia at home and abroad, to provoke confusion among the Yugoslav people and in the international working-class movement, and to disrupt the unity of the Party and weaken its leading role.

That evening *Borba* published the text of the reply together with the Cominform resolution. The plenum had decided to submit the facts to the people and let them have the final say.

I wrote the following in my diary:

We were the only ones to publish both texts. Neither Russia nor any of the other countries at the meeting in Bucharest published our answer. We also published all of Stalin's letters and our replies. We printed 450,000 copies which were sold in newsstands, so that people had a chance to use their own heads in deciding who was right and who was wrong.

However, in the Soviet Union, thirty-three years after the October Revolution, the citizens of the world's first socialist country were denied the right to think for themselves, nor were they given the opportunity to read our replies.

How much strength I drew from this fact! How it filled me with faith that we would endure and win, because we were not afraid of the truth!

That morning my mother asked me, "What is all this about?" When I told her, she said, "What a strange people we are. We are never afraid to say what we think to anyone's face, no matter how powerful he may be. I remember June 28, 1914, as though it were yesterday—the day that Gavrilo Princip assassinated Archduke Ferdinand. And look what your generation did when Hitler was at the height of his power! And then [in 1946] when the Americans seemed to be lord of it all, you brought down their planes. Now you have done the same with Stalin."

5.

The People—the Only Source of Resistance

Plebiscite in Prague ★

The first opportunity for a public plebicite was afforded us far from our borders, at the Sokol games in Prague, in which twenty-three hundred Yugoslav youths and seven hundred Yugoslav sailors participated.

Czechoslovaks have a great tradition in organizing this kind of athletic event, and this time they outdid themselves in preparations, building a stadium to hold 250,000 spectators—the biggest in the world. The members of our Physical Culture Federation trained for months in Ljubljana to take part. A special committee was set up of representatives of youth organizations, the army and navy, physical culture committees, and many experts.

The program was being drawn up just as Stalin's first letters against the Yugoslav Party were being sent, and so we hit on the idea of our participants stressing in their performance the role played by the Party in organizing the people's liberation war and building socialism in Yugoslovia. We had not the faintest idea what the result would be.

Special trains with three thousand Yugoslav gymnasts were on their way through Hungary when the Cominform resolution was published. My cousin Pavel was one of them and he sent me a letter:

> As we passed through Hungary we noticed Hungarian soldiers at each station to keep us from getting out of the cars. At every station, guards and soldiers were waiting who barely allowed a few of us to bring drinking water in pails and distribute the food prepared in another car. We had no idea what was going on. They guarded us as though it were a trainful of wild animals. The guards said nothing, gave no explanation. They were very strict (and fully armed), as though an invasion army were passing through their country and not gymnasts from Yugoslavia.

At the headquarters of the Physical Culture Federation in Belgrade we had organized a messenger service to bring the news straight from Tanjug as soon as it came from Prague. The first report was that our special trains had been surrounded by gendarmes and police in Czechoslovakia, just as in Hungary. Obviously, they feared contact between Yugoslavs and Czechoslovaks.

Although the state propaganda media in Czechoslovakia were already widely publicizing the Cominform resolution and the first sharp attacks on us, a second report told us that our young athletes had marched through the streets of Prague singing partisan songs and received a tumultuous welcome, traffic being stopped while the populace embraced our sailors and youngsters.

Carrying this report, I sped like a lunatic through the streets of Belgrade to the Central Committee building. I arrived all out of breath and put the report on Djilas's desk. "Look, it's the same as it was after June 22, 1941, when our Young Communist League members were the first in Belgrade to set fire to German lorries; once again the youth is the first to set an example."

In Prague the manifestations continued. The news agencies reported:

The meet began on July 3. After the Czechoslovak gymnasts came 700 Yugoslav sailors, sun-tanned, bare-chested, in white trousers and sailor's caps. During the first part of their exercises they portrayed the role of Yugoslav seamen in the war, and in the second part the sailors on their ships. At the end they formed the emblem of the Yugoslav navy, the five-pointed star, and the name of Tito.

A quarter of a million Prague citizens greeted this performance with thunderous applause.

The sailors were followed by the twenty-three hundred athletes. Their beautifully performed exercises depicted the struggle of the Yugoslav peoples. The spectators applauded even during the performance. In conclusion all the Yugoslav participants performed a big *kolo*—a reel dance—in the middle of the field. The spectators were so enthusiastic that the leaders of the meet asked the Yugoslavs to repeat it the next afternoon. But a diplomatic scandal ensued when the Soviet ambassador in Prague lodged a personal protest. Yugoslav ambassador Marijan Stilinović described the scene this way:

The stadium announcer broadcast the information that the Russian athletic team would perform, followed by the Yugoslavs, who would repeat their performance in compliance with public demand. In the neighboring Soviet box this was greeted with restless movement, murmurs, whisperings. There was a brief conversation in the box of the organizers of the rally. They showed the Soviet chargé d'affaires the program: as the Yugoslavs were being added at the last minute, they would naturally follow the Russian team.

At the same time, signs of nervousness were obvious in the central government box. The Czechoslovak ministers were leaning forward, whispering to one another. Minister of Internal Affairs Nosek glanced nervously at Gottwald, who had withdrawn like a snail, squinting like a petulant child, looking right and left, red in the face.

Over half an hour passed. The audience was restless and started whistling.

The senior officials of the meet dispersed, and paid no more attention to the Soviet chargé d'affaires. The announcer now said that the Yugoslav team would provide the next item on the program, at the general request of the public.

Quietly, without fanfare, our young men and women appeared on the field, several thousand of them, doing their exercises in a light dance rhythm—harmoniously, softly, faultlessly. The stadium fell quiet. I watched them as though mesmerized, until awakened from my trance by the ovations of the crowd. The applause had not yet died down when the sailors appeared, marching lightly. The crowd continued to applaud and, except for the Russians, the entire diplomatic corps in the boxes were on their feet. In the Soviet box the only one applauding was the ambassador's ten-year-old son.

At the request of the Soviet government, the Czechoslovak government quickly lodged a protest through Ambassador Stilinović against "the behavior of your team and their exploitation of our traditional hospitality. . . . Since they have been in Prague, your athletes have constantly provoked disorders and manifestations in the streets, and the Czechoslovak government will suffer this no longer." Stilinović replied immediately: ". . . Like all the others—except the Russians, who have been kept under lock and key by their seniors—our athletes walk around Prague. They are not to blame if the people of Prague applaud them, greet them warmly, and dance in the streets with them."

Some three weeks later, on July 27, the Czechoslovak embassy in Belgrade, acting on behalf of Foreign Minister Vladimir Klementis, issued an official communiqué expressing gratitude for the participation of the Yugoslav teams at the meet in Prague.

Four years later the courageous Klementis was sent to the gallows. No doubt his hangmen held against him the greetings he had sent us invoking the fraternity of our two peoples. But it had truly amounted to the first public plebiscite after the Cominform resolution.

Everyone Believes Yugoslavia Is Doomed ★

Few people outside Yugoslavia believed that Tito's government could survive Stalin's ultimatum. In my diary I noted what the leading Western newspapers had to say about the outlook for the Yugoslavs:

The *London Times* of June 29 said that it is hard to imagine how the present administration in Yugoslavia could continue to remain in power.

The *Manchester Guardian* of June 29, according to the French Press Agency, said "in its morning editorial that it thinks the Yugoslav government is probably already in the hands of others. 'Now the people of Yugoslavia,' wrote the newspaper, commenting on the Cominform communiqué, '. . . are openly urged to get rid of their leaders and change their Government. Probably this has already been done. Marshal Tolbukhin (how often a marshal of the Red Army appears at the critical spot, travelling innocently to Prague or Belgrade!) is known to be in Yugoslavia in an effort to deal with the trouble and one can hardly believe that any announcement would be made if he had failed. Tomorrow, perhaps, we shall hear that Marshal Tito and the other Yugoslav leaders named in the communiqué have been arrested and are facing trial as traitors to the people. (After all, they cannot all jump out of the window.)' "

Similar prophecies were heard in Washington. Reuters reported on June 29 that "a Washington correspondent of the *New York Times* says that informed persons in Washington do not see any break between Moscow and Belgrade and that Marshal Tito will either meet the Kremlin's demands or be replaced."

A telegram arrived through our Foreign Ministry that our counselor in Washington, Slobodan Lale Ivanović, had come out in support of the Cominform resolution and persuaded a number of younger officials to do the same. (Ivanović had become a Party member toward the end of the war, before which he had been prominent in the Farmers' Party headed by Dragoljub Jovanović.) We were informed that one of Ivanović's arguments had been as follows: he had taken a pencil and done some arithmetic. On one side was Yugoslavia with a population of 16,000,000. On the other side was the Soviet Union with 200,000,000, Poland with 24,000,000, Rumania with 16,000,000, Czechoslovakia with 10,000,000, and so on. That meant 16,000,000 against 280,000,000. "Why be a fool," he told a junior official, "the arithmetic is clear. Our Central Committee won't be able to hold out more than three weeks, and then we will have to give in. Anyone with brains will save himself while there is still time."

King Peter II and his former ambassador in Washington, Konstantin Fotić, beamed with satisfaction. On June 29 the Associated Press reported that the King's secretary, Brana Popović, had said: "His Majesty is enjoying this. However, he feels he cannot make any other statement as he does not for the moment know the facts in the case." In Chicago Fotić told the Associated Press: "Finally Tito has got what he was asking for. The iron curtain may clamp down even tighter and we may never hear what became of him."

That was the tone of most of the comments in the West. The same opinion was held in Eastern Europe. Stalin and Molotov reckoned that their strength would prevail over a small, poorly armed, backward, and economically isolated country. As he left Belgrade Yudin said, "You won't hold out three weeks. If you don't give in, the Western imperialists will swallow you up."

After the Cominform resolution Rakosi was again the first to forecast the prompt collapse of Yugoslavia. On July 2 he said: "In 1941 bourgeois nationalism caused a catastrophe in Yugoslavia and it will again lead to a catastrophe if the leaders of the Yugoslav Party continue along their present path. . . . But they cannot resist for long."

Ana Pauker also predicted a rapid collapse. She spoke of Yugoslavia's "conceited and bureaucratic leadership. . . . The liquidation of that regime is a matter of life and death."

I had occasion to see a confidential report on an address by Traiche Kostov to activists in Gornya Dzhumaya. Kostov spoke as follows:

> Tito and Kardelj write to Stalin, "We love the U.S.S.R., but we love Yugoslavia more." That is not the internationalist way of looking at things. It shows that in Yugoslavia socialism is becoming as narrowly nationalistic as it was in Germany.
>
> The merits of the present leaders of the Yugoslav Party cannot conceal the danger in which they have placed the Party and their country. Quite the reverse: their merits should not permit them to allow mistakes to go uncorrected. But they are trying to camouflage the actual situation by identifying themselves with the people. It seems to me that they are lowering themselves to the position of Louis XIV who said, "L'état, c'est moi."

Kostov had been informed how bravely our young people had conducted themselves in Prague, and that too found a place in his address:

> Whom do the present highest Party and state leaders in Yugoslavia serve? The entire democratic world condemns Tito, and the reactionaries are gloating. Unfortunately there are still people, especially young people, in Yugoslavia who believe in Tito, but when they are given the choice—Tito or Stalin, alliance with the Soviet Union and other democratic countries or with the imperialists, for socialism or for a bourgeois republic—they will see what road they have to follow.

During a discussion after the address, the first question asked, according to the report I received, was, "Does the attitude of the Yugoslav leaders have deep roots among the masses?" To which Kostov replied, "Of course it has, especially among the young people. Therein lies the difficulty in correcting their mistakes. I do not know how long the present leaders will succeed in maintaining themselves, but certainly the authority of comrades Stalin and Molotov will help clear up the present situation."

Another question was, "What will happen if the present situation does not clear up?" Kostov answered, "That would be terrible, but it must clear up."

The audience, most of them Pirin Macedonians, asked Kostov if the Cominform resolution had been published in Yugoslavia, and what repercussions it had among the masses. He replied, "The resolution was printed on four pages in the newspapers. They use empty phrases to try to refute all its assertions. How the people are reacting we still do not know."

Someone worked up the courage to ask why the reply of the Yugoslav Central Committee had not been published.

"Why should we publish it?" Kostov replied. "Why publish their conceited explanations, the curses they heap on us?"

In those difficult and fateful days after June 28, no one had remembered to tell our diplomats of either the first Soviet letter or the second, or of the fact that the conflict had broken out in such ferocity. We were still a nation run on partisan lines, with all the slipshod ways of the Bosnian mountain fastnesses. When the Cominform resolution was published and all the world's news agencies transmitted it, many of our official representatives were giving out the most energetic denials. The following Associated Press item came out in the Tanjug Bulletin of June 29:

The Yugoslav delegate to the United Nations, Joze Vilfan, stated on Monday evening that he does not believe that the Cominform has issued, in Prague, a communiqué accusing Yugoslavia of anti-Marxism.

"This must be the result of some confusion; the communiqué cannot be true," he said, after the Associated Press correspondent read him the text from Prague.

The Yugoslav delegate interpreted the case as anti-Yugoslav propaganda.

A Return to the Partisan Ethic ★

Shortly after the publication of the Cominform resolution a report came from Moscow saying rumors were rife that the Yugoslavs would be unable to hold out longer than three weeks: Stalin's authority was so great that the Yugoslav communists themselves would overthrow their leaders on July 21, the date of the opening of the Yugoslav Party's Fifth Congress in Topčider, a suburb of Belgrade.

Although Hebrang and Žujović were already in prison, Soviet propaganda had it that they would be in power in Yugoslavia by the end of July—Hebrang as Prime Minister and Žujović as Party secretary. As for Tito, during the initial period he would be Minister of National Defense!

Although the Yugoslav Party representative in Moscow, Puniša Perović, was told on June 29 to leave the Soviet Union, not all contacts with Soviet or other East European social and political organizations were broken off. In Prague, for instance, members of the Slav Committee of Yugoslavia attended a meeting of the Pan-Slav Committee. At these and other conferences throughout July, Moscow did its best to strengthen its position, lull us to sleep, or sidetrack us.

On July 7, for example, the Bulgarian academician and philosopher Todor Pavlov came through Belgrade on his way to the Pan-Slav Committee meeting in Prague. He was a well-known friend of the Yugoslavs. (In 1940, when the last Comintern mail was sent from Moscow to the Central Committee in Belgrade, Pavlov had been the main "connection" in Sofia; on instructions from Tito, I had sent a newspaperman from Belgrade to get from him the leather bag with the Comintern mail concealed inside.) He was met by Bulgarian diplomats and some of our Slav Committee officials, and quickly asked the Yugoslavs how the situation was shaping up. Our people politely replied: "Nothing special, everything is all right." But a Bulgarian woman, to everyone's surprise, burst out, "They are working and singing!"

Those days, the young people working on the New Belgrade development project often marched through the streets singing or danced the *kolo* on the Terazije, the main square.

But the Bulgarians did not share this opinion. They criticized Tito and the other Yugoslav leaders. Pavlov appeared to take a neutral attitude, but then said something that revealed the real Cominform strategy of making Yugoslavia bow to Stalin's authority. Interrupting a Bulgarian diplomat who was recounting some event, he said: "That is incidental; we must keep to the main thing. I have studied Stalin and I know how he reacts. Before coming to a conclusion he gets information in thousands of ways. He is above all of us. He is on the top of the Himalayas and we are in the foothills. Tito is the personification of the people of Yugoslavia, while Stalin is the personification not only of the people of the Soviet Union, but of all Slav peoples and all working people the world over. He loves all of us, and looking at us from above, he does not err." Thus did Pavlov unequivocally make the case: Stalin is infallible, bow to him.

It was in this atmosphere that the preparations for the Fifth Party Congress were made. The world press was alive with comments and guesses as to what the Yugoslavs would do, a majority believing that they had no alternative but surrender.

Andrei Vyshinski also let this attitude be known to us. In late June and early July he took part in a meeting of East European diplomats discussing the policies to be adopted at the conference on Danube navigation to be held in Belgrade that summer. On June 26—before the Cominform resolution had been adopted—Yugoslav representative Aleš Bebler reported that he had talked with Vyshinski about the draft of the Danube statute and had afterward inquired if Vyshinski wished to discuss general relations between the two countries. Vyshinski had said no, but an hour later (probably after consulting Molotov) he approached Bebler and very politely requested such a talk.

It appeared that the Yugoslav and Soviet delegations had

different views on certain minor issues of the navigation statute, so Vyshinski invited Bebler to a meeting on July 2, where he informed him that the Soviet government was ready to change its position and accept the Yugoslav suggestions. "This is a true Stalinist solution and I am certain that on this basis we shall work together successfully at the coming conference in Belgrade. And now let me hear your opinion of the Cominform resolution."

Bebler's response was "that our deeds would refute the accusations." Vyshinski remarked, "Apart from this it will be necessary to rectify actual mistakes," and developed the thesis that "Yugoslavia did not give the Soviet Union due credit for her liberation." Bebler denied this, but Vyshinski interrupted him, saying that as far as he himself was concerned "our personal relations, after the discussion of recent days and party differences, should not change."

But none of us saw things with absolute clarity in those days of July 1948 when the Fifth Congress met. Its decisions were, indeed, fateful. As the concise account in the *Encyclopedia of Yugoslavia* relates:

> The Communist Party of Yugoslavia offered unanimous resistance to the Cominform resolution, expressed particularly at its Fifth Congress (July 21–27, 1948, in Belgrade) and later at the congresses of national organizations of the Communist Party.
> The Fifth Congress analyzed the historical development of the Party, its emergence and activities during the prerevolutionary period, its role in organizing and guiding the liberation war and revolution, and in socialist construction. These analyses refuted and rejected as slanderous the assertions made in the Cominform resolution. The Central Committee was elected and Tito was re-elected secretary-general of the Party. The Party then had 468,175 members.

But this is only one view of that historic occasion. Actually it was both politically and emotionally a far more complex matter, fraught with general and individual tragedy. By his attack on Yugoslavia and his unjust accusations, Stalin had jeopardized the struggle of the oppressed throughout the world. I wondered what repercussions these events would have in India, which I had visited so recently. How would those millions of hungry, unfortunate people regard this conflict? Surely it would confuse them, perhaps weaken their ranks, and postpone their emancipation from poverty. For a moment it seemed to me that everything possible should be done to stop the conflict on behalf of those unfortunates in Calcutta—and there were many Calcuttas all over the world. But how? Hadn't it already gone too far?

With the help of his undisputed authority as the leader of the international proletariat, Stalin was spreading cheap, vulgar lies about our struggle, even about the course and proceedings of the congress itself. *Pravda* carried an article by its correspondent at the congress, Barzenko, who reported that among the guest delegations was a Trotskyist group from Switzerland. This insinuation notwithstanding, there were no delegates from Switzerland at the congress, as any of the two thousand participants could see.

We suggested to Tito that the report be publicly denied at the congress, and he agreed. The entire report was read out, and the Presidium called upon the congress "to condemn this falsehood and slander as yet another attempt to lower the prestige of our Party and the congress itself." All the delegates jumped to their feet and joined in the condemnation. It was the amorality of the men in Moscow that embittered them the most, I think. I asked Barzenko how *Pravda* could possibly have printed such a false item: it was, after all, the organ of the Bolshevik Party, and *Pravda* meant "truth." He replied in confusion that he had not sent that dispatch from Belgrade! He did not appear again at the congress.

The majority of delegates, including myself, were overcome by another sentiment: we must not give in, we must not let ourselves be used for lies. Here we were at this historic crossroads of the Balkans, between Europe and Asia, exposed on the one side to the attacks of the enormous Cominform organization with its tentacles reaching out to all parts of the world, and on the other side to the equally powerful propaganda apparatus of the West, partially uninformed and partially hostile to our country. There was Yugoslavia—a small nation with only 16,000,000 inhabitants, bled white during the war, devastated, now making a tremendous effort to stand on its own two feet, but without resources and without the experience needed to present its cause adequately.

Tito had no choice but to rely for support on all he had left—the people of Yugoslavia. That was why he decided that the entire congress, down to the very last word, should be broadcast over the air, so that it should be a truly open tribune where views were freely spoken and the people decided who was in the right.

Between the end of the war in 1945 and the Fifth Congress in 1948, the powerful self-initiative of the people which had carried the revolution to fruition had somewhat waned. There were a number of reasons for this: our bureaucracy was developing, Yugoslavia was a society not entirely devoid of contradictions, and we had accepted many Soviet ways of doing things. At the end of 1947 a childhood friend of mine, a communist, had said to me, "That great moral capital we communists gained during the underground struggle before the war and during the partisan war is being dissipated. We got our reputation because there was no difference between what we said and what we did, because of our applied ethics as partisans. And our people are not stupid. They see what we are doing now."

But the Fifth Congress was an important turning point: we were again given the opportunity to rely on the broad masses of the people—there was no other way out. If Rakosi or Gottwald had come into conflict with Stalin, they would have disappeared overnight. They were brought to power by the Soviets at bayonet point—they had not begun the way we did in 1941, first by saying that we had to fight the occupiers and then going out and doing it. And we, the communists, had always been in the front lines, always the first to sacrifice. Of Yugoslavia's twelve thousand prewar communists, only a quarter were alive at the end of the war; the others had died proving there was no difference between their words and their deeds. And what marvelous people they were—how the fighting men, the country people, and the city dwellers had loved them! There was in Serbia a peasant, a prewar revolutionary, Dragojlo Dudić by name, who had been the commissar of the Valjevo detachment and later became the first president of the People's Liberation Committee of Serbia. He had kept a diary, and it had been salvaged when he was killed in the first enemy offensive, brought down by a volley from a German tank somewhere along the Zlatibor road near Užice. In one place he described how his detachment had marched all day, how hungry the partisans were, and how finally at night a warm meal had been prepared for them, only he could not say what it was like because when he and the commander got to the caldron there was nothing left to dish out.

And with this ethic we had won. I remember the autumn of 1941, when I was commissar of the Kragujevac detachment. One evening our two-hundred-man force spent the night in a vineyard full of ripe grapes. We had had no food, but no one touched a single grape. In the morning the peasant owner appeared; tall, bony-faced, with a long white moustache—a typical man of Sumadija. He crossed himself and shouted: "I've seen many an army in my day, but never anyone like the partisans. The people will be with you and you will win for the simple reason that you are so honest!"

That is why the people stood by Tito in 1948, when the Cominform began to vilify the revolution. For they knew that it slandered a reality that millions of people in Yugoslavia had experienced; they were the principal witnesses to the fact and knew who was telling the truth and who was not.

The year 1948 saw the expansion of the People's Front. People outside the Party joined Tito—not anti-communists, but the ordinary man in the street who for one reason or another had not participated in political activities. They knew that this was a matter of life or death for the country—that the state, the future, their very existence was at stake.

The Chetniks and the Ustaši had their own line: Tito's regime would be brought down, their time had come. King Peter gloated, and Ante Pavelić's deputy, Božidar Kavran, entered Yugoslavia from Austria illegally, only to be arrested on the spot. When interrogated, he said he had come back to Yugoslavia because he believed that it was only a matter of days until Tito's collapse.

Thus we nipped in the bud all attempts by extreme right-wing elements to turn the clock back in Yugoslavia.

"I choose Tito, not as authority, but as revolution, as a guarantee that the revolution will continue. The revolution is the meaning of our struggle, and Tito is its standard-bearer and the symbol of resistance, just as he was in the war." That is how a friend of mine, an intellectual, described his feelings during the congress.

But this process of awakening perception was not a simple one, black and white. I watched the delegates to the Fifth Congress: they were for Tito, but they were ideologically encumbered by the past, for the Party had taught them to revere Stalin and the Soviet Union. Several years later Tito told me:

"Without question the whole conflict, especially the resolution, was a terrible blow for our people. Despite many suspicions, basically we had faith in the Soviet Union, in Stalin. . . . Before my very eyes, partisans in the war went to their death with Stalin's name on their lips. . . . Not in vain had we told our people, year in and year out, that the U.S.S.R. was the first land of socialism. . . . We needn't try to conceal or be ashamed of the fact that up to 1948 we looked on the Soviet Union with so much faith and love. On the contrary, we are proud of those illusions. They were positive and demonstrated our deep faith in progress and socialism. When Stalin so mercilessly and brutally trampled them underfoot, it was difficult for us but we did not lose faith in socialism; rather we began to lose faith in Stalin, who had betrayed the cause of socialism."

But this revelation of the historical truth did not proceed at the same pace and in the same way for everyone. Even during the Fifth Congress there were illusions to the effect that this was only a minor disagreement. Various Soviet maneuvers like those with Pavlov or Vyshinski raised false hopes that a compromise would be reached in the interest of the unity of the international proletariat and the struggle against imperialism. And the Russians also, as we have seen, tried to drag us into an ideological discussion, to make us compare our development with theirs and try to approach their model as closely as possible. Tito himself described how at the plenary session of April 12, 1948, he had warned that we should not fall into the trap of discussing dogma:

"Comrades, remember that this is not a matter of theoretical discussions, of errors by the Communist Party of Yugoslavia, of alleged ideological deviation. We must not permit ourselves to be dragged into a discussion of such matters. . . . This is above all a matter of relations between one state and another. . . . It seems to me they are using ideological questions to justify their pressure on us, on our state."

All of us had been infected to some degree by this bacillus of dogmatism. The cure was not equally rapid and effective everywhere, I would be the first to admit. When I look today at a speech I gave at the Fifth Congress, I find traces of that dogmatism:

Because of such a consistently anti-imperialist position by the Communist Party of Yugoslavia, because of the trouble we have given the imperialists, their propaganda machine has spewed forth against our country and Tito so much gall, so many lies and deceptions, that it can only be compared with the furious campaign against the young Soviet Republic in the days after the October Revolution. The imperialists are particularly provoked by the fact that Yugoslavia—the principal force, apart from the Soviet Union, in the anti-imperialist front—is the most consistent in defending the interests of a just peace. That is why we were labeled "Satellite Number One of the Soviet Union." We pride ourselves on our internationalist policy because we are firmly convinced that only such a policy suits the interests of our country and thus also the interests of the entire anti-imperialist front. We pride ourselves that those who guide our foreign policy, like those who guide the foreign policy of the Soviet Union, take as their point of departure the same ideological foundations in the struggle against imperialist oppression.

Or again, Djilas's report on his visit to Moscow in February 1948 had ended with the words: "However, there is no need to doubt for a moment the great love Comrade Stalin bears our entire Party, the Central Committee, and particularly Comrade Tito." During the struggle against the Cominform, Djilas was one of the severest critics of the Soviet social system and of Stalin himself, but in February 1948 he could write that because he was still obsessed by dogma and perhaps also by the cult of "the traditional ties between the Russian and Montenegrin peoples."

As I say, no one was immune to this mistake. In Belgrade a meeting of fifteen thousand members of the People's Front of the Fifth City District was held in honor of the Fifth Congress, and a telegram was sent to Stalin:

To our dear comrade, Josif Visarionovich Stalin:
  From our People's Front rally in the Fifth Belgrade District we send warm greetings to you and, through you, to the entire Soviet Union.
  Comrade Stalin, we have faith in you and believe you will do everything to remove the unjustified accusations made against our entire country, our Party, and our Central Committee.

Our affection for you, for the entire Soviet Union, for everything you have done for all mankind, is as boundless as is our faith that you will do everything to bring the truth to light soon.

Long live the indestructible fraternity of the Soviet Union and Yugoslavia!

Long live the person who taught us to love the Soviet Union—Comrade Tito!

Long live our great friend, Josif Visarionovich Stalin!

Most of the delegates shared these sentiments, and it was not by accident that Tito himself concluded the congress with, "Long live Comrade Stalin!" But when it was a matter of refuting the accusations leveled against us, of siding with Tito or against him, of defending the achievements of the revolution and our independence, the great majority cast their (secret-ballot) votes for Tito.

When I was writing Tito's biography, I had a talk with him about the gradual way in which the people of Yugoslavia were told about the causes of the conflict with Russia. I asked him why he had concluded the Fifth Congress with cheers for Russia and Stalin. My diary contains the following summary of his remarks:

It had to be that way. It was not bowing to authority, but because of our people. We had to move cautiously. Stalin undoubtedly enjoyed authority. If we had been too sudden about it, we would have cut ourselves off from the masses. If we had been too slow, the Russians would have got the better of us. . . . We could not allow ourselves to wallow in bitterness. Time and Soviet behavior would do the work for us, and the masses themselves would say, "Down with Stalin!"

If today, twenty years later, I ask myself who of the Yugoslav leaders was the most determined from the very outset in resisting Soviet hegemony, I must in all conscience acknowledge that it was Tito. It is true that he held the most responsible

post, but he also had in him the instinct of the oppressed, rebellious man of our soil, an instinct acquired from his native
district. I do not mean by this a racial or national quality, but
simply a characteristic, a gift certain strong personalities have
for feeling the condensed history of their people. And our
country, battlefield of the big powers, had for centuries felt
the oppressive force of the mighty, the violent death of multi-
tudes in the prime of life. Thus was born a feeling for truth
and justice, a conviction that we, too, had a right to equality
with other states, that we could and would rid ourselves of the
poverty and misery of centuries.

I do not think that such personalities alone make history.
But in crucial times, when many others think there is no way
out, no salvation, they have a way of knowing their destiny,
of finding the road to liberation, the solution that had once
seemed impossible. They set a stamp on the times and are
borne forward by the corresponding social forces. Tito felt
this in 1948 just as he had in 1941.

In 1952 I asked Tito: "How could Stalin, who is unde-
niably a clever man, misread the situation so badly that even
his first move failed immediately?"

"Russians take a stereotyped view of Yugoslavia. Their basic
weakness is that they did not perceive, and did not wish to
perceive, that Yugoslavia was creating something new; because
of this *a priori* attitude they could not grasp the essence of our
revolution, particularly one basic thing—the extent to which
the consciousness of all Yugoslavs had intensified through their
struggle, how aware they had become of the need to be independent and of the ties between leaders and masses. . . . Because of this belittling, stereotyped attitude toward Yugoslavia;
because of their intoxication with the victory in the war, and
the unintelligent approach of their agents in Yugoslavia—who
did not dare see what the new Yugoslavia was doing, but sent
the Kremlin reports designed to promote Stalin's good disposi-
tion and digestion—they did a disservice to the Kremlin, and
Stalin's mistakes in strategy resulted. Their reading of the situation was always wrong, so the means they used to settle mat-

ters to their benefit were already obsolete—not only as far as Yugoslavia was concerned, but everywhere. That is their basic weakness."

That the Yugoslav leadership could maintain itself simply by relying on the masses opened up possibilities for the vigorous reassertion of popular initiative. Tendencies toward greater democracy in all walks of life intensified. There also appeared the first criticism of government bureaucracy and a desire to achieve full socialism, where industrialization and a better standard of living must be accompanied by improved human relations—a new humanism.

But this process did not develop in a straight line, for even the Fifth Congress failed to relieve us of all our errors and dogmatism. Not so much in words as in practice we adopted the watchword, "Refute the accusations by our deeds." So throughout the second half of 1948 and most of 1949 we tried to prove ourselves by copying certain Soviet models—especially in the economy, as for instance the accelerated and even forcible collectivization of the land. Such practices simply alienated us from the masses.

But these were only temporary manifestations. Meanwhile the East threatened, the West blackmailed—especially with regard to increased economic ties—and the situation throughout the nation grew serious. Grave conflicts took place in the rural districts, where agriculture was stagnating and the state farms, as well as many members of the cooperatives, had to be given rations. The cities had large organizations for distributing supplies, and we had to strip the plants of their best personnel to staff them.

And so life itself forced us to rely on the only thing we had left—the people. The economy could not be revived unless the workers were given greater incentive; society could not be activated unless rigid bureaucratic forms were broken down. In this sense the Fifth Congress was a plebiscite not only for the independence of the country, but also for new roads to socialism. For the first time it was stated that revolutionaries were the servants and not the masters of the revolution. This was at the same time an appeal for a return to the partisan ethic of equality, truth, and justice.

A Deceptive Lull ★

The day after the Fifth Congress adjourned in Belgrade, the Danube Conference began, attended by representatives of the Soviet Union, other East European countries, the United States, Great Britain, and France. According to a decision of the 1946 Paris Peace Conference, the task of the gathering would be to adopt a convention regulating navigation along the Danube from Ulm to the Black Sea. This was duly done on August 18: the convention proclaimed that navigation along the Danube was free and open to all merchant ships and the goods of all countries, which were equal as to terms of navigation and payment of fees. A Danube Commission composed of representatives of the riparian states was charged with enforcing the provisions of the convention.

West and East clashed openly at the conference. The former invoked the so-called "acquired rights" which the big powers had won for themselves during the Crimean War and the Paris treaty of 1856, while the Eastern delegations defended the rights of the riparian states while recognizing the principle of freedom of navigation for all.

The Yugoslav delegation was fully in accord with this latter attitude, but in the spirit of the slogan "Refute the accusations by our deeds" went to the other extreme and voted unreservedly for all Soviet proposals, including one that the official languages of the conference be only Russian and French, not English.

The atmosphere of the conference was such that some of our diplomats could not see the forest for the trees. The Paris paper *Le Monde* on August 3 quoted one of the Yugoslavs to the effect "that relations between Yugoslavia and the Soviet Union had become very close since the Fifth Congress." I was then director of the Information Office and knew what a hue and cry would be raised over this optimistic statement. Tito had gone to Bled for a rest after the congress, but I received a message from him to find out whether or not the statement was authentic.

There was no respite from Soviet pressure. *For Lasting Peace, For People's Democracy*, which had moved from Belgrade to Bucharest, wrote that "Tito would quickly vanish from the political scene." Yudin was doing his best to distort the history of our people's liberation war, claiming that Yugoslavia had been freed by the Red Army, and even took to insulting Tito personally: "Tito is ridiculous when he tries to present himself as a military genius and great statesman. . . . [But] Yugoslavia has enough sound forces to prevent the betrayal of socialism and internationalism."

I was consoled by the fact that the Moscow press carried nothing about the congress during the first few days of August. But my cheer was short-lived, for the theoretical organ of the CPSU Central Committee, *Bolshevik*, soon carried an article by P. Fedoseyev, "The Marxist Theory of Classes and Class Struggle," taking Yugoslavia as an example of "deviation from Marxism" and repeating the Cominform resolution's accusations almost word for word.

But worse was yet to come. In July an attempt had been made in Rome to assassinate the leader of the Italian Communist Party, Palmiro Togliatti. Our newspapers had condemned this attempt and supported the demand of the Italian working class for an end to this kind of terror. Then, at the beginning of August, a Yugoslav was killed in Budapest, and the Yugoslav press attaché there was accused of the crime. In an article from that city *Pravda*'s correspondent equated the crime by the Yugoslav press attaché with the attempt to assassinate Togliatti. Our press attaché in Moscow commented, "So says that correspondent, and so think government people here. If they didn't, they would not allow it to be published."

The Moscow newspapers shortly thereafter carried regular reports on the Danube Conference.

Ana Pauker: Stalin's Chief Agent ★

I avoided all diplomatic receptions during the conference, but I did not avoid meeting Rumanian Foreign Minister Ana Pauker—swimming in the Sava River. Rafts belonging to the Serbian government were moored to the bank, and they had been placed at the disposal of the conference participants. I went there with friends to swim and practice skipping stones whenever we had a free minute. I had met Ana Pauker in February 1947 at the railroad station in Bucharest, where she was waiting to receive Kardelj, then on his way to Moscow for the foreign ministers' meeting about the Austrian treaty. I now greeted her but avoided conversation, because I had read in reports from Rumania that she was one of our fiercest antagonists.

That same evening I met the Bulgarian revolutionary Ivan Karaivanov, who had lived in Yugoslavia since 1945. He was closely acquainted with all the old communists in Eastern Europe, for he had long worked in the Comintern in Moscow. I mentioned in passing that I had met the stoutish revolutionary in a not very attractive bathing suit swimming in the Sava, and he began to tell me about her tumultuous life. The daughter of a very wealthy rabbi from Moldavia, she had started to study medicine before World War I, but had gone into teaching because she felt that she could thus better help the poor people of Rumania. She soon became a communist and had been the Rumanian Party delegate to the Fourth Comintern Congress. In 1923, when terror was launched in Rumania, she left for Russia with her husband, Marcel Pauker. She also lived in America for a while and then went back to Rumania to work underground.

A childhood friend of Ana Pauker was the redheaded Madame Lupescu, daughter of the richest Jew in Rumania and for many years mistress of the Rumanian King. From time to time, when Ana went to Moscow to submit reports to the

Comintern, she spoke of her old friendship with Madame Lupescu, once even boasting that she had used a car belonging to the King to go to a secret meeting with some members of the Rumanian Central Committee.

But her friendship with the lovely Madame Lupescu did not help much: in 1936 Ana Pauker was arrested and sentenced to jail. Meanwhile the NKVD discovered that her husband, who had remained in Moscow working with the Comintern, was an associate of Zinoviev and Kameniev. After the trial of the two old Bolsheviks, he was arrested and summarily executed. Upon her release from prison Ana Pauker returned to Moscow to learn not only of her husband's liquidation but of that of virtually all leading Rumanian communists living in the Soviet Union.

In 1945 she came back to Rumania with the Soviet troops. Karaivanov said that she helped Vyshinski establish contact with the Rumanian King Michael, to whom Stalin awarded the highest Soviet Order of Victory even before it had been given to any of the East European resistance leaders. According to Karaivanov, she was the dominant figure in Rumania and Stalin's most faithful agent there, although Gheorghiu-Dej was the official secretary of the Central Committee.

Warned though I was of her hostility to Yugoslavia, I would never have believed that this old-time revolutionary who had sat combing her hair on the shores of the Sava River that afternoon, would work so coldly and calculatingly to bring down the Yugoslav government. But at that very conference, while we did everything we could to prove our devotion to the Soviet Union and our neighbors, Stalin with her aid was preparing to strike again.

A telegram from Moscow gave us a hint of things to come: circles close to the Soviet government and Central Committee were certain that the disagreements with Yugoslavia would soon be liquidated, since an awakening of the "sound forces" was expected.

While the youth was united in its desire to defend Yugoslavia and Yugoslavia's own road to socialism, this was not the case with people encumbered ideologically with dogmatism. That is where Stalin did us the most harm. By his authority, he put all of us in a difficult position. Some of us got over it earlier, some later. The Soviet intelligence service worked hard to "buy" those whom we then called "dead souls"—people who were personally honest but ideologically confused. Others were frightened by the power arrayed against us, and still others—dissatisfied careerists—hoped to fulfill their ambitions by siding with the presumed victors.

After Žujović and Hebrang's rebellion was thwarted, a new plan was concocted for the second half of August. According to some reports, the Russians were even thinking of setting up a Yugoslav government-in-exile.

There were a number of candidates for this "government of sound forces." On August 7 *Pravda* published a letter of resignation from the Yugoslav ambassador in Bucharest, Radonja Golubović, to the Presidium of the National Assembly of Yugoslavia. The letter was completely in line with the spirit of the Cominform resolution, and *Pravda* gave it a great deal of publicity. It was *Pravda*'s first attack on our country after the Fifth Congress—and, for those who knew Soviet methods, a signal that a new offensive was under way. The "sound forces" began rallying.

On August 18 the Ministry of Internal Affairs issued a communiqué:

At one a.m. [August 12] in the Vršac district, three persons tried to cross the Yugoslav-Rumanian border. The border patrolman concealed there noticed four persons rapidly making for the frontier. When he tried to inform the commander of this, one of the men pulled out a revolver and shot at him. In self-defense the guard shot back, killing two of them on the spot; the other two fled in the direction of the Rumanian border.

Identification of the bodies showed that one of those killed was Colonel General Arso Jovanović and the other the director of the Sočica State Farm, Svetolik Arabjac, who, it was established, knew nothing about the intention of the

other three to escape. The third person, who evidently suc-
ceeded in escaping across the border, was Colonel Vlado
Dapčević, and the fourth, who was captured, was Major
General Branko Petričević.

It was later discovered tht Colonel General Jovanović,
Major General Petričević, and Colonel Dapčević had come
to the Sočica Farm on August 11 at about 10 p.m. on the
pretext of going on a boar hunt. However, according to the
confession of Major General Petričević, they had a plan to
escape across the border into Rumania, for which purpose
they took the director of the state farm along as a guide,
telling him that they were first going to check the border
guards on the way.

Colonel Dapčević was captured on September 2. The Ministry of Internal Affairs issued another communiqué:

> As the public knows, it was announced that on the occa-
> sion of an unsuccessful attempt to escape to Rumania by
> Generals Arso Jovanović and Branko Petričević, Colonel
> Vlado Dapčević, who was in the same group, probably suc-
> ceeded in escaping across the border.
>
> Since then, the public security forces have been searching
> for him. Thanks to the alertness of the border patrol, he did
> not succeed in crossing the frontier. Around 11 p.m. Sep-
> tember 2, he and his guide Dimitar Vukmirović were appre-
> hended by the border patrol on the Yugoslav-Hungarian
> border, where he had gone after failing in his attempt to
> escape to Rumania.
>
> Petričević and Dapčević have confessed and in their state-
> ments described the circumstances which led this isolated
> group to its treasonous behavior.

On the same morning that Yugoslav newspapers published
the communiqué on the death of Jovanović, Ana Pauker was
in the hall of Kolarac signing the Danube Convention. As
concerns her secret activities in Yugoslavia as an agent of the
Soviet intelligence service, I wrote the following in my diary
after a talk with Tito:

During her stay in Belgrade to attend the Danube Conference, Ana Pauker made the following statement: "All this will be over very quickly. . . . The Yugoslavs will not be able to resist."

Actually, Ana Pauker had given Arso Jovanović his instructions. But the Russians made a poor assessment of our ability to resist.

This debacle of the Soviet intelligence service spoiled Stalin's plans for quick liquidation of Yugoslavia's resistance. In his fury he ordered more stringent measures of economic blockade, and the first border incidents began. Tito ordered a note of protest to be sent to the Rumanian government on August 25:

The government of Yugoslavia considers it imperative to call the attention of the government of Rumania to . . . flagrant breaches of relations between Yugoslavia and Rumania. . . . Responsible government officials of Rumania are, in speeches and articles, calling upon citizens of Yugoslavia to rebel and overthrow the legitimate government of Yugoslavia. For instance, Madame Ana Pauker, Minister of Foreign Affairs of Rumania, has openly called for the liquidation of the present state leadership in Yugoslavia.

Russian Prescriptions for Soccer ★

Even sports activities between Yugoslavia and Russia represented a danger for Stalin. Indeed, it was precisely in the field of sports that a complete boycott of Yugoslavia took place at his orders.

First a ban was placed on the Balkan-Central European Athletic Meet to be held in Belgrade in October 1948. The present Yugoslav Army Stadium, then the stadium of the Belgrade Sports Club, had been expanded for the big meet, and a soccer game was in the offing: the Sparta Club of Prague was to play Belgrade's Partisan team. But the management of the Prague club sent a letter to the Partisan club on September

22 announcing cancellation of the game by their authorities.

My official involvement in the field of athletics had begun when, following a big argument with my good friend Svetozar Vukmanović-Tempo, chief of the Political Administration of the Yugoslav Army General Staff, I had become president of the Physical Culture Federation.

One day Yugoslavia's best soccer player, Rajko Mitić, came to tell me that he had been called to the Political Administration of the Army General Staff and ordered to transfer from his Red Star club to the Army's team, Partisan. He had explained, he told me, that he could not betray his club and his fans, and would not do so unless drafted.

I telephoned Tempo. He blasted away at me: had I no inkling that the Partisan team had to be the best in Europe, that the best players had to join it, that this was not his personal wish but a political matter? I gave him back an earful. "For God's sake, Tempo, soccer isn't the Five-Year Plan or the battle of the Sutjeska, it's a game. People choose their favorite teams for no particular reason. They put a lot of emotion into it, that's all."

Tempo yelled back at me, and I let go once more. "Look here, Tempo, when you were three years old you were already reading *Capital*. Well, I was born next to a soccer field. I'm telling you, if Mitić is forced to transfer from Red Star to Partisan, it will become a real political problem. People just won't understand."

We quarreled as never before in our lives. Mitić did not join the Partisan: some of the arguments I had used struck home. Instead of Mitić, center forward Jezerkić transferred from the Red Star to the Partisan team. At the next game between the two teams demonstrations broke out with fans booing the Partisan team. It was a real mess.

A few days later Tito called to ask me what I had argued about with Tempo. I explained the situation to him: that the Partisan team enjoyed privileges the others did not have, that its players automatically became army personnel, that they received salaries and did not do the work they were supposed to do—as for instance in the case of goalman Šostarić: "His only duty is to wind the clocks in the Central Army Club!"

Tito laughed heartily, then asked if I would like to become president of the Physical Culture Federation, if I thought I had any talent for that kind of job.

"I don't know if I have talent or not. When I was in Istocni Vračar grammar school, I was chosen to play right wing, but they took me out after half a game because I was too clumsy. Since then I've had a secret wish to prove myself, if only as an official." Again we had a good laugh, but it turned out not to be a joke because I did become president.

After Tempo and I had made up, he told me that Partisan had been set up exactly on the model of the Moscow Army team, the CDKA. Even in the field of sports, then, the harmful influence of the Soviet model was felt. And practice showed how damaging it was and what the political consequences were.

In delving more deeply into the activities of the Physical Culture Federation, I realized that Partisan was not the only product of the bureaucratic machine. Although it did enjoy a privileged position, many other clubs had also been organized on the Soviet model. For instance, in Moscow the main rival of CDKA was the Dinamo team, said to be backed by the Ministry of Internal Affairs and even Beria himself; right after the war, certain officials in our Ministry of Internal Affairs had set about establishing their own soccer teams. In some of our republics, junior officials (some of them in uniform) were sent out by jeep to collect the best players in the rural districts and bring them to the capitals. Some of these soccer teams were nicknamed "government clubs" by the people, and even today suffer because of their inglorious origins.

On June 28, the very day the Cominform resolution was made public, I was attending a session of the executive board of the federation. One of the matters on the agenda was a complaint lodged by the Proleter club of Osijek about a game with the Milicioner of Zagreb. The latter had good connections in Zagreb's top sports associations, which had taken some decisions to the detriment of Proleter and the benefit of Milicioner. We annulled the decisions and scheduled two new games. A storm blew up, with all kinds of interference. I refused to withdraw our decision—justice, I felt, was on the side of Proleter—and some of the highest officials of the Federal Ministry of Internal Affairs started to take an interest in the case. But the executive board of the federation refused to budge.

Other forums in the republics also wanted to have their own teams. Some high officials started rallying around the Red Star team, although previously they hadn't had the faintest idea whether Red Star was a soccer club or a marmalade factory in Krusevać. Order had hardly been restored in the Partisan when irregularities began creeping into Red Star. I was a Red Star fan, but when the Politburo of the Central Committee issued a directive banning government contributions to soccer clubs, I submitted a report that Red Star had received a substantial sum from the Serbian government. Two of my good friends refused to admit giving the money and almost made me out a liar. A year later I heard that Red Star was circulating letters among its fans asking for contributions, as it "had not received the sums promised it." I succeeded in getting my hands on one of those letters and sent a contribution to Red Star (and not such a small one at that, as I had just received my royalties from a book on Albania). I sent the letter to the Politburo to show who had been telling the truth.

It then occurred to me that I, too, should get out of sports, that sports should be left to the athletes just as the factories had been turned over to the workers. But I remained good friends with all the athletes. As a memento Rajko Mitić gave me his registration from the 1948 Olympic Games.

But the meddling of government and other officials did not stop. Aleksandar Tirnanić, captain of the state soccer team, once complained to me, "A high Foreign Ministry official called me up to tell me that the next game we played was of tremendous importance to our country and that I should take his advice in making up the team. I don't know what to tell him!" I gave Tirnanić a brief piece of advice. "Tell him the next time they choose an ambassador, they should ask you for advice. They know as much about soccer as you do about the staffing policy of the Foreign Ministry."

Vyshinski and a Glass of Vodka Percovka ★

In the autumn of 1948, as a member of the Yugoslav delegation, I attended the United Nations General Assembly session at the Palais Chaillot in Paris. Encounters with delegates from the Soviet Union and the other East European countries were highly embarrassing. On all the fundamental questions on the agenda of that meeting—Berlin, Greece, disarmament, the dedication on human rights—we voted with them; we had not changed our positions on international problems one whit, but the Soviet delegation refused to recognize this. When we met them, they simply pretended not to see us or turned their heads away scornfully.

That was not the way it had been in 1945 in San Francisco, or at the Paris Peace Conference in 1946, or at the foreign ministers' conference in February-March 1947. Vyshinski forgot what he had told our delegates on the eve of the Danube Conference in August: that differences in political views arising from the Cominform resolution would not spoil his personal relations with some of our people. The calculations were obvious: the Danube Conference had wound up exactly as the Soviet Union had wished, and the capitulation of Yugoslavia was anticipated immediately afterwards; but now three months had passed and the changes in Yugoslavia so ardently desired by Moscow had not taken place. Vyshinski now tried the different tactic of ignoring us.

I did not like him. During the Paris Peace Conference I had gone with Edvard Kardelj and the Albanian leader Enver Hoxha, then on a short visit to Paris, to call on Molotov and Vyshinski. They offered us drinks and I said I did not drink, that I was an athlete and also that the doctors had forbidden me to take liquor because of a serious head wound sustained during the war. Vyshinski refused to listen to me. He took a big tumbler, filled it to the brim with vodka percovka (the strongest kind of vodka, with a small hot pepper added), handed it to me, filled a much smaller one for himself, and said loudly, "To Stalin!" At that time I would still have given my life for Stalin, to say nothing of downing a glass of vodka. I drank it at a gulp, and after a few minutes collapsed into an armchair. I was sick for a number of days after.

In 1948, therefore, I replied to Vyshinski's scorn with scorn. But I felt sorry for the old Manuilsky, who had once told me that he kept a copy of my published war diary on his desk in Kiev, where he was the Foreign Minister of the Ukraine. In 1947 I had visited Kiev with Edvard Kardelj. That was one of the saddest journeys of my life: as we crossed over into Soviet territory at Jashi, all we saw was the devastation left by the Germans in their retreat. How great had been the losses and suffering of the Soviet people! That feeling of sadness overcame me once again in Paris as I looked at the graying Manuilsky. How much harm the Cominform had done, how much evil it had introduced into the relations between two countries that had suffered so much!

These memories made me particularly bitter and I spoke with extra sharpness in the discussions of the Economic and Social Council. On the last day of September we were discussing a protocol placing synthetic narcotics under international control. That protocol had originally been adopted by the League of Nations in 1931; Article 8 limited its provisions in such a way as to exclude the colonies under the control of various big powers. That meant that free trade in drugs was allowed in areas where more than 200,000,000 people lived. The Soviet delegate Pavlov submitted an amendment to change this colonial clause.

The delegates of the United States, France, and Great Britain were against the proposal. The United States was represented by Mrs. Eleanor Roosevelt, France by the famous lawyer René Cassin (otherwise president of the Association of Friends of Yugoslavia), and Great Britain by the Labourite

Christopher Mayhew. When I launched an attack against them, old Cassin nervously pulled his beard, raising his hand from time to time, while Mayhew left the room and only Mrs. Roosevelt sat quietly through the tirade.*

When the Universal Declaration of Human Rights came up on the agenda a few days later, I really let them have it. I castigated the Declaration for neglecting economic and social rights and the rights of minorities. In a long address on October 16 concerning the third article of the Declaration, which states that every person has the right to life, liberty, and the security of his person, I brought up the position of Negroes in the United States as a concrete example of the violation of these rights, and particularly the cases of lynching in the South.

A discussion developed. Mrs. Roosevelt had listened carefully and when the meeting was over asked me to tell her candidly why I had taken exception to her remarks that day. "When that State Department expert sitting behind you hands you a piece of paper with ready-made remarks," I said, "then what you say does not appeal to me; but when you yourself speak from the heart, that is another matter." Mrs. Roosevelt laughed and told me that my observation pleased her. "When the Russian delegate speaks of human rights," she added, "it seems empty to me, but you Yugoslavs have some faith. I am sure that if ever the matter of violation of human rights in the Soviet Union or even in your own country were discussed, you would tell the truth. And I see you have made a thorough study of the position of our Negroes."

"I have been acquainted with that problem since I was seventeen," I told her. "I went to New York to the World Congress of the YMCA with a group of young Europeans and Asians. We were full of idealism. But our American hosts immediately broke us up into two groups. The whites were accommodated in the YMCA on Thirty-third Street and the

---

* In our delegation Kardelj gave us considerable leeway and freedom of initiative. Questions were discussed in principle at meetings of the entire delegation, after which the delegates wrote their own speeches, consulting legal and technical experts if the need arose.

coloreds in Harlem. We had a fight right on the spot and asked if all Christ's children were not equal. That was in 1931 and I am very grateful to America. It opened my eyes. We saw so much injustice that not only I but a great many other young men concluded that there was no God. If there had been, how could He put up with such injustice? My mother taught me not to lie, and when I got back to Belgrade, I reported to the YMCA there about the World Congress and my trip to America, beginning with the words, 'There is no God.' "

Mrs. Roosevelt seemed interested in my boyhood experiences in her country, and asked me to visit her in the Hotel Crillon. We spoke about how various civilizations had stamped out heretics. I said Stalin's methods were the worst, and she smiled. "The Anglo-Saxons have a dangerous technique with nonconformists too. They are not killed, but are given the kiss of death. They are suffocated with flattery, and if they do not have enough backbone or enough faith in their nonconformism, they get lost in the shuffle."

For fifteen years I met Mrs. Roosevelt often at United Nations meetings or at her home. When she died, I wrote in the *London Tribune* and the *Paris Express* that I had found in her one of the greatest American rebels. The daughter of a millionaire, niece of one president and wife of another, she had nevertheless preserved her conscience as a rebel against the society in which she lived and for whose improvement she labored. With what enthusiasm she spoke, in 1960, of young students from the North going to the South to fight for the rights of the Negroes, some of them losing their lives in the process. The revolt of American intellectuals against the war in Vietnam fed on the seeds she had sown. When Russell's tribunal, sitting in Stockholm in May 1967, pronounced the first condemnation of American imperialism for war crimes in Vietnam, I recalled that good and noble woman. Her memory is with me still. As I write these lines, her picture hangs above me on the wall.

6.

Alone in a Hostile World

Communist Parties Against Yugoslavia:
the French Example ★

Walking along the Seine one autumn evening during the
United Nations session in 1948, I reflected that of the eighty-
odd communist parties in the world, not one had come to
Yugoslavia's support in her conflict with Stalin.

I had in truth not foreseen this. I had hoped, for instance,
that Secretary-General Ranadive of the Indian Party would at
least try to delve a little deeper into the dispute. But his reply
had made my blood run cold. The Central Committee of the
Indian Communist Party had agreed with all the Cominform
accusations, and Ranadive had rubbed salt into the wound by
remarking: "In our country, our Party had continually spread
the truth among the masses about the heroic struggle and
achievements of the Yugoslav people. At the Second Congress
of our Party, the delegate from Yugoslavia, while transmitting
his greetings, was given a big ovation by the Indian communists; however, the mention of the name of the Soviet
Union called forth even more thunderous ovations." Ranadive
added that he hoped our Fifth Congress would choose another
leadership which would reject the old "bourgeois-nationalist"
line, adopt a new line based on firm friendship with the

U.S.S.R., and apply Marxism-Leninism correctly to Yugo-slav conditions.

That night along the Seine I pondered the reasons behind this. I knew how unbearable was the condition of the Indian masses, and what this conflict meant for them. Perhaps Rana-dive had decided to agree with the accusations against Yugo-slavia simply to preserve for the Indian masses the symbol of Stalin as the principal anti-imperialist. That, I told myself, was the same mistake we had made in the most difficult days of the war, when partisans had gone to their death with Stalin's name on their lips.

Somewhat calmer, I returned to the ambassador's residence at No. 1 Boulevard Delessert, where we were staying. Our host was Ambassador Marko Ristić, with whom I had been friends since starting to work for the Belgrade newspaper *Politika* at the age of eighteen. Marko had been at school with the editors of *Politika,* Mima Dedinac and Dušan Timotijević, and it was through them that I met him and his wife Ševa. The poet-philosopher Koča Popović and the poet Rastko Petrović were also part of the same circle. I learned a great many things from the Ristićs and their friends—it was in their home that I drank English tea for the first time in my life! They were leading Yugoslav surrealists. I did not accept the tenets of surrealism, but I understood their efforts to protest against the older generation's conservative aesthetic concepts. Being with them was like taking courses in literature, languages, composition, and history. (Marko's grandfather was the famous Jovan Ristić, onetime Prime Minister, Regent, and Serbia's delegate to the Congress of Berlin in 1878.)

Marko Ristić became a kind of mentor to me when I started writing books. He not only gave me the idea of publishing my war diary in 1945, but edited it for me and helped me choose the title for the present book.

That evening I talked to Ristić about how troubled I was by all the communist parties taking sides with Stalin against us, although truth and justice were on our side. While I could to some extent understand this on the part of the Indian Communist Party, I could hardly see the motives behind a large West European communist party, like the French, doing the same. Ristić, not only as our ambassador but as a man intimately acquainted with French culture and particularly with progressive French intellectuals, was also obsessed by this problem, and during the next few years we discussed it frequently. When I began working on my biography of Tito, I made careful notes of these talks, and the French edition of the biography, *Tito Parle,* contained an appendix by Ristić himself summing up those talks of ours.* Later he continued to supplement his recollections of the French communists and the Cominform resolution.

My relations with Thorez were much more cordial than with Duclos. I had always had the impression that Thorez was not only generally more sincere, but personally more honest than Duclos. Duclos was really best summed up by an old diplomat who called him a *roublard*—a word derived from "ruble" and meaning in its narrow sense a cunning person who knows how to get money out of others, and more broadly a crafty schemer or trickster.

In his book *Une Politique de la grandeur française,* containing his addresses from 1936, 1937, 1939, and 1945 (not a word from the wartime period), Thorez wrote the following dedication to me on December 20, 1945: "To my friend Marko Ristić—in testimony to Franco-Yugoslav Solidarity—Thorez." Both the title of his book and the dedication are (politically) characteristic in the same way: the *national* and not the revolutionary element is in the foreground.

Many proofs, data, and texts could be cited, to which I could add my personal recollections of talks with Thorez, offering evidence of the same thing: with Thorez this emphasis on the national element, this French patriotism was not only tactical, but part of a policy fully expressive of his feelings, his over-all political concepts, and his temperament. I shall cite only one example:

At the November 10, 1946, elections the French Com-

* *Tito Parle* (Paris, 1953).

munist Party won more votes (5,473,033) than any other party, and the Politburo demanded that the premiership be reserved for a communist—i.e., it put Thorez up as its candidate, stressing that it was doing so "in the desire for closer collaboration with all republicans eager to implement, in unity and accord, with respect for the convictions and beliefs of everyone, a democratic, nonsectarian social policy that would guarantee the reconstruction of France." Thorez personally went much further in the same direction. In an interview with the *Times* [London] of November 18 he said that France could "avoid the stage of dictatorship of the proletariat" through which the Russian communists had had to pass, and that, thanks to the French workers' party, it could immediately create a "new people's democracy." The next day, in a statement to the American agency INS, he remarked that the French Communist Party was *not following the example of Russia* and that his party was associated with the communist movement which had existed in France since the mid-nineteenth century, emphasizing that if he became Premier, he would not immediately implement a communist program. "As I see it, the unity of the country is an indispensable condition for the reconstruction of France." (Thorez, although he was the sole candidate, did not get the necessary 310 votes in the Assembly.)

The bourgeois press considered Thorez's statements to be purely tactical, with the purpose of "dissuading and placating public opinion." My feeling is, however, that they reflected Thorez's sincere desire for the French Communist Party to go its own way, in line with specific French conditions, and not to be a copy, even less a tool, of the Soviet Communist Party. I had this impression also from a lengthy talk with Thorez on December 7, 1946, when he received me at the Hotel Matignon (he was still Vice-Premier in Bidault's cabinet, which was carrying on until December 16, when the provisional government under Blum was formed). Thorez repeated the ideas he had presented in his press statements—which he mentioned, asking me if I had noticed them. I told him about an article of Tito's called "What are the Specific Features of the Liberation Struggle and Revolutionary Transformation of the New Yugoslavia?"

published in the first issue of *Komunist* in October. Thorez felt that his views were in many ways similar to Tito's and asked me to send him a translation of the article, which he had not read. I did so, and when I visited Thorez again (on March 29, 1947) he expressed his approval of and admiration for the article, even repeating certain passages (for instance, Tito's refutation of senseless interpretations of the people's liberation struggle that ascribed its success to the high mountains and forests of our country, our fatalism, etc.). Breathlessly, with his light-blue eyes smiling in his snub-nosed round, somewhat childish face, waving his fleshy hands, he repeated Tito's arguments in somewhat simplified form with obvious satisfaction. . . .

The Second Congress of the People's Front of Yugoslavia was held in Belgrade towards the end of November 1947. Tito's address was given considerable coverage abroad. He spoke of the need "for all progressive elements in the world to unite increasingly in the struggle for peace." But, he stressed, the "process of internal development was specific to each country" and "what was happening in our country could not be transmitted schematically to others, and vice versa." "In some countries," he observed, "the people's fronts did not rise to the task on the eve of the war and during the great liberation struggle" because they had been established by agreement "from above," by the leaderships of various political parties—leaderships which had sometimes been "not only hesitant but even reactionary and traitorous." Thus those fronts were incapable of opposing "domestic reaction and the growing fascist war danger at any price." It was, therefore, understandable but not justifiable if communist parties in certain countries had not organized the struggle against the occupiers and created their own genuine democracy. They had not been in a position to move the broad masses to action in the very beginning and to lead those masses. When resistance had been offered to the occupiers later on, it was not unified, nor did it achieve the results it should have, results corresponding to the wishes of the people. The upshot was, naturally, that reactionaries again took power.

Jeannette Vermeersch, Thorez's wife and a member of the PCF's Central Committee, told me openly, at a lunch at our embassy attended by myself, Thorez, and Marcel Cachin on October 4, that this criticism of the mistakes and short-comings of certain communist parties, including primarily the French one, had met with disapproval on the part of certain leaders in the PCF. Thorez was as cordial as usual, and old Cachin was more than friendly, moved almost to tears as he always was with Yugoslavs ever since his trip to Belgrade to attend the May Day celebrations in 1946—his first meeting with our revolution and with Tito; his old eyes seemed to have retained an unforgettable vision of that May Day parade in Belgrade. Neither Thorez nor Cachin made the slightest allusion to Tito's address at the Second Congress, or the meeting in Poland at which the Cominform had been set up. The atmosphere at the luncheon was friendly and the talk lively, but no matters of political consequence were mentioned as far as I remember, except that Thorez and Cachin criticized certain shortcomings in *L'Humanité*. It was after lunch, when we went to the drawing room for coffee, that I found myself alone with Jeannette Vermeersch, and she asked me if I had seen that the reactionary press had quoted the passage from Tito's speech obviously referring to the PCF, and that the newspapers had emphasized this with particular satisfaction. She lamented that Tito did not take into account the effect his words might have in France, that they did harm to the communists and were grist for the mill of reactionaries. She did not want to accept my argument that Tito knew what he was doing and that the international significance of his address could not be judged on the basis of a passage taken out of context (she had not read the entire speech), still less on the misuse of one passage by reactionaries. She continued speaking, with obvious bitterness, of the French communists' difficulties and of the need for greater understanding of their position, especially on Tito's part. She made no mention of the meeting in Warsaw.

However, that meeting was actually uppermost in her mind. The next day—Sunday, October 5—the PCF paper published documents (the communiqué, the declaration, and

resolution) on the "informative conference." At the conference—and Jeannette Vermeersch must have known this
when she talked with me—the PCF had been criticized frequently, and Duclos and Fajon found themselves in a very
embarrassing situation. Having had to face that criticism
in person, they very probably came back from Warsaw furious. A number of PCF members—and those two above all—
never forgave the Yugoslavs for having taken an active part
in that criticism.

Their annoyance with us was all the greater as they already had an inferiority complex—for understandable reasons, as regards Yugoslav communists and particularly Tito.
But politically and psychologically the nuances of this feeling differed from one PCF leader to another. With Thorez
I have the impression that it was more a melancholy nos-
talgia for something that he had not himself achieved, rather
than envy: during the war Tito had been in his own country raising an insurrection and bringing about a revolution,
whereas he had been in Russia—a fact of which the bourgeoisie reminded him daily, in the press and in the parliament, calling him a deserter. (Stanoje Simić, Yugoslavia's
ambassador in Russia during the war, told me that once in
Kuibishev Thorez had complained to him that the Russians
would not allow him to go to France to lead the Resistance
because they feared spoiling their relations with the Allies.
He had pleaded with Stalin personally, but to no avail.)

Cachin did not have this feeling of inferiority at all: this
old, already slightly senile, but honorable fighter rejoiced
at the thought that there was a country where the revolution had succeeded, and headed by a man like Tito.

In Duclos' case this feeling was mingled with malice. He,
after all, had been in France during the occupation and yet
could offer no evidence of having played a decisive role in
organizing the struggle against the occupiers, or for that
matter of having played any role at all.

Jeannette Vermeersch's attitude was perhaps closer to
Duclos' than Thorez's, but for mostly personal reasons. The
character of this tall, bony woman with her rather lovely but
bold features, soft and hard at the same time, somehow
eluded me. In the light of later events, however, I have

reason to believe that her enigmatic personality played a harmful and even fatal role, and not only as regards Yugoslavia.

By the fireplace that day she must have been thinking not only of the conference in Poland but generally of the position of the PCF vis-à-vis Yugoslavia and Tito. Sentiments of grudging admiration were no doubt mixed with envy that the victory of Tito's party was inevitably set up as an example even by the PCF itself. These comparisons could not fail to detract from the prestige of Thorez's party, despite all the "extenuating circumstances" the PCF found for its failure. (One of these "extenuating circumstances"— namely, that action by the PCF was obstructed by the state policy of the Soviet Union and that the Russians had done everything they could to prevent the French communists from leading the Resistance—could not in any case be used publicly.)

At that time (late September and early October 1947) the PCF was involved in a big campaign to raise the circulation of *L'Humanité*. The attending publicity stressed the figure of Tito, who held a great attraction for the French masses. Posters were up all over Paris publicizing *L'Humanité*, and in the center of each, in connection with a series of articles by Simone Téry called "I Saw Tito," Tito's name appeared in big red letters. The first of these articles began on page one of the October 5 issue right under a slogan from the Declaration printed in bold red letters: "Defense of the national honor, independence, and sovereignty of their countries free from imperialist plans for expansion and aggression—that is the basic task of communist parties." The front page also carried Tito's photograph and the last page a photograph of the May Day parade in Belgrade.

This stress on Yugoslavia, and Téry's undoubtedly sincere but naively expressed enthusiasm, was in keeping with the admiration and sympathy which so many Frenchmen, among them most communists, not only demonstrated but really felt for Yugoslavia and Tito. But Stalin had already launched his underhanded intrigue to bring about a conflict between two of the biggest communist parties in Europe, the French and the Yugoslav. Even the establishment of the Cominform was probably a primarily anti-Yugoslav maneuver to bring all communist parties to heel and to use the Yugoslav Party, once in the yoke, to bridle other parties; if it could not be yoked, then it was to be compromised in the eyes of the others, particularly the French. In these Machiavellian schemes the Russians found fertile soil in the envy felt by certain PCF leaders toward Yugoslavia.

In 1947 Thorez was supposed to visit Yugoslavia. Not wishing a rapprochement between the two parties, Stalin succeeded in preventing him from coming. Instead of going to Belgrade, Thorez went to Moscow. . . .

The publication of the Cominform resolution had the effect of a bomb exploding. There was nothing singular about the case of the communist deputy who, although a member of the Central Committee, reacted with utter astonishment and disbelief to the first news about the resolution, saying that it was a *canard,* a "bourgeois provocation."

The effect of the [Cominform] resolution on French communists and sympathizers was one of great confusion and bewilderment, and even depression, as though at an unexpected defeat. As soon as it was published June 29 in *L'Humanité,* the PCF leaders, in order to satisfy their Soviet bosses, did everything in their power to mobilize their cadres and masses to give full approval to it, for they realized that it had provoked misunderstanding, anxiety, frequently disbelief, and even fear. A directive was issued instructing all Party cells, all mass organizations, and the Party press to explain both the resolution and the leadership's position on it. For neither was clear to the people: the actual significance of the resolution, or the tremendous fervor of the leadership in a matter which to the French masses seemed remote. The latter found it hard to grasp the charges leveled at a party, the Yugoslav Party, and above all at a single person, Tito, who far from being publicly criticized had on the contrary enjoyed the greatest possible prestige. In order to please the Russians, the PCF leadership's anti-Yugoslav endeavors had to be in direct proportion to the great prestige enjoyed by Yugoslavia and Tito in France. The arguments were of course confused and frequently contradictory, so that the masses could not understand the issue. All they could see was that the real reasons for the condemnation were not those set out in the resolution. Communists found it incredible that the Central Committee of the CPSU could err so greatly, but it was also hard for them to accept uncritically the sudden portrayals of the Yugoslav Party and Tito as quite the opposite of what progressive people had believed them to be. The PCF, in any case, vigorously carried out the directive, Duclos and Fajon in the lead. They of course had ample recourse to fabrications and lies from the outset. As always, systematic distortion of the facts and gross calumny had a certain effect—to which should be added the element of Party discipline and anxiety about disrupting Party unity or weakening the "democratic peace front."

I was able to reach these conclusions from the first talk I had, on July 1, with Gilbert de Chambrun (a deputy from the Pierre Cot group). In this conversation, as in the National Assembly, Chambrun considered it his duty to defend the PCF position in his refined way. However, he expressed great fear at the consequences, "dangerous for all of us," of a state of affairs which "provided the reactionaries with arguments and enfeebled the position of the people's forces in the world, especially in France." His only hope was that some sort of "compromise arrangement" would be found— by which he meant, although he did not say so openly, that we would give in. I replied that the only solution was to admit that an injustice had been done, that those who had erred would have to rectify their error, and that someone would have to pay the bill—but not Tito. It is interesting that at the end he admitted that the French communists had "gone a little too far," adding that he would "call their attention to the fact that this kind of writing in their press could only do harm to them and other progressive forces." *Sancta simplicitas!* . . .

It was obvious that the Yugoslav case, as an example (and proof) of interference by the Soviet Union in the internal affairs of a friendly country, had a devastating effect on all their sympathizers (who, like Pierre Cot, Yves Farge, etc., remained friendly to me for more than a year, until it became too dangerous).

General Petit—another member of Cot's group—likewise felt that he should not dissociate himself from the communists, since such a step might weaken the unity of the democratic front. Consequently, the poor well-intentioned general also had to refrain from visiting Yugoslavia with a group of progressive Catholics, although he told me privately that he did not at all agree with the attack on us or with the PCF intrigues against us.

Few of the Party intellectuals believed in the authenticity of the accusations against us; in their frequently opportunistic and frightened hesitations they looked for the most diverse explanations, then finally, sooner or later, bowed to the directives. It was no wonder that those elements in the Party who flirted with Trotskyism hastened to show they were the most fervent defenders of the Party line (although, naturally, they did not always succeed in accurately ascertaining what the line was). Thus Pierre Hervé, in a discussion over the French radio on the very day the resolution was published, accused Tito of blocking, by his extreme position, an agreement between East and West. In this, of course, he agreed with the assumptions of his friend Courtade but not at all with the official Cominform thesis that Tito "had joined the imperialist camp." (In any case, no matter how formulated, the accusations always contained essentially the same idea: Tito had to be liquidated because he was going his own way, taking into account primarily the interests of the Yugoslav peoples and not those of the expansionist policy of Russia.)

I do not wonder now, as I recall my own and others' 1948 illusions, why we believed that the resolution would have grave but in the end salutory consequences for the PCF, and that it could provoke a crisis from which that great party would arise reborn, purified, strengthened in its independence. I wonder even less that this did not occur. It may have seemed logical that grave consequences would result from the blind subordination of Duclos, Fajon, and other PCF leaders to Moscow; from the new, allegedly "internationalistic" policy the resolution stressed; and from the resolution's attitude toward the peasants. But Moscow's "embrace" was already so strong that the essentially opportunistic PCF would not wrench itself free of a political line imposed upon it against the genuine interests of the French people.

A few months later (in February 1949) I had a talk with Pierre Cot in which he called the attitude of the French communists toward us "absurd and idiotic." But, he explained, they *could not* have done otherwise; given its uncertain position in Moscow and its own internal situation, the Party could not dissociate itself from the resolution and thus disavow the CPSU. A few months before, the PCF had experienced an internal crisis that had threatened to disrupt it entirely. According to Cot, the reason for the crisis was the disagreement of certain Party leaders, even Thorez, with the tactics insisted on by the Kremlin, which in that conversation we half-jestingly called "Soviet Union First." In November 1947 Thorez was called to Moscow, where according to Cot he opposed that line. At the insistence of Moscow, Thorez gave in and said he would "try" to implement such a line in France, although he warned that it did not correspond to the French reality and that he didn't believe it would succeed. Active participation in the campaign against Yugoslavia was part of the "disciplined" implementation of that line, although, as Cot put it, many PCF leaders had never believed the resolution justified.

Togliatti, Stalin, and Tito ★

Why did the Italian Communist Party side with Stalin in his conflict with Yugoslavia in 1948?

The Italian Communist Party is the biggest communist party in Western Europe. It has always had a large number of members who thought of socialism above all as a creed for improving human values, and not merely as industrialization and development of the material aspects of life. For over three decades Palmiro Togliatti was the principal personality in that Party, a top Comintern official who, as he clearly stated in the last years of his life, believed there were different "roads to socialism."

Why then did he not raise his voice against the Stalinist dogma in 1948, or in 1949 when he submitted a report to the Second Session of the Cominform on "The Unity of the Working Class and the Tasks of the Communist and Working Class Movement"—a report in which he branded the leadership of the Yugoslav Central Committee "murderers" and "fascists"?

There are various opinions about this. Some point to Togliatti's great flexibility—reflected in his having maintained himself for so many decades, without loss of life or position, while preaching and even implementing his own brand of heresy. And it is true that after the first Cominform resolution, while Stalin and our Central Committee were still exchanging letters, certain high officials in the Italian Communist Party advised us to be flexible, go to Moscow, daub a little ash on our foreheads, then go home and do as we pleased. Critics of Togliatti claim that the 1948 developments were welcome to him because of jibes from the Italian right that he had been too easy on the Yugoslavs in the Trieste dispute; by supporting Stalin against Yugoslavia, he silenced the Italian chauvinists. There were also opinions that Togliatti was getting even with the Yugoslavs for their criticism of the Italian Communist Party at the first meeting of the Cominform. "You wanted to make the Cominform a court for beheading other parties; you were the first to dirty your hands, and now it is your turn to be subjected to the very principles you yourselves masterminded," said a leading Italian communist in the summer of 1948. However, apart from his speech at the Second Session of the Cominform, Togliatti personally did not participate much in the criticism of the Yugoslav Party; it was other communist functionaries who took up the cudgel (especially Vidali, in Trieste).

In 1964—six months before his death in the Crimea—Togliatti decided to describe and explain the position of the Italian

Party on the 1948 conflict. Having paid a short visit to Belgrade, upon his return to Italy he published an article* analyzing the situation thus:

> Much has been said about the origins and circumstances of the break of 1948, but it does not seem to me that everything is entirely clear even now. For communists in other countries, the decisive element determining their behavior was no doubt the profound traditional dedication to unity and discipline which had for virtually thirty years characterized our movement. Examination of the way in which unity and discipline could and should be maintained after the dissolution of the Communist International and in the face of a situation and tasks differing so greatly from those of the past, and differing also from one country to another, had not been carried out.
>
> The expulsion of the Yugoslavs from the Cominform was accepted without discussion.
>
> The absurd insinuations originating with the police—it was later said that Beria had thought them up—were not believed by those of our communists who had become acquainted with their Yugoslav comrades in Spain and during the war.
>
> But these insinuations circulated, creating orientations which were later condemned and shown to be extremely dangerous and harmful, above all for certain parties.
>
> But worst of all was the stagnation which the break and the polemics of 1948–1949 (naturally, together with other reasons) caused in the ideological and political development of our movement in many, indeed most countries.
>
> Concerning Stalin and his initiatives, which all the others followed, assessment is complex and discussion still continues. Certainly Stalin did not grasp how serious and firm the leaders in Yugoslavia were, and how strong their ties with the masses of the Yugoslav people. That was a very grave error which indicated a bureaucratic superficiality in assessing the facts and circumstances causing profound changes in the history of entire nations. But this error does

---

* "Visit to Yugoslavia," *Rinascita*, February 1, 1964.

not explain the basic motives of the break. These must be sought, as I see it, in the manner of evaluation, in the internal development of each country and in the international situation, in the realities and perspectives of the regimes in the people's democracies which appeared after the war.

It is worth recalling that even before 1948—that is, immediately after the war—an examination had begun of the new elements that the new type of socialist society had contributed in terms of political, economic, and social forms. But this examination was interrupted and everything settled by the scholastic formula that people's democracy was only a "synonym" for the dictatorship of the proletariat achieved in the Soviet Union.

Thus was the greatest historical theme of our time posed for the working-class movement—the theme of seeking new ways to socialism, building new forms of democratic power and, on that basis, organizing socialist economies in new ways dictated by subjective and objective circumstances. All of this, unfortunately, was virtually reduced to a problem in terminology. . . .

Today we cannot avoid posing and solving these problems, and they have persisted despite everything. But much time has been lost and mistakes have been made that could have been avoided.

Certainly it cannot be forgotten that in 1948 the cold war against the Soviet Union and against the people's democracies had broken out. International perspectives were uncertain. Many steps, many exacerbations, were unavoidable. But that makes it even more difficult to explain why Stalin, at precisely that moment, provoked a break with the Yugoslav state and the Yugoslav peoples the consequences of which could not be foreseen.

The problem posed here is therefore one of substance: that of programming and organizing relations between socialist states, maintaining simultaneously their indispensable solidarity at the international level and their imperative independence and autonomy.

Even before 1948 there had been discussion of relations between countries of the new democracy, and of relations between those countries and the Soviet Union; but the course of those discussions was not yet sufficiently well known to enable conclusions to be drawn.

It is a fact that cannot be denied that the magnificent military victories of the Soviet Union in the liberation war of 1941–1945 went to Stalin's head. He probably took all credit for them and thought that now he could do anything.

Togliatti's analysis throws much light on the conflict between Stalin and Yugoslavia, and recognizes some of his own mistakes as well. From his article we can also guess at the reasons for his attitude in the period 1948–1952, but as far as history is concerned his assessment of historical processes is the essential thing: that socialism was developing in a variety of forms and that even then the problem of relations between socialist states was posed very sharply.

It is a consoling thought that what was clear only to the Yugoslavs in 1948 is today, in 1968, after events in Czechoslovakia, clear to the great majority of communist parties. Does this not prove that history is, after all, moving painfully, sometimes slowly, but nonetheless steadily forward?

The Chinese Communists and the Cominform Resolution ★

The news that the Central Committee of the Chinese Communist Party had accepted the Cominform resolution in its entirety came as a shock. How could Mao Tse-tung so easily renounce the principle that every country had the right to pursue its own way to socialism, the principle of equality among socialist states?

Only after 1948 did I grasp the great difference between the Yugoslav and Chinese revolutions on the one hand and Stalin's dogmatic concepts of revolution on the other, and so understood what the former two had in common. In both China and Yugoslavia socialist relationships were instituted not by expanding the state boundaries of the Soviet Union, as Stalin had imagined would have to happen, but rather by persevering struggle and self-initiative on the part of the masses. As to the strategy and tactics of partisan warfare, how extraordinarily similar were the solutions found by Mao Tse-tung and Tito! The whole country—the rural districts where the majority of the population lived—had to be the base of the revolution, not just the urban areas. Strengthening partisan activity throughout the country also strengthened the influence of the movement in the cities. This strategy and tactics were developed by both countries, by both movements, although there had been no contact between them.

Then how could the Chinese communists agree to that disgraceful resolution directed not only against the Yugoslavs but against the principles upon which the Chinese revolution had developed and triumphed?

I searched for an answer in the situation they had to contend with in the summer of 1948. The Chinese were in the middle of an offensive against Chiang Kai-shek, who was getting all possible assistance from the United States. Perhaps taking our part would have strained relations with the Soviet Union at a crucial period in their revolution. But this involved the principle of equality among communist parties, of new roads to socialism, and *that* the Chinese could not renounce. I recalled what Stalin had told Kardelj, Djilas, and Bakarić in February 1948: that the Russians had wrongly assumed after the war that "conditions were not ripe for an uprising in China and that [the Chinese communists] should seek a modus vivendi with Chiang Kai-shek and disband their army. The Chinese communists agreed with us, their Soviet comrades, but when they went back to China they did just the opposite. They rallied their forces, organized their armies, and now they are beating Chiang Kai-shek."

Weren't the Chinese communists doing the same thing now? They had agreed to the Cominform resolution against us for tactical reasons, and now were doing as they saw fit, carrying out the revolution in the manner required by conditions in China.

But was that ethical? I was particularly enraged by an article by Liū Shao-chi, Number Two man in China, published in *Pravda* early in June 1949 under the title "Internationalism and Nationalism," in which he fully supported Stalin's position against Yugoslavia. I wondered if he had not undermined the foundations of the Chinese revolution itself by writing that article. I said to Djilas: "Tactics can be explained to some extent, but when someone tries to make a philosophy out of his own prostitution, that is going too far."

In spite of all this, Yugoslav communists retained a principled attitude toward the Chinese revolution. When it finally triumphed and the first Chinese people's government was formed, Yugoslavia was among the first to recognize it. (The Soviet Union recognized the People's Republic of China on October 2, 1949, and Yugoslavia recognized it on October 5, before North Korea, Outer Mongolia, East Germany, Albania, or North Vietnam.) The Western powers tried to talk us out of it, but we stuck to our principles. And when the question came up in the United Nations of recognizing the People's Republic and admitting it to membership, we consistently voted for that proposal.

In a *New York Times* interview of October 3, 1949, Edvard Kardelj drew a parallel between the Chinese and Yugoslav communists:

> Asked about the possibility that the Chinese Communists would follow a similar independent policy, he said that thus far they had supported the Soviet campaign against Yugoslavia "although the situation in Yugoslavia and our stand are completely unknown to them." He added that China and Yugoslavia had "gone through similar forms of development."
>
> He added: "They have liberated themselves with their own forces, they have specific forms in their state and other developments, different from Soviet forms, and so on, and this is the reason why certain publicists think that China will pursue her own road in her internal development and

will stand on the principles of equal relations with the Soviet Union, especially since China is a big country and not small, as Yugoslavia is."

Djilas said much the same in an interview in New York on November 5: "I feel that the people's democracy of China will develop in its own specific way, regardless of what kind of relations it has with the Soviet Union."

It was only after the death of Stalin and the first direct contacts between representatives of China and Yugoslavia that more could be gleaned about the reasons for the Chinese attitude in 1948. A Yugoslav trade-union delegation attending the May Day celebration in Peking in 1955 spent a full twelve hours talking about 1948 with members of the Central Committee of the Chinese Party. The Chinese wanted to know everything about the conflict, down to the last detail; they said they still stuck to their position and were "just talking to us about it." In the Park of Culture in Peking there is a huge map of the world with American bases marked in all the countries around the socialist states. Yugoslavia was represented as part of the imperialist world, with three American bases. Our people protested to the Central Committee and the next day the marks were removed.

A year later members of a Chinese parliamentary delegation visiting Yugoslavia opened their hearts in a talk with the Yugoslav representatives: "We cursed you and now you have the right to throw that back at us a thousand times over. . . . We were hard pressed, in the midst of a blockade, surrounded on all sides, and to be quite honest we did not know enough about the whole matter." When clearer signs of a conflict between the Russians and Chinese appeared, another admission followed: "The dogmatism of Li Li-san and Wang Ming [defenders of the Soviet line during the Chinese revolution] greatly harmed the Chinese Communist Party. . . . While that dogmatism held sway between 1931 and 1934 and those two were at the head of the Party, Mao Tse-tung was punished twenty times, thrown out of the Politburo and even out of the Central Committee."

I do not think it is an exaggeration to emphasize once more the internationalization of the conflict between Yugoslavia and the Soviet Union in 1948. It was not simply a clash between a big state and a small one, it was not merely Yugoslavia's independence at stake, but the principle of equality among socialist states, the right of each country to take its own specific road to socialism.

The Yugoslavs felt this in 1948, despite their own dogmatism, despite their blunders about Stalin and the U.S.S.R. Spat upon, attacked from all sides, we went our own way, defending that principle of equality which today, twenty years later, has become a fact of life from "the Adriatic to Japan," as an old partisan picturesquely put it.

Dmitrov and Stalin ★

Ever since the struggle for liberation and self-determination began in the modern history of the south Slavs, the most progressive elements in the south Slav countries have dreamed of a federation incorporating all the Slav peoples in this part of Europe.

From Austria-Hungary to Czarist Russia, the big powers bitterly opposed this policy and did everything they could to disunite the south Slav peoples so that such a federated state would never be formed. They often drew support from the dynastic and other conservative circles in each of the states concerned. Stalin, too, toward the end of World War II and immediately thereafter, applied the same method: divide and conquer. But in Yugoslavia and Bulgaria as well, there were strong forces headed by Tito and Dimitrov who wanted to create a south Slav federation.

Even during World War I, Georgi Dimitrov, as a socialist

deputy in the Sobranie, protested against the savagery of the Bulgarian soldiers in occupied Serbia—particularly in Toplica, where tens of thousands were put to death after the uprising of 1916. In 1923 he had to emigrate to Yugoslavia; when he came he was met in Niš by Serbian communists. Also waiting for him at the Niš railway station were the bishop and clergy of the city, who came to thank him for the help he had given the Serbian people in the war.

Later, as a high-ranking functionary in the Comintern, Dimitrov helped put relations between Bulgaria and Yugoslavia on firmer foundations. Stalin, however, did not find this to his liking. A letter which Moša Pijade wrote me about his meetings with Stalin showed this clearly:

I came into contact with Stalin only twice, and that within a span of three days in January 1945, when I was in Moscow as the head of the Yugoslav delegation preparing, together with the Bulgarian delegation, the final text of a treaty on Yugoslav-Bulgarian federation. . . . Stalin, during a visit both delegations paid him at the Kremlin, had supported the Bulgarian thesis of a dualistic federation—a federation in which Bulgaria would not be just one of seven south Slav republics, but one in which all six other republics would make up one unit and Bulgaria the other. . . . Although I was then completely under the influence of Stalin's authority and found it highly embarrassing to oppose him, I outlined my differing viewpoint briefly.

When we went to Stalin's for dinner two days later, he brought up the matter again, but now took the view that Bulgaria should be one of seven federal units. None of the Bulgarians dared go back to the idea of the dualistic federation, and I had no further reason to intervene.

Our first visit had been a courtesy visit, and I think it did not last more than a quarter of an hour. We stood the whole time, and the discussion about the federation was limited to only a few sentences exchanged by Stalin, Dimitrov, and myself.

At the second dinner two days later (at which we were served, among other things, an enormous frozen Siberian fish) we drank wine from liqueur glasses—a good thing in view of the Russian habit of giving one toast after another. This was a consequence of the dinner that had been held the previous evening for our economic delegation, headed by Andrija Hebrang, at which they had drunk from normal glasses with disastrous results. The host evidently thought it would be a bit much to repeat the drinking party of the night before. There were other Russians at the table: Malenkov, Bulganin, Vyshinski, Beria, and others.

During dinner we talked of all manner of things, even about various foods and beverages. Stalin asked the Bulgarian minister Yugov if the Bulgarians had good brandy. Stalin then rose from the table saying that as a matter of fact he had some Bulgarian brandy, which made the Bulgarian delegates, especially Yugov, very happy. Stalin left the room and in a moment returned with a few bottles. He showed us one, then another; they were not Bulgarian. Then he showed Yugov the third one; the label was Bulgarian, and Yugov melted with satisfaction—but only briefly, for Stalin asked, "Is it really Bulgarian or did you steal it from Yugoslavia?" Yugov's smile froze on his face, and I did not laugh at the embarrassing joke.

Later I felt even more embarrassed when Stalin insulted Dimitrov. Leaving the bottles on the table, Stalin drew his chair up to Dimitrov, who was sitting on my right. He started telling Dimitrov that at the next elections for the Sobranie some people from the opposition should be elected, and even if there were none, they should have about twenty fascists in the Sobranie as an opposition.

Some sort of short circuit occurred between them. Stalin repeated this three times, but Dimitrov kept on saying that Bulgaria had a Fatherland Front congress, probably meaning that an opposition was therefore unnecessary. I wondered why Dimitrov did not say something more relevant to Stalin's suggestion. An unpleasant smile was probably playing on my lips, for Stalin roughly said to Dimitrov, "You don't understand anything. Look at that one there, he understands!" and he pointed to me.

Dimitrov turned and saw he meant me. He blushed deeply, and I think he could see from my face how embar-

rassing I found the insult to him. It was something new to
me to see a man as important as Dimitrov treated that way.

I don't know why Stalin referred to me several times that
evening as Metternich, and then a few times as Talleyrand.
He said nothing to explain the allusion and it was not clear
to me, as we had spoken of nothing else until then except
the few sentences about the federation with Bulgaria.

In any case, of all the statesmen in the East European countries, Georgi Dimitrov was the most outspoken in opposition
to Stalin's hegemonistic methods, as applied not only to Yugoslavia but to his own homeland as well. He made this very
evident both before the eruption of the Moscow-Belgrade conflict and after. Right up to his death, Soviet agents completely
isolated him among the Bulgarians.

There is ample evidence of this. Josip Djerdja, the Yugoslav
representative in the Security Council Inquiry Commission
for the Balkans, went to visit Dimitrov in Sofia while the commission was there. Dimitrov received him cordially. Djerdja
started talking through an interpreter, but Dimitrov exclaimed,
"There is no need for interpreters between Serbs and Bulgarians. If anyone can get along without them, we can."

Djerdja presented Dimitrov with Tito's idea that the Yugoslav and Bulgarian delegations should adopt a uniform position
on the Macedonian question before the Inquiry Commission,
and Dimitrov agreed without hesitation. He told his secretary
to call the Bulgarian delegates, then asked Djerdja to repeat
his proposal to them. After Djerdja had done so, Dimitrov
said: "On the Macedonian question and on all other questions,
before the commission and elsewhere, the Bulgarians must keep
in step with the Yugoslavs on everything, but a little more
quietly, on a slightly lower key, as the prestige and moral
right of the Yugoslavs justify their pre-eminence, whereas we,
as a defeated country, are in a different position."

Various members of the Central Committee joined them—
Traiche Kostov, Minche Neychev, Damyanov, Chervenkov.
Dimitrov asked Neychev, who was then Minister of Education,

if the university decree was ready. Neychev replied that it wasn't, that he was having trouble with certain formulations, and so on. Bitterly, while looking at me, Dimitrov said: "There, you see how things are going in this country? For years I've been telling them not to do things the wrong way. They want to copy Soviet decrees and achievements, and naturally these things cannot be transferred to our country because the difference between us is too great, even if it were otherwise possible. We have the experience of our comrades across the border; they are considerably ahead of us already, but not so much that we could not take advantage of their experience, all the more so as other conditions are similar. But it is all in vain, these people of mine will not listen, they simply will not."

Even after the first hostile letters were exchanged between Moscow and Belgrade, Dimitrov continued to support the Yugoslav Central Committee. On April 19, 1948, he passed through Belgrade on his way to Prague. Waiting at the station to greet him (on instructions from the Central Committee) was Milovan Djilas:

> I found Dimitrov in a parlor car at the Topčider railway station in Belgrade. The only persons in the car were Dimitrov, myself, and another Bulgarian whose name I cannot divulge for obvious reasons. Dimitrov told me he knew about the letter of the Central Committee of the CPSU and that some of the things in it were accurate. Then he gripped me by the arm and said, "Be firm!"
> I told him that Yugoslavs were well equipped to do so and asked him what they were going to do. He told me that the main thing was for us to stand firm, and the rest would resolve itself.

When Stalin's second letter arrived and the conflict intensified, Dimitrov found an opportunity to demonstrate his sympathies for the Yugoslavs. On May 25, Tito's birthday, none of the Soviet or other East European leaders sent Tito the customary good wishes—except Dimitrov, from whom a telegram arrived with "Fraternal greetings and best wishes for your birthday." (He also appointed a young Bulgarian to deliver a relay-race baton to Tito in the name of Bulgarian youth!)

And when the gallows were being prepared in Bucharest, when Tito was getting urgent summonses from Moscow, Dimitrov again did not fail to support us. When, on *his* birthday, June 17, 1948, one member of a Yugoslav youth delegation in Sofia greeted Dimitrov and delivered a gift to him from Yugoslav youth, Dimitrov, visibly excited, embraced him and declared that he was happy to embrace a "representative of the young people living under Tito."

Dimitrov was seriously ill and the pro-Stalinists surrounding him took advantage of this. After the Cominform resolution Dimitrov was silent for a long time, but on December 25, at the Fifth Congress of the Bulgarian Party, he inserted a few sentences against the Yugoslavs in his remarks. A few months later, he was taken to Russia for medical treatment, although the medical services of his own country were excellent. He died on July 2, 1949. *Borba* and some of our other newspapers hinted that he had been poisoned. History must have its say on the matter. *Borba* carried a warm obituary written by Veljko Vlanović, and the town of Caribrod was renamed Dimitrovgrad.

Not long ago I had an opportunity to pay homage to Dimitrov. After the Soviet invasion of Czechoslovakia in 1968 Bertrand Russell, Jean-Paul Sartre, Laurant Schwartz, and I wrote an open letter concerning Bulgarian claims on Macedonia, the threats against Albania, and the movement of Soviet troops in Bulgaria. The letter was answered by a group of Bulgarian intellectuals, by *Literaturnaya gazeta* in Moscow, and by the Bulgarian ambassadors in Paris and London. The first of these said that Russell and Sartre had not written the letter but that it had been foisted upon them. Sartre was embittered by this—someone else writing his letters! Early in November we met for lunch at La Coupole, in Paris, and after our meal he began writing a reply in longhand on a slip of paper:

We have learned that a certain number of Bulgarian so-called writers and artists have contradicted our declaration of October 9. We maintain our positions without alteration. In addition, we take this opportunity to underline the fact that we denounced the annexationist tendencies of the Bulgarian government and cited a quotation which left no doubt on this matter. We could cite twenty more, of which the signatories of the Bulgarian "denial" cannot be unaware. It might be appropriate to state that the signatories to the denial, inasmuch as it tends to support the annexationist designs of their government, deserve to be called neither writers nor artists, nor socialists or intellectuals. They are an unhappy horde of propagandists, compelled by ambition and fear to servilely approve the Soviet aggression. And they have no political influence: they are puppets whose strings are pulled by politicians. In the same way the "philosopher" Panayot Guindev, who declared that "the unique form of socialism, such as is practiced in the Soviet Union, as well as the general principles of socialism, are obligatory for all countries," thus revives the Holy Alliance and is nothing but an imbecile who tries in vain, in the service of an illiterate dictatorship, to render coherent that which he does not understand.

Sartre stopped, thought a while, and said, "And now we shall tell them how an honest revolutionary should behave." He finished the letter with the following words:

For the honor of the Bulgarian people and in memory of Georgi Dimitrov, one of the few who could in certain decisive moments reconcile revolutionary fidelity with intellectual integrity, we hope that real writers, real intellectuals, real philosophers exist in Bulgaria who are now gagged and who, alas, could only be in the one place that the regime reserves for men of integrity: prison.

Yugoslavia and Albania ★

After the Cominform resolution I talked with Tito about a federation in Eastern Europe and the Balkans. On my visits to Moscow, Tito said: "I often asked Stalin and others how they imagined future relations in Eastern Europe, what they thought of a number of states' merging. "They should not merge. It is the duty of the peoples concerned to decide that," replied Stalin. But after my visits to the East European countries they got frightened and decided to subordinate those peoples definitively to themselves. Without question, the Russians decided to do this toward the end of 1947.

In the first few years after the war, Yugoslavia concluded a number of agreements on friendship and mutual assistance with her neighbors and other states in Eastern Europe: with Poland on March 18, 1946; with Czechoslovakia on May 9; with Albania on July 9; with Bulgaria on November 27; and with Rumania on December 19, 1947. The treaties bound the signatories to extend full military and other assistance if any one of them were drawn into military action. Each partner undertook not to enter into any alliance or take part in any action directed against the others.

But when Stalin launched his struggle against Yugoslavia, his sinister tactic was to have the smallest Balkan country, Albania, accuse Yugoslavia of the very errors the Soviet Union had committed, of pursuing the same hegemonistic policy that Russia had applied throughout Eastern Europe.

Stalin was exploiting the fact that the Albanians, as a small nation, were unusually sensitive about their independence, particularly since the bourgeoisie not only of the big powers like Italy and Austria-Hungary, but also of small neighboring states like Serbia and Greece, had frequently cast avaricious glances at Albanian territory. In areas where Albanians, Serbs, and Macedonians lived side by side, as for instance in western Macedonia or Kosovo and Metohija, one nationality was frequently suppressed by others. Prior to 1912, when these areas were under Turkish rule, both Serbs and Macedonians were subjected to unprecedented terror by the Albanian feudalists, while after 1912 Serbian chauvinists, replying in kind, wreaked vengeance upon the Albanians and Macedonians.

Like the Austrian government before it, the Soviet intelligence service worked mightily to exacerbate these conflicts and so destroy the great achievements of the people's liberation struggle, in which for the first time in history Albanians, Macedonians, and Serbs fought shoulder to shoulder against the occupying forces and their villainous supporters the Albanian feudalists, the Chetniks, and other obscurantists. During the war all those nationalities had their own detachments or mixed detachments with their own national flags, on which the red star symbolized new times and a common cause.

This sowing of dissatisfaction and suspicion was not the work of minor intelligence agents alone but of Stalin himself. In virtually all meetings with Yugoslav leaders Stalin brought up the question of relations between Yugoslavia and Albania. "How backward and primitive the Albanians are!" he said on one occasion. When Vladimir Popović, the Yugoslav ambassador to Moscow, replied that they "were very courageous and loyal," Stalin hastened to reply: "They can be as faithful as dogs, but that is a characteristic of primitives. In our country, the Chuvashes are faithful like that. The Czars used to use them as personal guards."

Or again later, during a meeting with Djilas in January 1948, Stalin had said, "The Soviet government has no designs on Albania. Yugoslavia can swallow it up whenever she likes." Shocked, Djilas had said, "Comrade Stalin, there is no question of any kind of swallowing, but of friendly and allied relations with Albania." To which Molotov replied, "Well, that's the same thing."

These Soviet opinions notwithstanding, economic relations between Yugoslavia and Albania in 1947–1948 had a far greater basis of equality than those between Russia and other East European countries.

Although itself underdeveloped, the Yugoslav economy was

nonetheless more advanced than Albania's. Yugoslavia might easily have exploited Albania had she taken world prices as a basis for trade, as the Soviet Union did. But Yugoslav-Albanian trade was based on Albania's selling Yugoslavia her goods at domestic Albanian prices, and importing from Yugoslavia goods purchased at prevailing Yugoslav prices. Yugoslavia made up the difference from a special fund established for that purpose. This made it impossible for Yugoslavia to extract excessive profits from Albania.

We have seen how Soviet representatives refused to set up the kind of joint-stock companies with Yugoslavia that would promote the latter's productive forces, preferring those from which profits could be made for the U.S.S.R. Furthermore, we saw that the Soviet Union did not wish to invest any capital goods in such companies. (This was even more evident in the case of Rumania, where the Soviet Union invested former German and Italian property as its own contribution to the companies.)

Yugoslavia, however, in setting up joint-stock companies at the request of the Albanians, concentrated on promoting Albania's productive forces. For example, a company was formed to build a rail network—something wholly lacking in the country hitherto. Whole factories were transported from Yugoslavia to Albania for this purpose. The Drač-Pećin line was laid, and preparations begun for construction of the Drač-Tirana line. Yugoslavia also sent equipment for a sugar factory in Korča; a fruit-and-vegetable-processing factory in Elbasab; a flax-and-hemp-processing factory in Rogozina; a fish cannery in Valona; a modern printing press, installations for an automatic telephone exchange, and machinery for a textile factory in Tirana. Although facing major economic difficulties herself, Yugoslavia managed to do all this in two years of cooperation with Albania. In the joint companies Yugoslavia also paid Albania land rent, unlike the Soviet Union in Yugoslavia. During these companies' three-year existence Yugoslavia did not take her share of the profits but reinvested in the enterprises. She even went further and approved credits for Albania amounting to some $40,000,000 in 1947 and $60,000,000 in 1948.

In 1949, in a book on *Yugoslav-Albanian Relations (1935–1948)*, I wrote in the conclusion:

> The question of regulating relations between socialist countries requires urgent and practical solution. Hundreds of millions of people are throwing off the imperialist yoke. Relations between socialist countries can be regulated only in the spirit of socialism, that is, through comradely and sincere cooperation based on the principle of mutual respect and equality, free from slanders, lies, provocations, and tricks of all kinds. In its attitude toward the Soviet Union and all people's democracies, and particularly toward the People's Republic of Albania, Yugoslavia has demonstrated in action its profound respect for that principle.
>
> Renouncing such a principle would not only be uncommunist and deal a grave blow to the cause of revolution and socialism in Yugoslavia, but would have far-reaching and harmful consequences for the further success of progressive forces struggling against imperialist oppression.

My book was full of shortcomings, but I think the conclusion stands. It has been confirmed by the history of the past twenty years.

A New Year's Eve with Tito ★

I spent New Year's Eve of 1948 at Tito's house in Belgrade, where about thirty friends and their wives had gathered. When my wife Vera and I arrived, the atmosphere was serious. Everyone was talking about the radio address Tito was going to give that evening. Unintentionally, I made them change the subject.

Tito had not seen my wife for a long time. "Don't you recognize her?" I asked. "This is my daughter Milica."

"Of course I know Milica. Once in Zemun, in the house of your mother Olga, I even took care of you. You were an infant, not even a year old, in a baby carriage.—Time passes!"

I burst out laughing at the success of my joke, and Tito, realizing his mistake, also laughed. It was perhaps the only gay moment of the evening.

We were all keenly aware of the gravity of Yugoslavia's situation. Economically we were in desperate straits: the Five-Year Plan had already been launched, many factories were half built, but machinery expected from Poland, Czechoslovakia, and the Soviet Union would not be forthcoming. Kidrić said that many of these projects were doomed; some would even have to be dismantled despite the considerable progress to date. Trade with Russia and other East European countries died out quickly. We were supposed to get 3,166 tons of cotton from the East, but nothing was coming in. The mills were idle. Yugoslavia would have to seek urgent help from the West, but there too the Russians were obstructive. Moreover, Yugoslavia's new trade agreement with the Soviet Union was eight times smaller in volume than the previous one. Rumors were rife that a special organization of all the East European states was being set up to pursue the economic blockade against Yugoslavia. Some of Tito's guests said that at the trade talks in Moscow we had been asked to raise our export quotas of lead and copper and to reduce imports of cotton and petrol.

For more than six months officials in the Foreign Trade Ministry had been inquiring about the possibilities of expanding trade and economic cooperation with Western countries, but the results had been virtually nil. Certain circles in that part of the world were simply trying to blackmail us. The time had come, they said, to twist Yugoslavia's arm, to make us pay dearly for the nationalization of foreign property. They were not satisfied with having sucked our blood for decades; now they wanted to make us pay twice the price that their obsolete machines were worth. Someone said it would be cheaper to let them cart the old junk away and build new factories with modern machinery. But where were we to get the new machines? For that you needed gold, and we had none.

I pointed out that in the West many statesmen thought our dispute with Russia fraudulent. That was the general impression in Washington, for instance, and in London. Those who believed the opposite were few in number and felt we could not hold out long. Charles Bohlen, a top Soviet expert in the State Department, had stated on June 29 that the Russians would crush us in three weeks' time. French experts held the same opinion.

"And now that we have held out half a year, they are reverting to the theory that there is actually no conflict, that we made up the whole business to deceive the West. During the U.N. session in Paris I met an American diplomat who spoke Russian and who had accompanied Roosevelt at meetings with Stalin. He had Marx, Engels, Lenin, and Stalin at his fingertips. He spent an entire evening trying to prove that our conflict with the Russians was a fiction, that something like that could never happen in international communism, that it was impossible."

"And what did you tell the genius?" Tito asked.

"I said: 'Let us pray God that this should be! It would be wonderful if the conflict were unreal.' "

Tito was surprised that American diplomats could be so obtuse, so ideologically narrow-minded as to be victimized by their own internal propaganda. Had they forgotten George Washington's slogan, Trade with everyone and alliance with none?

Ranković said that as soon as the Cominform resolution had been published, certain Americans had immediately set about intriguing. An American correspondent in Moscow had visited our cultural attaché to talk about the resolution and had spoken of the possibility of Yugoslavia's joining the Marshall Plan—which, he said, would cause a change in the nations of Eastern Europe that only Yugoslavia could trigger off. Our chargé d'affaires in Moscow had received word that this was a simple provocation, and all officials in the embassy were cautioned not to be taken in by this sort of thing, no matter what the source.

Simultaneously, as we have seen, Soviet intelligence was making a tremendous effort to lure into its service key Yugoslav government officials. Toward the end of 1948 the entire Budapest embassy, together with the Tanjug correspondent there, had resigned and come out in support of the Cominform resolution. (The only exception was the chargé d'affaires, who was in Belgrade at the time.) In the Foreign Ministry itself, Soviet intelligence had made great efforts to enlist the largest possible number of officials who knew the codes and had access to important documents. A number of Soviet agents were discovered in the East European Department alone. One group was arrested, and when their replacements were similarly corrupted, they were arrested too. (In that single department more than twenty agents were discovered during the first two years of the struggle; all confessed.)

Scarcity prevailed. Food and manufactured goods were rationed, and belts drawn tighter than ever before. The rubble of war had barely been cleared away when the economic blockade started. "In my next speech," sighed Pijade, "I shall have to quote Heine: 'The friends I loved and adored, those have done me the most harm.'"

Tito best summed up the situation in his speech that night: "The going is tough. But when have we had it easy? We are used to hardships, and they cannot cause us to waver, to say nothing of breaking us. We believed in victory and fought when all Europe was groaning in the fascist gloom, when many people had lost all hope and had begun to believe that evil had triumphed for a long time to come. We do not waver even today."

The talk turned to the Yugoslav apprentices in Czechoslovakia. Right after the war about three thousand boys had been sent to Czechoslovakia to learn trades in various factories. When the Cominform resolution was passed, the Czechoslovak authorities had pressured them to take a stand against their country. Few succumbed, though a number of Yugoslav teachers came out for the Cominform and gave their pupils special lectures on the subject. The apprentices wanted to go back to Yugoslavia, but the Czechoslovak authorities prevented it, hoping they would give in. In mid-September the apprentices started a protest strike; the police intervened and some one hundred eighty young boys were arrested. Ordinary Czechoslovak citizens helped the boys as much as they could, and in several Czechoslovak towns the situation grew tense.

One of the teachers who had opted for the Cominform told the children they would be arrested upon returning to Yugoslavia. He promised to take them to Moscow if they refused to return to their country. Later he lost patience and started threatening them. "If anyone says he wants to go back to Yugoslavia, I'll knock his teeth in—wait and see! I'll be going back to Yugoslavia in a month and when I do I'll drink the blood of any who insist on going back now."

Other teachers did not share his opinion, and were arrested by the Czechoslovak authorities. The apprentices were then locked up in their dormitories, where they went on a hunger strike. The police surrounded the buildings and cut off their power, telephones, and water supply.

When the Prague officials finally realized the extent of the apprentices' resistance, the latter were allowed to go back to Yugoslavia. All but ninety apprentices gathered their belongings and returned—yet another plebiscite among Yugoslav youth in favor of Tito and the truth. Crowds came out on the streets of Maribor, Sarajevo, and Novi Sad to welcome them back.

The ninety who remained broke ranks. In mid-December another group of twelve returned and sent Tito greetings. Tito read us their letter that New Year's Eve. It had set him thinking about the significance of ethics in our people's struggle for existence—not only now but in centuries past. He expressed these thoughts in his address:

Those who expect to force us, by slanders and falsehoods, to say that the truth is not the truth, must know that it cannot be done. In our country, dedication to truth and justice is a force that does not permit us to be spineless.

We have inherited this quality from our ancestors and consider it the most positive characteristic possible, to which not only every communist but every honest person must adhere. That is how we must educate both the members of the Party and our younger generation. We believe that this time, too, truth and justice will prevail. Otherwise, the outlook for the world would be a very gloomy one. Those who say, to calm their consciences, that the end justifies the means, should realize that this slogan was particularly well known to the Jesuits during the Inquisition. Great things cannot be built by foul means and in a dishonest way. Great things are created in an appropriate manner and by appropriate means. We shall always adhere to this, for otherwise we should disgrace the blood shed for the victory of a just cause in the great liberation war. Those who use dishonest methods against us today will one day have to desist, for the consequences to the progressive movement in the world could be fatal. This also concerns those people who disseminate the most fantastic lies and calumnies about us in the press and elsewhere.

Half a year of struggling against Stalin showed us that the only way out was to rely on our own people, to continue the traditions of the people's liberation war. Our conflict with Russia had already taken on international proportions—that is, it was a conflict not only between Stalin and ourselves, but between Stalin and all East European states, between Stalin and the international working-class movement. He was taking advantage of the conflict with Yugoslavia to impose his hegemony on everyone. But at that stage we still were unable to get help from any quarter. All the East European states, all their leaders, all the heads of the communist parties had fallen prey to the cult of Stalin. All of them invoked the need for unity in the international working-class movement in the face of mounting assaults by imperialism. Some of them even went so far as to insist that although we were in the right, we should sacrifice ourselves to the interests of unity.

But we in Yugoslavia did not lose hope that others too would eventually see Stalinist hegemony for what it was, that they would realize the need for a variety of roads to socialism. The struggle for equal relations among socialist states was at the same time a struggle for equal relations among all states, therefore part of the struggle against imperialism.

That New Year's Eve and afterward we had long discussions about measures to overcome Yugoslavia's isolation. This phase of the battle against Stalin was described by Tito:

> They are continuing the economic blockade of Yugoslavia in order to create economic chaos here, the more easily to implement their plan of conquest. Simultaneously, they are exploiting Yugoslavia's isolation so as to put even greater pressure on Yugoslavia as a state and on the Yugoslav communists. [Our] ties with all workers' and democratic organizations in the world are being disrupted. We are being branded as Trotskyists. Relations between Yugoslavia and neighboring countries are being exacerbated.

At one time Tito voiced the opinion that our young revolution was finding the going tougher than the Soviet revolution in 1918, when eight states sent troops to Russia to defend the Czarist regime: "The Bolsheviks had it easier. They had the support of the international working-class movement." Which was true: at the call of their leader Bevin, English dock workers had refused to load ships carrying reinforcements, food, and ammunition to the interventionists in Russia; on French navy ships the sailors mutinied; and in Yugoslavia mass strikes had been called to help the young Soviet state.

A number of political and organizational measures were taken to break Yugoslavia's isolation. On December 30 Edvard Kardelj, the new Foreign Minister replacing Stanoje Simić, submitted to parliament the five principles on which Yugoslavia's foreign policy was to be based:

1. Strengthening the United Nations.

2. Fighting for the democratization of the United Nations, and particularly against the West's voting machine.

3. Disarmament and the banning of atomic weapons.

4. Cessation of all economic discrimination.

5. Independence and sovereignty for each state and non-interference by the big powers in the internal affairs of smaller states.

The Information Office, of which I had been director since its founding, was assigned new tasks. It had to provide complete information about Yugoslavia, about our efforts to build socialism, our struggle for equality among states. And more effective ways had to be found of disseminating that information in both East and West.

We began, therefore, to have regular press conferences for the foreign and domestic press—both "on the record" and "off" —where officials from the various ministries made statements and replied to questions.

We also published special information bulletins and foreign-policy documentation to acquaint Yugoslavs with international and domestic developments. But progress was slow and cautious. We were still dogmatic, despite the six months of struggle behind us. I myself was such, as the following incident shows. A foreign-policy publication had printed a statement by former Vice-President Henry Wallace:

Marx—the communist God.
Lenin—the communist Jesus Christ.
Stalin—the first communist Pope.
Tito—the first communist Martin Luther.

Although I had taken the initiative in having this quotation published, I changed my mind. I did not like the bold type it had been set in, and the bureaucrat in me was concerned. The result: I almost banned my own publication. My associates dissuaded me; although they did not share the views expressed and the comparison was obviously vulgar, they felt our foreign-policy documentation should print what people thought of us no matter how strange their opinions might seem. So finally I yielded, and the issue was not withdrawn.

Vili Jager, editor of the documentation, literally wiped the sweat from his brow as he left my office.

Despite this, I was one of the more forward-looking bureaucrats, so it may be imagined what went on in the minds of the less progressive. At the turn of the year the idea had spread that the Soviet Union would yield, that it would agree to a compromise. One of our diplomats even made a statement to this effect to *Le Monde* (and the next day, at Belgrade's insistence, denied it). Those who believed this, bolstered their thesis by citing the fact that after the first letters Stalin had not once attacked us publicly. *Bolshevik, Pravda,* and *Izvestia* battered away, though, as did the other Soviet leaders, and on November 7, the Soviet national holiday, Molotov had once again called upon the people of Yugoslavia to rebel. But Stalin said nothing—neither in a *Pravda* interview of October 30 accusing the Western states of wanting to attack the U.S.S.R., nor in an International News Service interview of January 31, 1949, in which he stated that he would conclude a peace pact with the United States and lift the Berlin blockade.

This boosted our hopes. On December 21 *Borba* celebrated the Russian leader's birthday with a long editorial on "Sixty-nine Years of the Great Stalin," with Stalin's picture over three columns. Then, on January 20, the anniversary of Lenin's death, we wrote that our Party had been governed by the "teachings of Lenin and Stalin and had won great victories." Stalin's collected works were on the publication schedules of all our major publishing houses. And, paradoxically, one of the most Stalinist measures in Yugoslavia's postwar political life was introduced precisely during this period, when, toward the end of January, the second plenum of the Central Committee passed a "Resolution on the Basic Tasks of the Party in the Socialist Transformation of the Villages and the Promotion of Agricultural Production," providing for accelerated collectivization on the Soviet model.

Most Yugoslav communists truly wished to "refute the accusations by our deeds," and one of the Cominform accusations had been that we had abandoned the villages to the kulaks. Now at that time we had not worked out any doctrine, nor had we had any experience of our own in implementing socialism in production and in the rural districts. Since we had the Soviet example and nothing else, in our desire to build a socialist system as quickly as possible we fell into the Soviet groove.

But we shortly found ourselves at a dead end, and concluded that we could rescue economy from chaos only if the workers were granted broader rights. Thus did the Yugoslav system of self-management emerge from necessity. But during almost all of 1949 we had to fight against the fatal Stalinist influence over our minds and our environment, despite the fact that we were combating Stalin's attempts to subjugate our state.

The question arises as to when Stalin decided to threaten us with troop movements on the borders. In my biography of Tito I wrote that upon receipt of the first Russian letter of March 27, 1948, Kardelj had stated:

"There is no turning back. I know the Russians well. I know their logic. They will even declare us fascists in order to win moral-political justification before the world for their struggle against us. If they could, they would liquidate us by force. I believe they will not decide to use it, simply for foreign-policy reasons."

I recall that Djilas, Kidrić, Moša Pijade, and I discussed this matter once at Bled during preparations for the Fifth Congress. We had been put up in some lake-front cottages and were writing reports. Pijade worked day and night and was almost out of his mind from exhaustion. He even wrote a letter to Kidrić, who was staying in one of the other cottages, which he began "Dear Moša" and signed "Yours, Boris." We all laughed about this, and Boris suggested we all go to see Moša for coffee. He spoke of the possibility of an attack, and Moša agreed with him.

Svetozar Vukmanović-Tempo has confirmed in his memoirs that there were discussions of such a possibility: "Would other measures of economic or military pressure be undertaken? We all feared that such pressure would come, although we knew that it was unthinkable in relations between socialist countries."

We talked about it endlessly. A few days before the congress Pijade, Blagoje Nešković, and I met to draft the Party statute to be submitted. As we had already agreed to take the Soviet Party statute as a basis, we finished our work quickly. Then we began talking about the pressure from the Soviet Union. Naturally we wondered if they would use arms against us. I remember saying, "If they attack us, I'll fight just as I did against the Germans."

Nešković responded quickly and brusquely: "What's that you say?"

"Just what you heard."

"But that is the Red Army."

"As far as I'm concerned, if they attack us it won't be the Red Army any more, but an aggressor just like any other. If they attack, we will defend ourselves. Although we care about the Red Army, we must say this openly so as to stop those who would compromise it in an attack on a socialist country emerging from a grueling revolution."

Pijade got up and said excitedly, "What could we do but fight? Just let them attack and see! There can be no question about it. Hesitation could be fatal to the cause of socialism!"

The West too was counting chickens before they hatched. News was constantly spread about Soviet troop concentrations on our borders, even when this was not the case—as for instance immediately after the Fifth Congress, toward the end of July 1948. (Later, Soviet troops did mass on our borders.) On July 29 *Le Monde* published a United Press report from Istanbul under the headline "Does Stalin Intend to Use Force?" According to Turkish sources, the Soviet Army was concentrating troops on the Yugoslav border and sending reinforcements through Rumania. After attacking Yugoslavia, the Russians were going to replace Tito with General Peko Dapćević.

I showed the report to Pijade. He raised his spectacles to his forehead, sighed, and answered in the traditional Belgrade way, with every fifth word a pungent curse:

"Damn their Russian hides. This is their black propaganda at work. They want to frighten us. And look at the intrigue they are starting with Peko. That's what makes me think they're at the bottom of it, although the whole thing could also have been cooked up by the West."

Early in January 1949 similar reports came in about troop concentrations along our borders with Albania, Bulgaria, and Rumania. And the same stories recurred in March. Jean-Jacques Servan-Schreiber, then a correspondent for *Le Monde*, arrived in Belgrade and asked me for an off-the-record interview. I agreed, but on March 23 *Le Monde* published the information on page one, attributing it to an unnamed official —he had taken me in.

Djilas upbraided me and wondered how I could have been deceived by such a young journalist. I tried to justify myself. "It's the hand of God," I said. "When I was a young newspaperman I used to do the same kind of thing. On the Croatian coast near Novigrad, in 1936, I disguised myself as a fisherman and interviewed Edward VIII. *Politika* gave it front-page coverage. Now I'm being punished for my sins."

The severe look on Djilas's face melted in a laugh. "It's a lucky thing you didn't tell Servan-Schreiber more!"

In line with an agreement with Kardelj and Djilas applying to all foreign newsmen, I had said "no" when asked if Yugoslavia expected an attack: no military preparations were visible on the other side of the boundary; the whole world expected something like that to happen, but the Yugoslavs were not nervous. . . .

No such denials were issued in the Soviet Union. In April again the world press was full of reports about troop concentrations. Once more I wrote a denial which *Borba* published as its own: this was a creation of Western newspapermen to discredit the Soviet Union, to present it as an aggressor and identify it with the imperialist states. I then added that it was strange that Tass had said nothing; when similar news appeared about Soviet troop concentrations on the borders of Norway or Turkey the sparks really flew, but now there was nothing.

Clearly, Stalin was still counting on his fifth column in Yugoslavia, on our "honest fools" mentality, on our alienating the people with unpopular (Stalinist) measures. The reports about troop concentrations served to frighten us, if nothing else. Only later, when this fell through, did he really begin thinking of an armed attack, carefully weighing the possibility of keeping it strictly localized.

Meanwhile, slowly but surely, we were breaking out of the isolation he had imposed on us.

Moscow Sells Slovene Carinthia for Dollars ★

Stalin was not a Russian but a Georgian, a member of a small national group. As a revolutionary he had devoted himself to the nationality question and had even written a special study on its emergence and development in history.

Czarist Russia had been a "prison of peoples," but they had all been emancipated by the October Revolution. Lenin consistently implemented the principle of the self-determination of peoples, including the right to secession. All nations, peoples, and ethnic groups had been given the opportunity to develop fully in the Soviet Union. But when Stalin took the helm, it was a horse of a different color. Great Russian hegemony began to be reasserted.

Lenin had noticed this tendency and on one occasion remarked that in his Great Russian sentiments Stalin, like all converts, tended to overdo things. This observation is worthy of note. Jovan Cvijić, the Yugoslav sociologist, has noticed the phenomenon of social mimicry among various Balkan ethnic groups who, after the arrival of the Turks, adopted the newcomers' national costumes, language, customs, and religion in order to survive under the terror perpetrated by them. Psychologists have established the manifestation of identification with the aggressor—that is, how converts become the cruelest proselytizers of a new religion, imposing on their brethren, with fire and sword, the viewpoints of the new masters. Stalin, who had total and absolute power, developed this phenomenon to the highest degree. "Power corrupts, and absolute power corrupts absolutely."

His disdain of small nations was particularly noticed by us in his attitude toward the Slovenes of Carinthia. At the end of the war, when the statesmen sat down at the round table with their maps to decide the fate of nations—especially small nations—Stalin was ruthless in using the Carinthian Slovenes to bargain for some $50,000,000 of German property in Austria.

The position of the Carinthian Slovenes, and of the Slovenes generally, has something tragic about it. The westernmost of the south Slav peoples, they are under pressure from powerful neighbors. Their ethnic boundary to the north has been moving steadily southward as the northern glacier bears down upon it. According to official statistics, in 1880 the Slovenes in Carinthia represented around 30 per cent of the population, but due to the pressure of Germanization the figure by 1910 had fallen to 21 per cent. This process is still going on.

There is a similar tragedy in the history of the Macedonians. And the better we of the larger south Slav nationalities understand this, the better we will all get along.

As a small boy, just before the end of World War I, I went with my mother to Ljubljana. My young Uncle Jovan was dying in the hospital there of tuberculosis. Ever since we had moved from the Bosnian mountains to the plains of Belgrade, tuberculosis had been striking our family, and now it had killed my Uncle Jovan too. One gloomy night as I was returning with my mother and her friends from the hospital, sunk in reminiscences of my beloved uncle, I heard a song in the distance:

Oh, Slovenes, where are your borders
Oh, Slovenes, where is your blood
There, at Gorica, there are our borders
There, at Celovec, there is our blood.

I asked my mother what kind of a song it was and why it was so sad. She and her friends explained who the Slovenes were, how they had once occupied a much larger area, far beyond their present boundaries to the north and west. But they had never been able to unite with the Slovenes in other states, and the wave of Germanization from the north had been swallowing them up.

When I grew up I translated Prežihov Voranc's novel *Pozganica*. I also read reports of how the Germanizing of the Carinthian Slovenes had intensified since Hitler had occupied Austria; how the Slovenian intelligentsia was being forcibly evacuated; how the Slovene language had been prohibited, as had all Slovenian cultural and economic organizations; and how the Slovenes' property had been confiscated.

During the war, news of the first partisan battles in Carinthia was received with great joy in our Supreme Headquarters. The Carinthian Slovenes were the only people within the prewar boundaries of Hitler's Reich who fought for their liberation with gun in hand. It was terribly difficult to wage a partisan war in Carinthia, and their forces were scattered many times, but they always rose from the ashes. When the forces of the Third Army and the Fourth Operational Zone broke through the old Yugoslav-Austrian borders into Carinthia, the Carinthian partisan detachment already held all Carinthia south of the Drava. On May 9, 1945, it entered Celovec (Klagenfurt) together with British and American troops.

However, the big powers wanted things their way. In Potsdam, where the future of the world was mapped out, it was decided that Austria should be occupied only by troops of the big powers; units of the Yugoslav Army were ordered to withdraw, and toward the end of May did so with a heavy heart.

In January 1947 the Yugoslav government sent a memorandum to the Council of Ministers of France, Great Britain, the United States, and the Soviet Union officially requesting annexation of the territory of Slovene Carinthia by Yugoslavia. Our principal arguments were the objective ethnic situation and the fact that the Carinthian Slovenes had taken an active part in the people's liberation war.

In March 1947 the Big Four conference on the Austrian treaty was held in Moscow. The Yugoslav delegation was headed by Edvard Kardelj, whom I accompanied. Molotov and Vyshinski told Kardelj that there was not the slightest chance of Yugoslavia's territorial demands on Carinthia being accepted. Gloom settled over the delegation. We learned other things too.

Soviet representatives had often stressed that they considered the main problem in the treaty to be the German property in Austria, which the Soviet Union wanted for itself. The Americans, British, and French realized, therefore, that the Russians would concede a point on the border question—that is, they would drop the issue of the Carinthian Slovenes—in return for an agreement to their liking on the German property. Kardelj telegraphed Tito to this effect.

But Stalin did not wish publicly to take the responsibility for selling the Carinthian Slovenes down the river. Accordingly, Molotov and Vyshinski asked our representatives to draft maximum and minimum demands as regards Slovene Carinthia, "so as to enable them to bargain better with the Western statesmen and try to get as much as possible." As yet unaware of the game being played, we drew up such proposals.

But the fate of the Carinthian Slovenes had been settled long before. Without the knowledge of the Slovenian Liberation Front leaders or the National Committee of our Anti-Fascist Council, Stalin had sent the following letter to Austrian Chancellor Renner, leader of the Austrian social democrats, in May 1945:

Esteemed comrade,
    I thank you for your communication of April 15. Please

do not doubt that your concern over the independence, *integrity*, and progress of Austria is my concern as well.

I am ready to extend any help that Austria might need, to the extent of my ability and possibilities.

Please excuse the tardy reply.

J. Stalin

As Pijade put it later, "the right to self-determination by the Carinthian Slovenes was traded for $50,000,000 over and above the $100,000 that the three Western partners had earlier been willing to grant their Eastern partner." And we the Yugoslav communists—Stalin's "honest fools"—had not the faintest hint of all this, and went on pledging our loyalty to him whenever the occasion arose.

The Soviet Ultimatum of August 19, 1949 ★

In the summer of 1949, the battle between Yugoslav security forces and Soviet agents in Yugoslavia was drawing to a close. All the Russians' secret organizations had been broken up and their members arrested. Among those apprehended were Russian White Guards who had moved to Yugoslavia after the Russian Revolution—some of whom had acquired Soviet citizenship after 1945. Others taken into custody had worked for the Gestapo, whether secretly or openly, during the occupation. (Petar Oranski of Kragujevac, for example, had taken part in the Germans' mass execution of seven thousand workers, high-school students, and others in his home town on December 21, 1941.)

The Soviet embassy lodged sharply worded protests about these arrests and exchanged several notes with our Foreign Ministry. But the climax was reached on August 19, 1949, when Molotov sent the Yugoslav government a veritable ultimatum. The note was delivered to the porter of the Foreign Ministry building in Kneza Miloša Street at three a.m. Ivo Vejvoda, the head of the East European Department, read it

about seven-thirty and sent it immediately to Kardelj. A half
hour later, Kardelj telephoned Vejvoda and asked him what
he thought of it. "It could be worse," said Vejvoda.

"But it is the worst so far!" answered Kardelj. And with
that he called Djilas, Kidrić, and Vukmanović to his office to
discuss the note. Tito, on Brioni Island, was informed of the
contents.

The note stated, among other things, that the arrested White
Guards "like all Yugoslav patriots, do not approve of the generally known and impermissible behavior of the Yugoslav
government, which has deserted the camp of democracy and
socialism to join that of international capital, now endeavoring to harm the Soviet Union to the greatest possible extent
so as to win the plaudits of representatives of international
capital and thus satisfy its ambitions."

It went on to say that the White Guards had freely expressed their political convictions. But "the free expression of
democratic views is not considered a crime in any country
except those with fascist regimes." The Yugoslav government
was then compared with the Tsaldaris government in Greece
and Franco's regime in Spain.

One need only observe everything going on in Yugoslavia
to know for certain that there is no longer any question of
a people's government or a democratic and socialist order
in Yugoslavia.

Indeed, what kind of a socialist system is it in Yugoslavia
when the country has been placed under the control of
foreign capital and the leaders of the Communist Party of
Yugoslavia are at war with the communist parties of the
whole world? . . .

Apparently, the Yugoslav Government does not intend to
take any measures against those guilty of these fascist practices.

If this is so, the Soviet government must assert that it
will not reconcile itself to such a state of affairs and that
it will be forced *to resort to other more effective means,* in-

dispensable for protecting the interests of Soviet citizens in Yugoslavia and of calling to order the fascist thugs who have gone too far.

A reply arrived from Tito in Brioni. He assessed the situation as serious. A few days before, news had arrived of Soviet troop concentrations in the neighboring countries and of the creation of a special Cominform army group to attack Yugoslavia. Each of those present at the meeting with Kardelj, therefore, began to "carry out the task assigned him earlier by the Central Committee," as Vukmanović described it in his memoirs. "As I had been appointed commander-in-chief of the partisan detachments of Yugoslavia, I immediately took all necessary measures to alert the entire organization. We informed Tito of everything, and he agreed with the steps taken. Orders were issued for military maneuvers in the north, where we expected an attack."

Djilas, telling me that day of the contents of the note, also informed me that food stores, archives, and factory equipment were being evacuated from Vojvodina further south, especially to Bosnia and Herzegovina.

How awful is the suspense of waiting for an enemy offensive! We knew it well from the war. Once it starts, the going is easier—you see the main line of attack and maneuver accordingly. But until then you are up against a wall and waiting for the enemy to shoot when he feels like it.

Kardelj called me and told me to take special care that our press did not give Russia any excuse for an attack. I kept my eyes wide open. But the devil never sleeps. In the *Literary News* of September 6 an article entitled "Krylov or Aesop?" appeared:

A diplomatic note is a devilish thing. You write it, you see how elegant it looks, and you think, "No one is as clever as I! Who could go this one better?"—especially if you are a lawyer by profession.

But the bad part is that usually you get a reply. Well,

well, look at the way he is replying. Just as though he were
thinking: "Boy, did I fix him!"

There are famous notes. And there are even more famous
replies. For instance, the note from Austria-Hungary to
Serbia in July 1914, in which foxy Austria asked for a number of things: changes in Serbian textbooks, and so on; in
addition, they wanted Austrian courts to investigate the
Sarajevo assassination and interrogate Serbian citizens in
Austria. The note is famous—famous for the insolence with
which the great power Austria-Hungary tried to interfere
in the internal affairs of the small state of Serbia, famous
for leading to World War I. But if the Austrian note was
famous, the reply of the Serbian government was doubly so.

The Serbian government—the government of a small
country whose capital lay on one bank of the Sava and
Danube, while from the other bank, belonging to Hungary,
you could cast stones at Belgrade—this Serbian government
agreed to all of Austria-Hungary's demands (demands to
which it would not have agreed had it been a big power—
but then such impudent demands would not have been
made of it), and refused only the demands that the Austro-
Hungarian authorities carry out an investigation on its territory. Thus did little Serbia refuse to allow the great power
of Austria-Hungary to violate its sovereignty. The little dog
dared to bark at the big elephant—so goes [the Russian
writer] Krylov's fable. The elephant died and the little
Serbian dog got a big chunk of the elephant. A big power
disappeared from the map of Europe as though it had never
been. True, little Serbia disappeared, too, but its place was
taken by a bigger Yugoslavia. The end of the story was not
taken from the Krylov fable. . . .

It is far stupider when modern diplomats—those who brag
loudly, like circus barkers, about their monopoly over Marxism-Leninism—dole out lessons about Marxism in diplomatic
notes, having nothing better to do than fly in the teeth of
Krylov's fables. . . .

I looked to see who had written this marvelous article and
found the name "Psić Zubatović" (Toothy Houndson). Sweat
broke out on my forehead. I called Djilas. "Look at the *Liter-*

ary News and read the article by Pijade. He has signed his pseudonym, one he used before World War I when he was working on the *Pijemont*."* That same day the public prosecutor's office banned this issue of the *Literary News*. I consoled Pijade while we were at the movies, watching a western. "Never mind, old man. That's the best article ever to come out of our fight with the Cominform, and I'll bet that some day it will enter the *First Anthology of Yugoslav Journalism*."

"Damn that Stalin. Who does he think he is, threatening us!" growled Moša in reply.

---

* The *Pijemont* was a paper of the Serbian secret military society the Black Hand, headed by Colonel Apis.

7.

Inquisition in Eastern Europe

Trials in Budapest, Sofia, and Prague ★

On September 28, 1949, the Soviet government delivered to the Yugoslav government a note in which it unilaterally canceled the treaty of friendship and mutual aid between the two countries:

> During the trial which ended on September 24 in Budapest of the state criminal and spy Rajk and his accomplices, who were agents of the Yugoslav government, it was revealed that the Yugoslav government had for some time been engaged in extremely hostile and subversive activity against the Soviet Union, hypocritically masked by false declarations of "friendship."
>
> The trial in Budapest also showed that the leaders of the Yugoslav government have been pursuing and continue to pursue [these] hostile and subversive activities not only at their own initiative but also on direct instruction from foreign imperialist circles.
>
> The facts revealed at this trial further showed that the present Yugoslav government is completely dependent on foreign imperialist circles and has been transformed into an

instrument of their aggressive policy, which was to have led, and actually did lead, to liquidation of the independence of the Yugoslav Republic.

All these facts testify that the Treaty of Friendship, Mutual Assistance, and Postwar Cooperation between the U.S.S.R. and Yugoslavia concluded on April 11, 1945, has been brutally violated by the Yugoslav government.

On the basis of the above, the Soviet government states that the Soviet Union considers itself released from the obligations stipulated in the afore-mentioned treaty.

By order of the Government of the U.S.S.R.

Deputy Minister of Foreign Affairs

A. Gromyko

This note clearly illustrates the goals Stalin wished to achieve in his battle against Yugoslavia. The trial had been designed to present Yugoslavia to world public opinion as a state with hostile designs on her neighbors, thus justifying aggressive Russian behavior toward her as an "imperialist base" in the Balkans and Central Europe.

As soon as the Soviet Union had done so, the other East European countries canceled their treaties of alliance with Yugoslavia: Poland and Hungary on September 30, Bulgaria and Rumania on October 1, and Czechoslovakia on October 4. The entire action had obviously been co-ordinated by Moscow.

The trial of László Rajk, Hungary's Minister of Foreign Affairs, involved a number of codefendants: Dr. Tibor Szónyi, a member of the legislature; Gyorgy Palfi, a Lieutenant General in the Hungarian Army; Lazar Brankov, former chargé d'affaires of the Yugoslav embassy in Budapest; and others. It was not the only one of its kind. The first such trial had taken place in May 1949 in Albania, when Koci Xoxe, Vice-Premier of Albania, was placed in the dock. Then in Sofia, in December, Traiche Kostov, former Vice-Premier of Bulgaria, and a few others were accused. The wave of trials spread through all Eastern Europe, the last significant one being held in Prague in November 1952, when the accused included no less than eleven prominent Party and government officials: Rudolf

Slansky, secretary-general of the Czechoslovak Party's Central Committee; Bedrih Geminder, chief of the International Department of the Central Committee's Secretariat; Vladimir Klementis, Foreign Minister; André Simon, editor of the Party newspaper *Rude Pravo;* Jozef Frank, deputy secretary-general; Bedrih Reicin, Deputy Minister of National Defense; Karel Svab, Deputy Minister of Internal Affairs; Rudolf Margelijus and Artur London, Deputy Ministers of Foreign Trade; Oto Fischl, Deputy Minister of Finance; and Vavro Hajd, Deputy Minister of Foreign Affairs.

The historical documents indicate that all these trials were organized in one place: Moscow. After Stalin's death, which sparked off a series of "rehabilitations," the materials published offered clear evidence that one and the same hand sent these many high-ranking officials to death. If a comparison is made of the indictment and testimony of the accused, it is also obvious that the trials were planned in one place. The goal was to represent Yugoslavia as acting on instructions from American, British, and French imperialists and menacing the independence and social order of the states concerned.

According to Rajk's indictment, Yugoslavia had organized a spy network in Hungary as far back as 1945 for the purpose of overthrowing the socialist system and bringing down the government. Instructions were also allegedly sent out from Belgrade for the murder of prominent Hungarian leaders. These plans were accelerated, according to the indictment, by Tito's visit to Hungary in December 1947. In October 1948, after the Cominform resolution, Aleksandar Ranković, then Yugoslav Minister of Internal Affairs, went to Hungary secretly. In the vicinity of Paks, in the hunting preserve of Horthyite landowner Antal Klein, he supposedly met Rajk to give him final instructions for the coup d'état, at which time he was accompanied by Karlo Mrazović, Yugoslav ambassador in Budapest, and a good-looking Hungarian woman named Györgyi Tarisznyás.

The indictment also claimed that Rajk had been a foreign spy while in Spain with the International Brigade. After the

Spanish war he established contact in the concentration camps of Gurse, Vernet, and Saint Cyprien with Yugoslavs who had fought in the Brigade. The indictment further claimed that more than one hundred fifty Yugoslav veterans of the Spanish war had been agents of foreign intelligence services and were taken on by the Gestapo, which sent them back to Yugoslavia secretly in 1941, when the uprising broke out. Among the Yugoslavs so named were Aleš Bebler, Ivan Gošnjak, Božidar Maslarić, Kosta Nadj, Karlo Mrazović, Svetozar Vukmanović-Tempo, and Svetislav Stevanović—although the last two had never been to Spain, and Bebler, Maslarić, and Mrazović had never been in the concentration camps cited. (Maslarić had made his way from Spain to North Africa and thence to the U.S.S.R., while Bebler and Mrazović had been evacuated to Paris because of their grave injuries, and from Paris returned to Yugoslavia.)

Similar indictments were submitted in Tirana, Sofia, and Prague. Yugoslavia was supposedly getting ready to conquer Albania and divide it up with monarcho-fascist Greece. Kostov was accused of plotting to use the south Slav federation (an "imperialist idea") for annexing Bulgaria to Yugoslavia. He was described as the ringleader of the plot in Bulgaria; as an intimate and confidential associate of the Yugoslav leaders, through whom he established contact with imperialist intelligence centers; and as a villainous, bitter enemy of the Russians, opposed to "Dimitrov's policy of rapprochement between Bulgaria and the Soviet Union."

Kostov's indictment further claimed that Macedonian political and cultural organizations in Pirin Macedonia were "agents of the Yugoslav state security administration" and responsible for the wish of the Pirin Macedonians to unite with the People's Republic of Macedonia. The indictment stressed that the imperialists were to blame for the Pirin Macedonians' desire, which Kostov had supposedly encouraged. At the trial itself all the accused, with the exception of Kostov, confessed guilt on all counts. As we shall see, the same methods used against the old Bolsheviks in the Soviet purge trials of

1935–1938 were revived during the trials in the East European countries.

Soviet propaganda media raised a storm against Yugoslavia not only in Eastern Europe but throughout the world. In London, for instance, James Klugman, one of the top people in the British Communist Party, used material from the Rajk, Xoxe, and Kostov trials to write a book entitled *From Trotsky to Tito*. In it he stressed the alleged ties between Belgrade and the British and American intelligence services. He could not have done them a greater favor: these lies ground out by the Moscow propaganda machine were very useful to the Western secret services, which gained free publicity and profited from the intensified fear of their activities in Eastern Europe.

I had known Klugman before the war, when he worked with Lola Ribar in international youth peace organizations. During the war he had been a British intelligence officer in Cairo maintaining ties with resistance movements in Europe. Today he is the official historian of the British Communist Party. He no longer mentions *From Trotsky to Tito*, since after Stalin's death the Soviet and all other East European governments publicly disclaimed the accusations made at those trials.

Marshal Voroshilov Repents ★

Man feels the full impact of evil when it strikes him personally. I have been persuaded of this on several occasions, one of them my trip to attend the U.N. session in New York in 1949. At a station near Cherbourg, where we were to embark on the *Queen Elizabeth*, I got off the boat train to buy a newspaper. In it was a report of the indictment of László Rajk.

Our whole delegation was on that train: Kardelj, Djilas, Bebler, Veljko Mičunović, Milan Bartoš, Janez Stanovnik, and others. We started to talk about the article. How could Stalin have fallen so low as to use such base methods, fabricate such monstrous lies? Someone—I no longer remember who—said,

"Now I understand how the old Bolsheviks must have felt during the purge trials in 1936–1938."

I remembered a most instructive folk tale about a priest and the plague. The terrible disease had struck at a certain village, carrying away a number of souls each day. The people bewailed their fate to the priest, who told them, "People are dying here and there, but the village remains." When the plague struck his own wife, he fled into the street wailing, "Help, help, the whole village is dying."

Although I had not been a Party member during the Moscow trials, I could not help linking up the truth about Stalinism in 1935–1938 with the truth in 1949, when Stalin "started his mass export of gallows," as Moša Pijade put it in one of his articles. And I was tortured by the same thoughts one summer day in 1962 when I was studying the Trotsky papers in the Houghton Library at Harvard University. What I was looking for was material on his ties, if any, with the Young Bosnians and other secret youth organizations in the years before 1914, when he had spent some time in the Balkans. But I could not resist looking over his archives from later years after he had been expelled from Russia, especially those of 1936–1938.

Trotsky received *Pravda* regularly, and his copies dealing with the trials and the accusations that he was an imperialist spy caught my eye. He had read and underlined every second or third line with a red pencil. His discomposure is evident from the fact that the red pencil seems frequently to have broken, leaving only a deep indentation on the paper; he must have been pressing very hard.

I have not changed my views that Trotsky's doctrine was very authoritarian: he was the first in Russia to create an efficient state machine, the backbone of the later bureaucracy. But that summer day in the Houghton Library I grasped the full weight of Stalin's crimes against the old guard of Bolsheviks and Trotsky himself, who was tracked down in Mexico in 1940 and slain in cold blood.

I started to link up the purges in the U.S.S.R., which began in December 1934 with the murder of the old Bolshevik Sergei Mironovich Kirov, secretary of the Leningrad Regional Committee and member of the Politburo, with the purges in the East European countries in 1949. (According to some sources, Stalin had Kirov killed so as to create the pogrom-like atmosphere needed for executing his infernal plan of murdering revolutionaries in the U.S.S.R. en masse.) For the indictments authored by Vyshinski in 1936–1938 clearly served as a model for the trials in Budapest, Sofia, and Prague in 1949–1952. The methods were the same: interrogation of the accused, their "softening up" before the trial, their "confession" of everything they were supposed to confess.

In 1969 I spent New Year's Day reading materials from the trials of Rajk, Kostov, and the Czechs Slansky and Klementis. I was deeply immersed in them, and my head spun with the horror of it all. Just then the Bosnian writer Rodoljub Čolaković, an old revolutionary, sent me the second volume of his book *The Story of a Generation,* covering the period from early 1933 to the end of 1936, during which Čolaković spent much time in the Soviet Union. He was there when Kirov was killed, and in his book writes of the slaughter which followed when so many lost their lives, including Yugoslav revolutionaries who had fled the terror in their own country.

It was a long time since I had devoured a book as I did Čolaković's, so strongly imbued as it was with a sense of truth and justice. How warmhearted were his descriptions of meetings with the Russian man in the street! How he loved him, how he loved Russia, and how he admired the Russians' great effort to put an end to their historical backwardness, foster industrialization, and raise human relationships to a higher level! Openly and honestly, Čolaković squares accounts with Stalinism, its murder of the human soul, its slaughter of the human body. Expressing his pain at the loss of one of our most admirable revolutionaries, Rade Vujović, Čolaković exclaims: "Stalin killed more good communists than the bourgeoisie of the whole world put together."

No calculation has yet been made of how many people were killed in the purges in Eastern Europe, or how many were cast into prisons and camps between 1948 and 1953. (In Czechoslovakia the number of arrested ran into tens of thousands.) Only with the period of rehabilitation after Stalin's death did we begin to learn more about this ghastly period.

Traiche Kostov was rehabilitated on April 11, 1956, when Todor Zhivkov, first secretary of the Communist Party of Bulgaria, stated at a meeting of Sofia Party members that the accusations against Yugoslavia and the Yugoslav leaders made at Kostov's trial had been unfounded.

Two weeks earlier, in Hungary, Rakosi had declared that a Supreme Court investigation had shown the accusations against Rajk to be "fabricated." Rajk's solemn public rehabilitation took place on October 7, when the victims were buried with ceremonies in the presence of Hungarian dignitaries—a strange bit of hypocrisy. Deputy Premier Antal Apró spoke: "Never have we had a more tragic duty than this one, as we rehabilitate our dead comrades whom we cannot resurrect. We regret profoundly that we believed in the malicious slanders which took these comrades to their martyrdom. All those to blame for their deaths will be held responsible for their misdeeds. Never again will such a grisly thing be allowed to happen."

In Czechoslovakia rehabilitations were slow in coming. Novotny agreed only to revoke the accusation that Slansky and Klementis were Yugoslav agents. It was not until after his demise in January 1968 that the rehabilitation process got under way—only to be interrupted by the Soviet invasion in August.

No one can make the dead rise again. But Stalin's purges also destroyed many lives they did not kill outright. In his book *The Life of Josip Broz*, Vilko Vinterhalter has described how various high-ranking Soviet functionaries repented what they had said and done, at Stalin's orders, against Yugoslavia between 1948 and 1953.

Marshal Voroshilov had been highly respected by the Yugoslav partisans. A hero of the Russian Revolution and civil war, his name was even woven into a song from the villages of Montenegro sung when fateful battles were being fought on the Eastern Front:

> Three marshals
> On three fronts
> All three sworn
> To strangle capitalists
> Voroshilov in the north
> Destroys Hitler's bands.

But when Stalin launched his campaign against Yugoslavia, Voroshilov was sent from one East European country to another to say the cruelest things about Yugoslavia. For instance, on August 22, 1949, in Budapest: "How sad is the fate of the present leaders of Yugoslavia who have fled from the camp of socialism and democracy to the camp of capitalism and reaction. These traitors to socialism are restoring the capitalist system in their country, liquidating the democratic achievements of the Yugoslav people, and introducing bloody fascist terror."

Stalin died in 1953, and in the summer of 1955 Khrushchev and Bulganin arrived in Belgrade to repent of their deeds. A year later Tito went to Moscow, and Voroshilov was among the first to greet him: "In greeting you, Comrade Tito, the Soviet people greet friendly Yugoslavia and the peoples of your country, to whom the working people of the U.S.S.R. are bound by firm and strong friendship."

At dinner the old Marshal wept: "What a dunce I am. What stupidities I had to mouth at Stalin's orders! How ashamed I am! Forgive me, please."

How strange that Stalinism was able to distort even that legendary hero of the battlefield, Marshal Voroshilov. . . .

But in the hard times of 1948, when threatened on all sides, the Yugoslav man in the street did not lose his faith that truth and justice would prevail. On September 5 *Borba* published a resolution passed by the workers of the Slavija Construction Company in Belgrade concerning the Cominform attack: "Our collective energetically refutes the lies and slanders and is certain that the truth will prevail and that the slanderers will one day blush when their people ask them why they did not tell the truth."

Kostov, Klementis, and André Simon ★

At the Moscow trials of 1936–1938 and the East European trials of 1949–1952, almost all the accused confessed to everything in the indictments. Old revolutionaries, men of courage whose fate had hung in the balance for decades, who had no fear of death, suddenly agreed to take the blame for actions, to confess to crimes which, as history has shown, were totally fabricated. How is it possible to explain this phenomenon?

The problem has tortured me to this very day. I knew personally some of the men who were tried in the 1949–1952 period—as for example André Simon, editor of the Czech Party newspaper *Rude Pravo*. We had seen each other frequently during the Paris Peace Conference in 1946, and in 1947 he had visited me in Belgrade in the company of the world-famous journalist Egon Ervin Kiš, the most talented correspondent I have ever known.

Simon had told me that Kiš loved wild duck, so on the eve of their arrival Djilas and I went hunting in Srem, near the Opovo monastery. I had no luck, though I shot constantly, but Djilas brought down about a dozen birds. As we were going home, Djilas said: "I know Boro [my son] asked you to bring back wild-duck feathers, so take a couple of ducks so he won't be disappointed. And I know you have guests for dinner."

Dinner with Kiš and Simon lasted until the small hours, almost until dawn. I had the same impression of Simon as before: he was an honest revolutionary, intelligent and courageous.

I was all the more shocked, therefore, to hear in 1953 that

he had confessed his guilt at the trial in Prague and asked to be hanged for his misdeeds. How had they broken him? What could have happened to make him confess to the most horrible crimes, which he had never committed, particularly as he was truly a man of culture?

The same thorny question tormented me in connection with Vladimir Klementis, whom I also had known, although not as well as Simon. We had met a few times during the Paris Peace Conference, and I recalled some of our chats. Once he asked me if I had known any prewar Czechoslovak revolutionaries. I told him that a little before the war broke out I had been a courier for our Central Committee and had helped Jan Šverma get through Belgrade and out of the country. Klementis was glad to hear this and a sentimental smile lit his face. Šverma had been the hero of the Slovak uprising of 1944, during which he had lost his life.

Even after the Cominform resolution, Klementis did not break off personal ties with me. In the autumn of 1949, when Stalin's campaign against Yugoslavia was at its peak, the Rajk trial under way, and the Cominform preparing another resolution, we were on the *Queen Elizabeth* together—heading for the United Nations session in New York. On the ship I went in for sports as usual. As a former ping-pong champion (in 1930 I had won the Queen Marija prize—a fountain pen) I played in all the tournaments and came away with all the prizes. One morning I was playing a hard match with a young American when Barbara Castle, then a British Labour M.P., appeared, her beautiful red hair shining in the sun. "Come up on the sun deck, Vlado," she said to me innocently. "We're playing deck tennis and we need a fourth for doubles."

I left the American and went on deck with my English colleague. When I saw who our partners were, I realized that her charm masked the calculations of a politician. They were none other than the British State Secretary in the Foreign Office, Hector MacNeil, and—Vladimir Klementis. Thinking it awkward for Klementis to be seen playing with me by his fellow delegates, I was about to ask to be excused, when he

said, "We two Slavs will beat the dickens out of these Brit-
ishers!"

We did, in fact, beat our British friends, Barbara Castle
complaining bitterly about my lobbing. I begged her pardon.
"You understand, I know how a gentleman should behave,
but deep inside me there is a Balkan male animal who won't
permit me to be gallant and lose the game to a lady."

I did not see Klementis again. But when I read that he too
had confessed to everything, my blood ran cold. How had they
made him do it?

Traiche Kostov I had also known personally, and his case
was really the most astonishing of all. With a few other Bulgarians he had visited Belgrade immediately after the liberation, and I had accompanied them to nearby Avala Hill,
where I explained the battle for the city in October 1944.
Kostov had listened attentively. That evening Aleksandar
Ranković told us that Kostov did not favor a Bulgarian-Yugoslav federation on a basis of equality; Kostov had told a Yugoslav: "We Bulgarians are more or less intelligent and you
Yugoslavs are more or less rich, so each will bring to the
federation that which he possesses."

The Yugoslav Central Committee did not have a very good
opinion of Kostov, nor did the old Bulgarian revolutionary
Ivan Karaivanov. Kostov was criticized for unsatisfactory behavior when caught by the fascist police during the occupation.
(Karaivanov even said he had been an agent, because many
Bulgarian Central Committee members caught during a raid
had been executed, whereas Kostov had come out alive.) Then,
after the Cominform resolution, he was, along with Chervenkov, among the first Bulgarians to join the attack against us.
When Kostov was arrested in 1949, Tito stated in a speech
that the Yugoslavs had known he was a police spy.

When the trial in Sofia began on December 4, 1949, as
director of the Yugoslav Information Office, I held a press conference about it. I was certain it would end as the trial of
Rajk had, with Yugoslavia the butt of the accusations and
Kostov confessing everything.

But I was shamefully wrong. I trained my guns on Kostov, calling him a spy of Czar Boris and everything that went with it. Then I received the first report from Sofia: Kostov was admitting nothing.

The main points of his indictment were that he had capitulated to the Bulgarian fascist police, that he was a spy of the British intelligence service, and that he had plotted with Yugoslav leaders to create an anti-Soviet Balkan federation. But all he would admit to was anti-Soviet activity; a lack of vigilance that had enabled agents to infiltrate the Party and state apparatus; and "individualism" and personal ambitions impermissible in a leader of a communist party of the Bolshevik type.

After Kostov made this statement the judge hastened to cut short the proceedings, so that they could give him a working over, but when the trial was continued Kostov stuck to his guns. The next morning *Pravda* angrily reported: "As soon as Kostov uttered his first few words, it was obvious that the court was faced with a cunning, experienced, and calloused criminal who had set himself the task of deceiving the court in every possible way and distracting its attention from the basics, so as to ward off the blame for what he had done."

Sitting at my desk in the Information Office, I banged my head with my fist: "Oh, Vlado, what an ass you are! You have accused this man publicly of being a police spy, and now see how bravely he is conducting himself." The same day I held another press conference and admitted my blunder. It was the least I could do under the circumstances.

Almost twenty years have passed, and I am still wondering how Kostov managed to stand up under torture, why he refused to do what Rajk, Slansky, and so many others had done. Finally, why had the others behaved as they did: was it fear, false promises, sincere belief?

Without access to primary historical sources—that is, to the documents of the investigations and trials themselves—it is impossible to formulate a reliable opinion about the motives behind these political murders.

After the assassination of President Kennedy I was asked by various American magazines and television networks to submit my opinion, as an expert on the 1914 Sarajevo assassination, as to whether Lee Oswald was the murderer and what his motives could have been. My reply was that I had drawn my conclusions about the motives of Gavrilo Princip and his comrades primarily from the records of the investigation and trial. Austria-Hungary had been guilty of many sins, but it was nevertheless a *Rechtsstaat,* a law-abiding state, and during the interrogation and the trial itself gave the assassins and would-be assassins an opportunity to explain their motives. The records have been preserved, they are available to historians, and the necessary conclusions may be drawn.

In appraising the trials and resultant political murders in the Soviet Union in the period 1936–1938 and the similar crimes committed in Eastern Europe in 1949–1952, we must also have available to us authentic papers from the investigations and trials; in addition, we must know something about the ties between political organs and executive authorities, the directives handed down, who issued them, and what their purpose was.

The fact that many of the old Bolsheviks executed in the thirties were "rehabilitated" by the Soviet government after Stalin's death is without question proof of their innocence, of their being victims of political murder. Simultaneously, these acts of rehabilitation undoubtedly reveal the motives of those who ordered the murders. But not all the necessary documents are accessible to research workers.

In the case of those unjustly executed or imprisoned in Eastern Europe, rehabilitation has not been carried out in all states. For instance, in Albania Koci Xoxe's execution is still upheld. And in the states where rehabilitation has been proclaimed, the number of these judicial murders and the motives behind them have not always been fully elucidated. In Bulgaria Kostov was formally rehabilitated, but no details were given as to who sent him to his death (was it only the Bulgarian authorities or was it also someone else in Moscow?). The Hungarians made a rather serious attempt to arrive at the full truth about the murder of Rajk, but they also did not dare go too far in investigating who ordered Rakosi and Gerö to accuse Rajk and his companions of those particular crimes and have them executed.

It is more than obvious that all these East European trials were on the same model, that they had the same purpose and were organized in one place. Moreover, it cannot be ignored that the men brought before the courts were revolutionaries who had remained in their own countries during the war, sharing the fate of their people, and not those who came from Moscow to take power after the Red Army had liberated their countries. The question must therefore be asked: what was the involvement of leaders brought from Moscow in the judicial murder of those revolutionaries who had striven not for a blind imitation of dogmatic Soviet formulas, but for more humanitarian forms of socialism?

In this respect the rehabilitations in Czechoslovakia—particularly those occurring after the demise of the Novotny regime in January 1968—give an insight into the background of the Stalinist plots, the methods of interrogation and obtaining forced "confessions," and—most significantly—the extent to which Soviet police directed the slaughter. It is highly probable that one of the reasons the Soviet government decided to invade Czechoslovakia in August 1968 was to prevent the awful truth from being fully revealed.

If we ask why the old Bolsheviks and the East European revolutionaries confessed to the senseless accusations against them, it must be stated at the outset that the same techniques of investigation and interrogation were not applied everywhere.

It has been said that drugs were used to force the victims to confess, but scientists claim that such drugs have not yet been perfected. Khrushchev declared that Stalin issued directives to the interrogators to "beat, beat, beat." But physical torture alone does not explain the results of these trials, for the accused had bravely withstood police terror in the bourgeois courts. Also mentioned are the deceptions practiced by the interrogators: it is reliably reported that Rajk's confession was obtained by a promise that his execution would be faked, and he and his family sent to live somewhere in the Soviet Union; he is said to have howled as he was taken to his execution, realizing that he had been duped. The officials had even brought his wife to his execution to observe him thus!

But none of these factors can be considered decisive in explaining the behavior of the accused; to do that one must enter into their minds and understand their devotion to the cause of revolution and their attitude toward Stalinist dogmatism. The old Bolsheviks posed the greatest threat to Stalin because they were the standard-bearers of all that was humane in the revolution of 1917. By the same token, those communists who had been in their own countries during the war and who proposed more humane and civilized forms of transition to socialism than the Soviet one were hated by him. For Stalin substituted loyalty to the Party for the idea of fidelity to communism. The Party was everything, it made and broke individuals; blind obedience to the model of the U.S.S.R. under Stalin and to his absolute power was required of all. During the investigations the interrogators engaged the defendants in discussions of lofty goals and the external dangers threatening the U.S.S.R. (and those dangers were real), asking them to admit their sins for the sake of a cause that was beyond their personal interests. Thus were their souls destroyed before their bodies, or, to put it scientifically, thus were they made to identify with the aggressors against themselves.

In bourgeois prisons the certainty that they were not alone, but a part of the awakening masses, had given these revolutionaries the moral courage to withstand torture. But that was not the case in the Stalinist prisons, at least not for the majority of prisoners. There had been no mass revolutionary movement in Eastern Europe from which these men could have emerged. Among them were leaders sufficiently intelligent to realize that no more progress could be made by Stalinist methods. Many of them felt that Yugoslavia was no better a model for national development than the Soviet Union because she herself had begun by accepting many forms from Moscow. They held the Yugoslav revolution in esteem, but reacted neurotically to it and felt pangs of conscience about not having been able to generate the same kind of revolutionary processes.

Into this mental climate, this atmosphere of dogmatism, the interrogators insinuated the accusation that Yugoslavia was a traitor, that there was something more to the conflict with Yugoslavia, something that only Stalin—"that Himalaya in the international working-class movement"—was aware of.*

Such opinions were also to be found in Yugoslavia in 1948 among certain honest but overly dogmatic persons. There were those who wanted Yugoslavia to go to the Cominform meeting in Bucharest because "we all feel that what we have been accused of so far is not the essential; surely there is some plan that we from our vantage point cannot perceive; we cannot imagine that anything could bring the interests of our country into conflict with the interests of the Soviet Union and the anti-imperialist bloc."

An example of this misguided dogmatism was Rajk himself, who believed there were certain loftier goals behind Stalin's accusations of Yugoslavia which he, as a good revolutionary, should support. When the skillful interrogator exploited this belief, then promised that his life would be spared, Rajk fell into the trap and confirmed all the monstrous accusations against Yugoslavia as well.

Stalin's interrogation methods were unquestionably influenced by the Christian tradition of indoctrinating heretics and by the experience of the Czarist secret police (which had itself learned a great deal from the Catholic Inquisition). Stalin simply improved upon those terrible methods of the past. But it would be methodologically erroneous to ignore the nature of the twentieth-century society and state in which these medieval

* The phrase is that of the Bulgarian philosopher Todor Pavlov.

methods were applied. And here we run into the Stalinist concept that confines socialism to industrialization, thus neglecting
human values and the still-unresolved interrelationship between the individual and society in all its aspects (including
the national question), and disregarding the individual for the
sake of an imaginary social good.

So to fall back on the "personality cult" alone to explain
these trials would be to take an idealistic position as a point of
departure for elucidating social transformation.

The Mysterious Death of Louis Adamic ★

One July day in 1945, after the Yugoslav delegation had
returned to New York from the United Nations meeting in
San Francisco, the American writer Louis Adamic, of Slovenian
descent, invited me to spend a few days on his farm near Mil-
ford, New Jersey.

I wrote about my meeting with Adamic in my diary:

I met Adamic a few days after arriving in the United States
in the company of General Žujović and Ambassador Simić.
We spoke mostly about the work of the powerful organization
called the United Committee of Americans of South Slav
Descent, which had done much to inform the American public of the struggle of our peoples. It was headed by Louis
Adamic and Zlatko Baloković. I told Adamic how we had
heard the news of his stand against Draža Mihailović and
Fotić [the royal Yugoslav ambassador in Washington] on the
eve of the Fourth Enemy Offensive, and how much it meant
to us.

All of our encounters were short, although a few of them
lasted as much as four hours, but short in the sense that after
each one of them I felt that my conversation with Adamic
was unfinished, that it had only just begun. So we agreed
that I should come to his farm for a few days.

We arranged to meet at noon in Adamic's hotel and I
arrived right on the dot. Adamic laughed: "Yugoslavs are

usually late, but I see that Tito's officers are exceptions to the rule."

We wanted to catch the first afternoon train out, for the heat from the sun-drenched walls of New York's skyscrapers was such that one felt barbecued. It was not just ordinary dry summer heat: it was damp and depressing, giving your pores no chance to breathe. The clean shirt I had put on before leaving my hotel was soaked in a few minutes.

In a cab we sped across Manhattan, through the hustle and bustle of the city streets and finally down a dark tunnel to Pennsylvania Station. In a twinkling we got out and grabbed our bags; a second and then a third taxi disgorged their passengers right behind us. Here the heat was even worse, for the hot air mingled not only with exhaust fumes but with the acrid smell of coal smoke.

Adamic left me in a corner of the enormous hall while he went to buy the tickets. As I waited I watched this anthill beneath Manhattan with its thousands upon thousands of people rushing toward the long lines of trains arriving and leaving every minute. There was so much commotion that one was overcome by a desire to shut one's eyes and get away from the pressure. Through the cacophony, which to my tired mind seemed to be intensifying from one moment to the next, came a young girl's voice announcing the arrival and departure of trains—a soft voice, speaking each word slowly and clearly. In that awful noise and damp, it was a balm, a swallow of cool brook water after a long, wearying partisan trek in the mountains, or like the feel of new-mown hay after a six-hour march at night.

Adamic came back with the tickets and managed to get me a cup of cold water. Then he led me through tunnels and halls, through a mass of pressing people, until we reached the train and took our seats. The train made its way through the tunnel under the Hudson River and I felt pressure on my eardrums, but when we were in the open where there were no overheated skyscrapers or roasting sidewalks, a fresh wind blew. I filled my lungs and felt revivified.

For the first time, I had a chance to observe Adamic a little more closely: an unusually high forehead and powerful chest were his two most outstanding features—particularly the chest, which showed that he had worked as a physical laborer in his youth. But Adamic could never be observed at rest, for he was always in motion, taking out of his attaché case letters from acquaintances and magazines with various articles marked in red.

He asked me what I thought of New York's skyscrapers and began to talk about them himself, about the fantastic technology, about how our people could also make the same kind of progress thanks to their enterprise, vigor, and perseverance. He said it would be a good thing to start collecting books in America on engineering, medicine, and agriculture and to send them to Yugoslavia so that the people could raise their level of technological know-how. . . .

I realized there was great logic and method in everything Adamic said. Indeed, the same two characteristics had been present in all our earlier meetings, and in all the letters, telegrams, clippings, and books he had sent me every two or three days while I was in San Francisco. He was a man who had imbibed the practical American spirit—not a minute was wasted, he had organized his work to an enviable degree. But every once in a while that practical American spirit was interrupted by something from the old country, from Slovenia, from us—a certain élan or enthusiasm. That quality was present when he spoke of our country industrializing, of our having to train experts and specialists right away.

We were so immersed in our subject that we did not notice the passage of time, and when we reached our stop I again felt that our conversation had only just begun.

We were met by Adamic's wife Stella, a small, fragile American woman. She was wearing trousers, her hair was tied up, and she looked very simple but tastefully dressed. My glance went to her hands, which showed traces of housework, and this somehow made me feel closer to her.

We drove to Adamic's farm—past hills, woods, a river meandering through a valley. It reminded me strongly of Dolenjska and the Krka River valley near Rog, along the way from Soteska to Toplice and Novo Mesto. I told Adamic this and he smiled. I think he too had had this in his mind when he decided to buy the old-fashioned farm with its hundred acres (mostly forest) a few years before. We passed by the house of Adamic's neighbor, an old farmer, who waved to us, and then went on to Adamic's own house—a sturdy stone building almost a hundred years old. Adamic had spent quite a lot of money adapting it to his needs. We visited the garden, where the beans were growing tall. An old man, bony-faced, slightly bowed, a spade in his hands, looked up from his work. Adamic greeted him and, when he explained where I was from, the old man wiped the soil off on his overalls and shook my hand: "My name is Andrej Križ-mančič, and I am from the Trieste area!"

Old Andrej blinked and seemed a little excited. He took his leave quickly and disappeared among the bean stalks. Adamic explained that the old man had been in America many years and was now working for him, caretaking and tending the garden. Since the Yugoslav army had liberated Trieste, Andrej had had no peace. He wanted to go home.

We started talking about Trieste, about what it meant to Yugoslavia, especially to Slovenia, to the Slovenian people. No Yugoslav nationality was so disunited as the Slovenes. Almost two-fifths of them had been forced to live outside Yugoslavia by the unjust boundary lines that had been drawn, and now for the first time they had an opportunity to live together in a free state.

Adamic spoke with vigor and warmth. The fate of Trieste was as much a concern to him as to old Andrej, to all of us.

In May and June, when almost the entire American press assumed a completely hostile attitude toward us on the question of Trieste, the first voice heard in our favor had been Adamic's. In an article for the liberal newspaper *PM* he set out our rights and hit particularly hard at British policy.

As we came in from the garden, Adamic spoke of the infamous statement of Field Marshal Alexander, in which he compared us with Hitler, Mussolini, and Hirohito. Adamic was beside himself: "How can he say that about a people who have displayed such courage and perseverance in the face of the enemy? But I don't think Alexander thought that one up—Churchill probably told him to say it. . . ."

Adamic started talking about British policy, about the position of its empire, about Churchill's visit to President Roosevelt in the autumn of 1943, when Adamic and his wife had been invited to the White House for dinner and he had told Churchill himself what he thought about things.

Twilight had fallen, a night breeze wafted in from the woods, and Stella called us to dinner. We sat down at a table set in front of the house and were joined by Adamic's mother-in-law, a gentle and silent elderly lady. The stout cook—in a white apron, dress, stockings, and shoes—stood at the door and banged on the gong. This was a signal for Andrej to drop his work and come to dinner. . . .

The next morning I was awakened before dawn by the chirping of a multitude of birds and could not for a moment recollect where I was. . . . For a long time I gazed at the forest, breathing in the fresh air and listening to the birds. I fell asleep again and was awakened about nine o'clock by Adamic calling. We spent the morning talking about literature and Adamic's writing. He explained his approach to writing books and how he collected material for them. . . .

I had to return to New York the next day. Adamic and Stella took me to the station. As the train drew away, I thought about the letter I was taking with me from Adamic's farm. Early that morning someone had knocked on my door. Andrej's bony gray head appeared from behind the door. In his hand he held a letter, and for a long time he went on apologizing for waking me. Finally he gave me the letter and asked me to take it to Marshal Tito. The letter was entitled:

The Voice of the People of Trieste

I, the undersigned, a former Triestino from Primorska, congratulate the Liberation Front, Marshal Tito, and all the partisans who fought so bravely and triumphed over Nazism and fascism.

But the victory was not complete, and you still must fight a diplomatic battle to have Trieste and all Primorska joined to Yugoslavia.

I should also like to add the following:

Death to Nazism and fascism, life and liberty for the people.

                    Andrej Križmančič, c/o Louis Adamic
                    Milford, New Jersey

I shook hands once again with Andrej and as he stood in the doorway, he said: "Tell Comrade Tito that we are grateful to him for defending the just cause of the Slovenes!"

I did not visit America during the next four years, but I kept up a correspondence with Adamic. Then in January 1949 he came to Belgrade to gather material for his new book on the conflict between Russia and Yugoslavia, a book published only after his death in 1951 and entitled *The Eagle and the Roots*. In my book *Notes on America* I had described my first meeting with Adamic; now he, in this book of his, described a meeting with my wife Vera and myself early in February 1949:

Between two and three-thirty on Saturday, I lunched at the Dedijers' and met Vlado's second wife, Vera, a pretty, quiet young woman from Slovenia, where she played a part in the resistance and the revolution. Vlado's first wife, Olga, a physician, died a heroine in the mountains of western Yugoslavia in 1943.

"Vera and I had a fight last night because of you," Vlado said in English when Vera went into the kitchen. "Well, not really a fight—a squabble. She wanted to go out and beg, borrow, and steal to give you the kind of lunch she imagines you're accustomed to in America. My argument was: 'To hell with him! If he doesn't like what we have here, he can go back where he came from.'"

Vera didn't understand why Vlado and I laughed so heartily. I explained to her that the phrase "go back where you came from" is used by super-patriots in the United States to put "furriners" like me in their place.

"I told Vera," Vlado went on, "that at your home in New Jersey we ate in the kitchen and I helped myself from the refrigerator. Unless she went back on her word, you won't get anything special."

I said I was grateful for that.

"I agreed to only one extravagance," Vlado continued, "that this room be heated," and he put a hand on the tall green tile stove in the corner. "Usually in winter the kitchen

is the only warm room in the house. The children stay there
most of the day."

"Why don't we eat in there?"

"Too small. Also, no refrigerator full of milk, butter,
eggs, fruit, ginger ale, Coca-Cola, and ice cubes. Come,
look"—and, to Vera's distress, Vlado ushered me into the kitchen. The children's toys and the crib of the youngest were
there.

As Director of Information, Vlado's rank was about equal
to a deputy minister's and, under the system of privileges
then in effect, he was entitled to extra food allowances.
These were accorded officials primarily so they could enter-
tain foreign visitors. Vlado said he left the house at seven
in the morning, returned at two for half an hour, when he
could, for lunch; and when he came home again, it was late
evening and he had no time or taste for social life—a dis-
qualification for his job.

"What's that American gag? Oh yes, I say it's spinach and
to hell with it! Anyhow, like a good many others, Vera and
I don't need or want the privileges."

I asked if the privileges were abused.

"By a few," said Vlado, "and there's plenty of talk which
makes it unpleasant for the many who live modestly and
isn't helpful generally. There's quite a struggle going on
inside the Party against the privileges. It's not a simple matter, though. Some of the *drugovi,* like Tito, Kardelj, Kidrić,
and Bebler, have nice homes—by our standards—and enough
fuel and food: they must; for they have foreign visitors all
the time. If Tito didn't have all that the No. 1 man in a
country should have when guests come, even the people who
now prattle about the 'luxurious living of the higher-ups'
would protest because he permitted strangers to see our
backwardness and poverty." . . .

Lunch at the Dedijers consisted of *ričet,* a Slovenian dish
of barley and beans and pieces of pork, potatoes, dark bread,
substitute "coffee," and *palačinke*—rolled pancakes with fruit
jelly.

"This is the only special," was Vera's aside to her scowling
husband as she brought in the pancakes.

"Where did you get the butter and eggs?" asked Vlado,

giving a good imitation of the "Western" conception of a Balkanite bullying his wife.

Vera smiled and placed her forefinger on her lips.

After lunch, Vlado and I sat alone awhile. . . .

Before I left, Vlado took me into his small, unheated study to show me his library. He pointed to a collection of anti-Tito literature which appeared in the United States during 1946–1948.

"Fantastic stuff," he said. "Some of it is hilarious. Do you know how many copies any of these books sold?"

I was sure the sales figures were very low.

"Since you brought down those planes in '46," I said, "Yugoslavia and Tito have been so unpopular in America that even anti-Yugoslav, anti-Tito books don't sell." . . .

Vlado Dedijer, whom I hadn't seen since Saturday afternoon, related he had spent the evening and all of Sunday talking with a number of *drugovi,* who were in town for the congress, as part of his job of research on the Communist Party in Serbia, particularly in Belgrade, since 1937. He had been working at it, on and off, during the last two years. A terrific story—of courage and martyrdom, he said; of patriotism and solidarity with the international working-class movement. He planned to put it into a book some day if he ever got the time. He fell silent for a spell, thinking of his material, perhaps. . . . [He then asked:] What else had I been up to?

I told him . . . and said that everything I had seen and heard in the last few days was impressive and disturbing, and that I felt the current Yugoslav scene was at least mildly terrific too.

"During the last five or six years I've read possibly a couple of million words on Yugoslavia," I said; "now I discover I know almost nothing about it. And some of that may be your fault. You're sitting on the story, or somebody is. What kind of Director of Information are you, anyhow?"

"Lousy, to be exact," said Vlado. "I'm glad you agree, and when you see Stari [Tito], tell him so, will you? . . . Seriously, I'd like to be relieved of this job and do nothing but delve into our recent history and write as many volumes as it takes. Tito, Kardelj, and Djilas keep saying they need me on this job, and I stick to it. I'm supposed to be a disciplined communist; also, poor as I am at it, there's probably no one better for the job right now. We're very short of qualified people."*

That February Adamic waxed more and more enthusiastic about writing a book about the clash with the Cominform. I offered to help him as much as I could, and he got the same promise from Tito, Kidrić, Kardelj, and Bebler. He was also aided by Vili Jager, my faithful assistant in this sort of work.

Early in May Adamic wrote me from Opatija:

Dear Sambo,
Don't miss the editorial in the *London Times* of April 29.
In a few days I will send you the outline of my book. You will really have your work cut out for you.
I arrived in Opatija dead tired and sick. After only three days, I feel better already.

L.

Jager and his staff threw themselves into the work and sent Adamic everything he asked for, either to Opatija or to Slovenia, where he spent most of that spring. He had talks of several hours each with Tito, Kardelj, Djilas, Ranković, Kidrić, Tempo, and others. And he traveled all around the country talking with peasants, workers, and young people.

Then he went back to America to write. Sometimes he was angered when my replies to his endless questions did not arrive promptly. Here is part of his letter of January 3, 1950:

Not a word from you. I sent you several letters and chapters, etc., to Paris. Did you get them?
It would be useful if you piped up from time to time. . . .
I suggest you write me at least one line. That you *must* do. . . . Your stock with me has fallen to 0.06 per cent.

* Louis Adamic, *The Eagle and the Roots* (New York, 1952), pp. 59–62 passim, 74.

He was in better spirits in a letter of February 4:

> The book won't come out before mid-June. I can't come to
> Paris now. Perhaps I'll fly to Belgrade in April, when I finish
> the book. . . .
> In the meantime, please read all the chapters and return
> them immediately with suggestions. . . .
> Please check to see if I have recorded accurately all my
> talks with Tito and the others. . . .
> Jager is an excellent worker. Please tell him so. I have
> received everything he sent.

Adamic published parts of his book in his magazine *T and T*,
where they made a profound impression, especially on American progressives. But the reaction from Moscow was violent.
Adamic was subjected to all kinds of pressure not to write the
book. The *Pittsburgh Press* reported that Elizabeth Bentley,
a former member of the American Communist Party, had come
on her own initiative to testify before the House Un-American
Activities Committee that Louis Adamic had been a Soviet spy
during the war. Adamic complained that he could not sue her
for libel and slander as she had made the statement in a Con-
gressional committee hearing. He suspected that Elizabeth
Bentley had been told by the Cominform to provoke him for
not agreeing to stop publication of his book on Yugoslavia.
On New Year's Eve (1949–1950) Adamic sent me a short note:

> I am terribly tired. This is an awful job I have taken on
> myself. Why wasn't I born in Norway!
> I have had a talk with Jože Vilfan who will tell you all the
> details of what is involved. The idea is for you to come to
> the USA at the end of February or the beginning of March.
> That will get things moving faster. Also it will be less
> obvious if you come here, rather than that I go there.

On January 4 another note: "Perhaps I will not finish the
book before the end of March. It might be a good thing for
you to come to the U.S.A. in the middle of March."

Adamic worked away steadily on his book. He had so much material he decided to publish it in two volumes. There was some difficulty about his talks with certain of our leaders who wanted him to publish their words verbatim. This slowed down work on the book.

In April 1951 I received a very sad letter from him in New York. Threats against his life had increased. (Even in late 1949, when I had last been in New York with him, he had told me of such threats: "It's the Russians and the American right-wingers. I am a thorn in the side for both.") But Elizabeth Bentley's provocation had been futile. (Adamic decided to include this Cominform maneuver in his book, in a footnote.) There were family troubles. His mother-in-law had died, and his wife Stella was not well. Old Križmančič had also died. More and more frequently, Adamic was at his farm alone.

Toward the end of July I received a report from a Yugoslav official in New York of a talk with Adamic in which he had said that he felt his life was in danger. I noted this in my diary and give it in its entirety here, as it may offer certain indications as to how that brave man met his end.

On July 17, 1951, I had a lengthy talk with Louis Adamic (about four and a half hours). It was rather intimate in nature.

Adamic told me at length how certain people were threatening him in connection with his book about Yugoslavia. He said that he had told this only to Bebler, Rogel, and myself.

In 1949 Adamic had received warning from a Cominform agent, J. V. Adamic knows him well. V. had come to Adamic to warn him that he would become an enemy of the people if he supported Tito. Although the warning was rather sharply worded, Adamic did not feel that V. was capable of doing him any violence.

In 1950 V. again visited Adamic and again warned him that he was becoming an enemy of the people. Their conversation was rather acrimonious.

(It is interesting to note that both times V. visited Adamic on a Wednesday, when his wife had gone to the doctor, so that Adamic was alone in the house.)

In October of last year (a little after the arrival of our delegation and after the talk Adamic had with Kardelj and Bebler), four men drove up to Adamic's house in a car with Michigan license plates. Adamic was at home alone that day. (His wife had gone to the West Coast.) He was in the garden. The car stopped in front of his house. The men got out and came toward him. They started asking him how his book was getting along and where the manuscript was. (Adamic replied that the manuscript was in New York.) They told him it was going to be a poor book and it would be better for him if it were not published. Adamic said they started threatening him. Then the dry cleaner's truck pulled up. Adamic took advantage of this to go into the house. He picked up the telephone but could not call the police as he had a party line and the other person was talking. But he pretended to be calling the police, shouting loudly, "Tell the police to come here right away," so that the four men would hear. A few moments later they got in their car and left.

(Adamic says that he stupidly forgot to take down the license number. He only remembers that the license plate was from Michigan.)

The incident troubled Adamic and he did not dare sleep at home, but stayed with friends in the neighborhood. Then he decided to go to his wife on the West Coast, and placed the house under the supervision of the state police. (He intends keeping it under their supervision.)

Once on the West Coast he rented a small bungalow on the shore. He did not go about, so as to avoid talk and not attract attention to himself.

He has the habit of working at night. He sleeps two hours, and then takes a short walk along the shore, works two hours, goes to sleep again, for a walk again, to work, and so on. Walking along the shore at two in the morning, he was suddenly attacked by two men. They struck, slapped, and punched him so hard that he fell to the ground. They cursed him and said it was a disgrace that he was writing such a book. They asked for the manuscript, but after beating him up and cursing him out, the two unknown men disappeared.

Adamic told nothing of this to the police. Nor did he tell his wife about it (or about the other cases) as he does not wish to cause her anxiety. He told her only that he had tripped and fallen.

All these threats and then the physical attack on him have frightened him badly. He has the feeling of constantly being followed—a feeling that has grown so powerful that he went to a psychiatrist to see if he was all right. The doctor said he was.

From this talk with Adamic and from his behavior I got the impression that Adamic is living in constant fear that someone is going to assassinate him, to murder him. (For instance, during our talk in the hotel the electricity went off for a minute and Adamic got very nervous.)

Adamic feels the threats originate with the extreme right-wing, the Ustaši, and so on.

A short time before I received this report, Adamic had sent me a copy of the full text of his two-volume book. The first volume consisted of an introduction and nine chapters, the second of five chapters. Each chapter was in a separate folder on which Adamic had written in his own hand the title, as well as personal notes and suggestions as to which of our magazines might be able to use certain chapters. For instance, the following note may be found on the cover of chapter 9, volume 1: "If the *Literary News* or some other paper wishes to use some of this material, I suggest they begin with my reference to John Gunther on page 97 or to Lekić on page 68, and then all the way up to the second book."

In my diary I wrote:

On the evening of September 4 I was in my study reading Adamic's manuscript. Everything was quiet when all of a sudden the phone rang. Tanjug informed me of the following: "Adamic has been found dead in his gutted house."

I was struck dumb. Who was the murderer? He had re-

cently told some of our people that someone was threatening
to kill him because of the book. I immediately cabled Stella
Adamic and she wrote back on September 18:
"Dear Vlado,
"My warm thanks for your telegram. I know the news
must have upset you terribly.
"Louis's book will be published. I think that it is a good
book, an honest book.
"When you visit America again, I should like to see you.
"Best wishes to you and yours,
Stella"
The letter was written on airmail stationery that was
burned at one end. Stella added a postscript: "This paper
was in Louis's room—that is why it is burned."
I have kept the letter as a memento, but sent the manu-
script of Adamic's book to the Slovene Academy of Arts
and Sciences, as a present.

The secret of Adamic's death has still not been revealed. I
did not see the records of the investigation, and can say nothing
precise about it, but I read carefully everything the American
press wrote about Adamic's death. He had been found in a
seated position, in his bedroom on the second floor, when the
firemen broke into the flaming house. There was a bullet hole
in his head, and a rifle in his lap.
New York Times correspondents reported that Adamic had
been murdered. Their assumption was confirmed by Fire Chief
Ellis of Ridgeville, Pennsylvania, who with his group of volunteer firemen was the first to arrive at Adamic's house after the
alarm had been given at four-twenty a.m.
Though Ellis did leave open the possibility of suicide, he
pointed out that the interior of the house had been so soaked
in gasoline that the firemen could barely make their way inside. Why should anyone do that and then shoot himself, he
asked.
Adamic's secretary, Mrs. Sharp, told the *Daily News* that the
preceding autumn four men had threatened to kill Adamic,
warning him that "the book had better be the right kind of

book, or else. . . ." He did not know the men but knew who was behind them. Adamic told them he was determined to write the book as originally conceived. "I have to finish the job and I am going to finish it to the end," he said.

Mrs. Sharp had been typing Adamic's manuscript and working on it for three years. She had visited Adamic at his home on Friday evening and remained there three or four hours, reading and talking with him about the international situation.

Chief Ellis made yet another statement to the *San Francisco Chronicle* to the effect that he was sure the house had been set on fire, and the New Jersey police also called the fire suspicious. The house is across the way from a corn crib which, it has been established, was set fire to first. Ellis added that the fire could not have spread that far without someone's help. He also pointed out that the rifle was a long one and he could not see how Adamic would have reached the trigger with the gun pointed at his head. Other papers wrote that the autopsy showed no other cause of death and that no disease was observable that might have made Adamic commit suicide. Moreover, two rifle bullets were found in Adamic's head. How could he have discharged the second when he must have lost consciousness after the first?

Adamic left no letter, either to his wife or to friends. He had received a considerable sum of money on loan from a friend, and fifteen years after his death that money was found in the ruins of his house. Adamic was a considerate person; had he intended to commit suicide, he would have returned the money first.

The only thing found on Adamic was a newspaper clipping referring to Elizabeth Bentley's accusations before the House committee.

The theory that it was a suicide was supported by Adamic's wife; because of her illness, as he had explained to me, he had not wanted to burden her with the news of the threats made against him.

It was reported in Belgrade that the FBI refused to investigate Adamic's death.

8.

Breaking Through the Russian Blockade

The Case of Marshal Rokossovski ★

There are days when you get up on the wrong side of the bed and go through the day with a chip on your shoulder. This happens to me rather frequently, at which times the frown on my face makes friends and acquaintances scurry for cover.

That is the way I felt on November 11, 1949. In New York for the U.N. General Assembly, I was driving from downtown to Lake Success, an hour away, where the U.N. was temporarily housed. The traffic that day was heavy and we were going to be late. Nervously, I leafed through the *New York Times*. A news item from Warsaw caught my eye: Marshal Rokossovski, a Soviet marshal until that morning, had just become a Polish marshal and, topping that, Poland's Minister of National Defense.

The General Assembly's Third Committee was that day discussing the problem of refugees. My adviser, a lanky Dalmatian called Ratko Pleić, sent a note telling me that the Chetnik commander Father Djujić was in the audience. I told Pleić a protest should be lodged with the State Department for allowing a war criminal like Djujić to make provocations on U.N. premises. As I was doing so, the Polish delegate, a small man with a big nose, got up to speak. There was nothing about Yugoslavia on the agenda, but he started talking about "Tito's clique" and how Tito was an American stooge, Dedijer another, and so on—in true Cominform style.

I went pale, then asked for the floor on a point of order, and so was able to speak immediately without waiting for the long line of others ahead of me. I scribbled a few notes and as soon as I got to the floor, struck out at that Polish flunky: "You accuse us of being the satellites of a foreign power and of simply repeating their delegation's position. I can tell you that you are doing so out of jealousy of the independence enjoyed by Yugoslavia. You accuse us because we have not agreed to become the satellite of the Soviet Union, as Poland has done."

I felt Pleić's firm hand on my shoulder. At this indication of his support and agreement, I continued even more sharply: "You have directly attacked Marshal Tito because he is our Marshal, our very own, a real one, a man of our own country. In Poland recently you were forced to accept a foreign marshal, Marshal Rokossovski."

Silence fell over the hall, and the chairman raised his gavel to interrupt me, but I went on for all I was worth: "We don't like to import or export marshals or be marshalized in any way whatsover, even *à la russe*."

The Soviet delegate, Ambassador Panyushkin, leaped from his seat as though struck, while the Pole hid his head. Shortly after, the chairman adjourned the meeting. I gathered up my papers. One of our delegates, a diplomat, stood palely behind me: "You shouldn't have made things worse, you should have controlled yourself."

The next day there was press coverage of the incident. *Le Monde* carried a strange version under the headline "Yugoslavia Is Not Poland: U.S.S.R. Can Keep Its Marshals to Itself." The article said that Ambassador Panyushkin had called me a representative of "Tito's clique" and that I had retorted: "Yugoslavia is proud of Tito, who liberated the country from the enemy. Our Tito is a real marshal, and if the Soviet Union should wish to offer us one of its marshals to manage our affairs, as it has done in Poland, our answer would be: *Non, merci*."

Actually, our committee sessions were poorly attended by newsmen. It was only later that they heard there had been an incident between us and the Russians over Marshal Rokossovski, and so reported it.

Here I must beg Panyushkin's pardon for a trick I played on him. Comrade Panyushkin was not exactly quick on the uptake. His nemesis was the simultaneous-translating equipment. On the dials, each number represented a different language, and 0 served to switch the equipment off. The Soviet delegates sat near us, only two or three seats away. When going from the speaker's lectern to my seat, I had to pass them, and would quickly turn the Russian equipment to 0. Then I would whisper to Pleić: "Now watch the Russian again!"

The session would begin and Panyushkin would raise his hand, asking for the floor on a procedural matter: "Mr. President, the equipment is not working." Technicians and secretaries would rush to adjust his earphones to number 3, for Russian, while we would have a good laugh. I did this a number of times, always with the same result. When he was named Soviet ambassador to Peking, I thought to myself he would not be much use there.

In any event that evening, November 11, I could not fall asleep. I was staying on the seventh floor of the Hotel Lexington, in a room with Veljko Mičunović. Outside our window the hotel's neon signs blinked on and off every few seconds, and the light penetrated even through the curtains. It was like an electrical storm on Mount Durmitor. I was thinking about writing a book on Yugoslavia that would acquaint the world with the development of our revolution—an idea that came to me after my duel with the Polish delegate. Big countries had powerful media for getting across their ideas, whereas we had none.

Mičunović could not sleep either. Lying on his bed smoking in the dark, he talked of guerrilla warfare in Montenegro in the winter of 1942, and then about his U.N. work and the meeting that morning.

"Hey, I've got an idea. . . ."

And so that night, or rather that morning, the idea of writing Tito's biography was born. Mičunović, like every good Montenegrin, was cautious and careful; he went over all the possible difficulties in the project, but he was not pessimistic. Our talk ended after dawn, when the neon sign had been switched off.

Next day our sessions were not due to begin until the afternoon. In our delegation's headquarters on Fifth Avenue that morning I finished off my work in an hour, then told Pleić that we should prepare a reply to the Russian delegate.

"Wait a minute, Vlado. How can we do that when we don't even know what he's going to say?" protested Pleić.

"Well, I know how the Russian mind works. They'll say this and that, I'll bet you. Now you prepare an answer to all their points, and then we'll be ready to reply when they start firing away at us."

My prediction as to how the Soviet bureaucratic mind worked turned out to be ninety per cent correct!

Before lunch I walked to the New York Public Library, my favorite spot in that anthill of a city. There you had to buckle down to work whether you wanted to or not—with all the hustle and bustle and everyone busily rushing to and fro, you could not possibly just sit back and be a lazy Balkan. In the library I worked on the third volume of my wartime diary and leafed through the *New York Times* of 1943 and 1944 to see what had been written about the battles in Yugoslavia. But a son of the Balkans remains a daydreamer even in that mechanized beehive, and I stopped working and started drafting an outline for a biography of Tito to see how it would look chapter by chapter. I worked on it until two o'clock, forgetting about lunch and some meetings I had.

I went back to Yugoslavia on the *Queen Mary*. Every day I took a walk on deck with Milan Bartoš. I told him my plan for the biography, and we would go into the salon to jot down some new points to be included, working late into the night. Bartoš was wonderfully methodical, and I was more than satisfied with what we accomplished.

In the meantime Tito had received two offers for his memoirs from the United States. When I got home I immediately put a call through to him and requested a meeting. I told him my plan.

"If foreigners write it, we'll slave for them collecting materials, then won't be satisfied with the results. Why don't I have a try? I wouldn't bother you too much with questions."

Tito winked: "You'll give me no peace, you'll smother me with questions! And why are you looking at me like that?"

"How am I looking at you?"

"As though you were seeing me for the first time."

"It's true, I've been looking at you for thirteen years and I still can't decide what you look like. Sometimes your features seem very gentle and sometimes sharp. Your face keeps changing. No wonder no one has succeeded in doing a good likeness of you."

We got down to serious talk. He agreed to let me write the book. I told him I would sell the book abroad for good money, because that would be the best way of assuring a wide distribution. Westerners feared propaganda, but this way publishers would vie with each other for the book, and the publisher who got it would do his utmost to get a good return on the deal. In a word, I would take advantage of "capitalist contradictions." Tito found this highly amusing.

We said nothing about the plan for the book or its contents —neither then nor ever. He left all that to me.

Yugoslavia's Election to the Security Council ★

The Rajk trial in Budapest, the concentration of troops on our eastern boundaries, the growing number of border incidents, the threatening note sent by Molotov at the end of August 1949, news of the detonation of the first Soviet atomic bomb—all these events induced our Ministry of Foreign Affairs to propose that Yugoslavia apply for membership on the Security Council at the fourth session of the United Nations. The decision was kept secret and no other state was informed of it until our delegation arrived in New York. When, however, we publicly submitted our candidacy, the Soviet Union immediately named Czechoslovakia as a rival candidate. A dramatic and intricate struggle began—not only on the floor of the U.N., but in the lobbies and corridors also, as well as in the press. There was also recourse to "black propaganda."

Our self-appointed "Big Brother" did everything he could to frustrate our nomination. Vyshinski, heading the Soviet delegation, in his first address made no mention at all of the conflict between his country and Yugoslavia. His attitude was that Yugoslavia belonged in the Soviet sphere of influence: it was a Soviet hunting ground, and what happened there was no concern of the U.N.

But the head of our delegation, Edvard Kardelj, in an address on September 25 came out with the real facts of the case and gave a full history of the dispute. He pointed out that between July 1, 1948, and September 1, 1949, alone there had been 219 armed incidents on Yugoslavia's eastern borders. He ended by saying:

> In his address Mr. Vyshinski sharply condemned warmongering and the policy of using the threat of war. He also stressed that the Soviet government has always supported equality among states. In that spirit he submitted a resolution to this Assembly in which the Soviet Union emphasized its dedication to the solution of all disputes by peaceful

means. However, the Yugoslav delegation must emphasize that the government of the U.S.S.R. is under the obligation to apply this in practice, above all where it can most easily do so: that is, toward a country which is not in any bloc, which threatens no one, and which is not far from the Soviet Union—that is, toward Yugoslavia. All the more so as Mr. Vyshinski again stressed in his address that the U.S.S.R. wished peaceful cooperation on a footing of equality with all countries which desired to cooperate under those conditions. The Yugoslav delegation wishes to stress that Yugoslavia is interested in precisely that kind of cooperation and only in that kind, and is always ready to cooperate.

Vyshinski immediately started using all his diplomatic skill to foil our nomination. He shrank from nothing. For instance, he got word to the Security Council that if Yugoslavia were elected, she would vote with the Soviet Union, just as Czechoslovakia would—thus adding grist to the mill of those Americans who still believed that there was no dispute between Russia and Yugoslavia, and that it was all dust in the eyes of the West. Conversely, however, Vyshinsky's "black propaganda" also spread the idea that if Yugoslavia were elected to the Security Council, the Soviet Union would leave the United Nations.

Vyshinski pinned his hopes particularly on the secret spheres-of-influence agreements among the three big powers at the war's end. These agreements had also related to the United Nations. Although it had a Labour government by then (1949), Great Britain still adhered to those secret agreements and supported Czechoslovakia for the Security Council. Vyshinski was so confident of success that he even publicly acknowledged that geography determined the candidates for the Security Council. As the U.S.S.R. was master in Eastern Europe, it had the right to pick the candidate from there; he invoked the gentlemen's agreement among the big powers on this point, and added that Yugoslavia's election to the Security Council would be illegal in that it would violate that agreement.

Our delegates—especially Kardelj, Djilas, and Bebler—had

their hands full making press statements on all the issues raised by Vyshinski's "black propaganda," while at the same time submitting a number of constructive proposals to the U.N. For instance, on October 5 we delivered to the Secretary-General the draft of a Declaration on the Rights and Duties of States specifically designed to regulate diplomatic activities that could be used to menace the sovereignty of small states.

Interestingly enough, the Czechs themselves—probably under the influence of Klementis—did very little to get themselves elected. Later on he ran into grave trouble over this.

Soviet "black propaganda" also resorted to a technique favored in American politics—compromising individuals by revealing secrets of their private lives.

When I was in San Francisco in 1945, Orson Welles had shown me his great film *Citizen Kane*, based on the figure of William Randolph Hearst, who had been a candidate for governor of New York prior to World War I. Shortly before the election, Hearst's opponents arranged to have him caught with a girl in a hotel; scandal ensued, and Hearst lost the election.

Only a few days after Welles had shown me the film, the Chetniks involved me in just such a plot. In the Fairmont Hotel in San Francisco, where our delegation was headquartered, two women of Montenegrin descent visited me and asked me to take some letters for them to Montenegro. I was slightly suspicious and told them to take the letters to another member of our delegation, a Montenegrin (as I am not) and a man who had been a Yugoslav diplomat before the war. At the Assembly session the next day our young secretary rushed into the hall and handed me a copy of Hearst's newspaper the *San Francisco Examiner*. On the first page big headlines screamed "Furious Husband Catches Titoist Diplomat with Wife." What had happened? The Montenegrin women had arranged a meeting with the diplomat in question to give him the letters. She had come at the appointed time, hung herself around his neck, and after a moment in barged the husband, detectives, and newsmen. The whole thing had been cooked up by Konstantin Fotić, former King Peter's ambassador in America.

The Soviet delegation wanted to use the same kind of trick against us in 1949. One of our diplomats was called to the telephone. A woman's soft voice said she had heard him speak in the U.N., was enchanted by him, and must see him or her heart would break. The unfortunate fellow fell for this and arranged a rendezvous. But our guardian angels learned of the trap—and from Soviet sources at that! The big scandal, depicting Yugoslavs as marriage-wreckers and people who go against public morals, fell through. We took the intended victim to see Kardelj fifteen minutes before the date, and the girl was stood up, left waiting at a bar. We observed her to see whom she was with. Five or six big men were there, waiting for our would-be Romeo to show up so they could create a scandal. Just to prove we weren't Simple Simons we photographed all of them for our historical record.

Vyshinski's final effort was to let the Americans know he "would make important concessions to them in the Balkans if they refrained from voting for Yugoslavia." The American press made a big thing of this. On October 8 the *New York Times* had an editorial about it, asking that the "sellers come out with the whole assortment of goods they have to offer."

Election day finally came: October 20. Before the voting, Vyshinski once again ascended the podium to plead for adherence to the spheres-of-influence and "gentlemen's" agreements.

A two-thirds majority must be obtained in the General Assembly vote in order to become one of the three rotating members of the Security Council. On the first ballot Ecuador received 58 votes, India 56, Yugoslavia 37, Czechoslovakia 20, Afghanistan 1, and the Philippines 1.

We were, therefore, one vote short of the two-thirds needed. But Yugoslavia received it in the second round with 39 for us and 19 for Czechoslovakia.

We were absolutely overjoyed. Our Washington ambassador

Savica Kosanović, a rather frail man, came up to embrace me and I hugged him back. All of a sudden his breathing failed. We had to set him down in an armchair and call the doctors and an ambulance. At the hospital it turned out that in my excitement I had broken two of his ribs. I was mortified to think I had done such a thing just as we had won a great victory in breaking out of the international isolation Stalin had imposed on us.

My University ★

Every year between 1948 and 1953 I spent two to three months at United Nations sessions. Nowhere else did I ever learn as much as in those years. What I had learned in schools gave me a general concept of things and helped me to inform myself further. But at the U.N. we discussed not only purely political matters but also the scientific aspects of social problems; I had to get to the bottom of each issue, study for months in advance, and in discussions with other delegates from all over the world—men of different ideologies and persuasions—test my positions to see how right they were and to what extent they corresponded to the realities of the world we lived in. Those U.N. sessions were my real university education.

During those years our Council discussed two major questions: the draft of the Human Rights Convention and a number of drafts for the convention on freedom of information. There were points of contact between these matters and the work of the other committees, especially the Economic, Trusteeship, and Legal, so I was constantly in touch with the Yugoslav delegates on them. I thus established a close working relationship with Leo Mates, Josip Djerdja, and Milan Bartoš, and learned a great deal from all of them. The memory of our work together is a pleasant one.

The national question, the right of peoples to self-determination, the relationship of political to economic rights, and especially the right of each people to utilize its natural resources

—all these crucial issues were discussed in our committee during those years.

Conceptions differed. Representatives of some of the medium-sizéd and smaller West European states advanced their old social democratic ideas about the European peoples' right to self-determination and Europe's leadership of economically underdeveloped parts of the world—a point on which I often engaged in lively polemics with the Belgian socialist Professor F. Dehouse. The British Labourites praised the solution of the national question in Yugoslavia and Yugoslavia's resistance to Soviet hegemony. We were grateful for their support, but had to remind them that Yugoslavia was struggling for equality among peoples all over the world, in both East and West.

I presented a summary of Yugoslav policy on the national question in an address on November 18, 1952. A British delegate had just been arguing that the term "self-determination of peoples" was vague and therefore difficult to apply in practice. Following him, I talked of the various forms of classic (that is, military) occupation of colonies, and the emancipation of peoples oppressed in this manner. I then posed the question whether this kind of oppression included all types of violation of the right of self-determination:

First, the new way of suppressing a state is to allow it to be ostensibly sovereign, but to keep its state organism under the absolute control of the conqueror and its economy an appendage of his. This form is characterized by its snuffing out of the independence of nations with developed state and social systems and its reduction of them to the level of colonies. That is the system whose victim Yugoslavia was to be.

Second, the great powers consider themselves authorized to decide the fate of all peoples on a certain territory which, although not theirs, they concede to each other without consulting the people concerned. This practice had long been condemned in theory, but unfortunately was repeated in World War II and is still the cause of many tensions and conflicts. That is the system of spheres of influence.

Third, the advanced states exploit the misfortune of underdeveloped countries and take advantage of their own economic potential to increase the small state's dependence. First the economy and then other aspects of the life of the nation pass under the control of the stronger state, so that the people lose the right of self-determination on all matters where such independence would not be in the interests of the controlling state. It is frequent that the stronger states assume this position under the guise of defending the liberty and independence of various continents.

Fourth, there is no better way of helping the aggressor, he who strives for world mastery, than to deny other peoples the right to self-determination. Not for a moment do I underestimate the effort to develop material means of defense against an aggressor, but unless it is backed by the awareness of the people in all parts of the world, the awareness that each nation has the right to free and unobstructed development, that everyone has the right to live in his own way within his own state, material means of defense alone will not suffice to ward off an aggressor. Slaves cannot defend anyone, nor do they have anything to defend. Only free people who know why they are fighting and who have something to defend, can stand up to an aggressor, regardless of his material superiority, regardless of his cunning.

We discussed various solutions of the national question in different parts of the world, including the Soviet Union. Our delegation had gathered some material from Soviet sources and the Soviet press. I observed that the national question in the Soviet Union during Lenin's time had been approached and solved in practice so as to serve as an example to the rest of the world. But now Great Russian hegemonistic tendencies were on the rise; administrative measures were being used to wipe out the autonomous republics, and entire nations were being resettled elsewhere:

In the U.S.S.R., the national question is not being solved in the sense of searching for ways to enable various peoples to live side by side in peace and equal cooperation. Rather, the small nations are left at the mercy of the leaders of big nations who are in a position to deny them the right to exist, even to wipe them from the face of the earth."

I referred to the decree of the Supreme Soviet of the Russian Republic abolishing the Chechen-Ingush Autonomous Soviet Socialist Republic and transforming the Crimean autonomous Soviet Socialist Republic into the Crimean Region. The most recent edition of the Constitution of the U.S.S.R. also made no mention of the Kalmyk Autonomous S.S.R., the German Volga Autonomous S.S.R., and the Karachai-Cherkess Autonomous Region. Even the nationalities to which the Soviet Constitution conceded the right of having their own republics, as members of the Union, were not and are not on a footing of equality, suffering ever-increasing restrictions on the right to national developments:

In Byelorussia, there were twenty Byelorussians to every Russian. However, according to official statistics, in the Supreme Soviet of Byelorussia there were 278 Byelorussian and 78 Russian deputies in 1951, which is 3.5 Byelorussians to every Russian. The situation was even worse in Kirghizstan and Kazakhstan. In the former, there were 66.6 Kirghiz nationals to 11.7 Russians, whereas in its Supreme Soviet there were 77 Russian and 184 Kirghiz deputies. In Kazakhstan the ratio of Kazakhs to Russians was 57 to 19.8, although in the Supreme Soviet there were 134 Russians as against 218 Kazakhs. The situation in the Ukraine was worst of all, and I cited the Soviet Constitution's provision that the central government in Moscow concern itself with all Ukrainian affairs; the Ukrainian government did not even have the right to manage its own universities, to say nothing of its industry.

The Czechoslovak delegate had been charged with replying to these facts. He was all red in the face and didn't have the nerve to look me in the eye, but he breathed fire nevertheless. He particularly took me to task for having said that, after

World War II, the Soviet Union began applying the same oppressive methods to the peoples of Eastern Europe.

I could hardly control my anger:

> I think the Czechoslovak delegate has the right to pride himself on his chains, and to tell the whole world that he is satisfied with them. But he certainly has no right to recommend those chains to others and to attack other countries for defending their own independence.
>
> I do not believe that my government is immune to mistakes, either in domestic or foreign policy. But I think that all of us here, the representatives of all sixty nations, will agree on one thing, and that is that the present Yugoslav leadership has for the past ten years steadfastly defended the independence of Yugoslavia—first against the German, Italian, Bulgarian, and Hungarian invaders in World War II, then against attempts to frustrate our free and independent development, and finally, after 1948, against attempts by the Soviet Union to encroach upon our independence.

I said that everyone, including the representative of the Soviet Union, was aware of this. Since 1948 the Soviet Union had been openly endeavoring to subjugate my country. And because the Russians burned their fingers in the attempt they began to yell and howl, to curse and engage in mud-slinging of all kinds, calling us Gestapo or imperialist agents, and so forth. "The reason for their fury is obvious. We are your conscience, my dear Mr. Representative of Czechoslovakia, the conscience that you yourselves have lost."

At a delegation meeting that evening my associates told me they thought well of my reply to the Czechoslovak. One colleague asked me jestingly, "You said that our government was not immune to mistakes. Does that mean that you would also criticize your government if you felt that it had made a mistake?"

"Coming forward at this international tribune and dispensing lessons to others places a tremendous obligation on the conscience. . . ."

Nightmare at Oplenac ★

Early in 1950 I left the Information Office, but there was no letup in my work. I was appointed secretary of the Foreign Policy Committee in the National Assembly, and secretary of the International Commission of the Party Central Committee.

It was the press conferences in the Information Office that had most interested me. At one of my last ones, at the end of December 1949, one of the foreign newsmen had asked me if Yugoslavia would celebrate Stalin's seventieth birthday. This was right after the Rajk and Kostov trials and after the second Cominform resolution in which we had been labeled murderers and fascists. I replied: "It would be utterly hypocritical to celebrate it after all the slanders that have been directed at us." Since in the East European countries the celebration of Stalin had been transformed into idolatry, I was fiercely attacked for this statement by the Cominform press and radio. On December 23 Radio Budapest said: "While hundreds of million of toilers throughout the world, including those in capitalist countries, celebrated with profound and sincere sentiments of gratitude and love the seventieth birthday of Comrade Stalin, Tito's band of spies did not miss the chance to vent its venomous hatred against the Soviet Union and Comrade Stalin. At a press conference in Belgrade on December 21, Stalin's birthday, the American spy Vladimir Dedijer, stated that . . ."

One of the reasons I left the Information Office was to have more time to work on Tito's biography. This project, in which I was assisted in collecting materials by Vili Jager, Slavica Fran, Dojčilo Mitrović and Vuka Bugarčić, was progressing satisfactorily. But it was tough going interviewing people in the field. Many of them wanted to embroider on the facts of Tito's life, and I had to be on the alert.

Toward the end of April 1951 I went to Oplenac, to a Serbian government resort once occupied by King Alexander Karageorgevich as a summer residence. A discussion was then under way in Belgrade about privileges—who had the right to an automobile, to supplies from the diplomatic stores, and so on—all of which pointed to a crucial dilemma in the ethics of socialism. I had come to Oplenac with Krcun Penezić, then Minister of Internal Affairs of Serbia, the two of us charged with a special task. Aleksandar Ranković had asked me to write a historical account of how Draža Mihailović had been apprehended in 1946. Krcun had brought all the materials along, we had long talks, and I began to write. I completed the text quickly and gave it to Krcun. "Keep a copy for yourself. Ranković said you should," said Krcun.

I put the copy in a white envelope, sealed it with red sealing wax, and put it into my diary. The work had excited and upset me, and I was not feeling well in any case. Also, Krcun had forced me to drink a glass of red local wine. That night I had a nightmare—a reflection, actually, of thoughts that had been tormenting me in the daytime and of our heated discussions on social equality.

Krcun had gone off somewhere alone and I was sleeping in the small summer house of King Peter I, across the way from the church of Oplenac where the old king lay buried with his son, King Alexander.

My arm was completely numb. I could not get to sleep. Something seemed to be suffocating me, the wine had gone to my head, and the dizziness was aggravated by my old head injury and my exhaustion. I fell asleep and then started up. My glance fell on the white wall, all lit up. To me it looked like the white blanket with which we had covered Olga the day she died on Romanija Mountain in 1943. The cover rose and Olga's black hair appeared.

I always saw the same apparition whenever an attack was coming on. Olga was saying something, her hand raised under the white cover. I tried to wake up but sank again into the nightmare.

Something whistled about, like the wind howling in the juniper trees that night in June 1943 when we dug Olga's grave with our bare hands and little knives. My palms were damp with the blood dripping from my head wound into Olga's open grave, hands which had been damp with blood a few nights before, when I had had to slice pieces of meat from a mule and hand them around to my fellow soldiers.

Something banged, and I woke with a start. The wind had slammed the window shut. I was wet with perspiration and slowly came to my senses as I watched the light on the wall. I got up and went out. It was after midnight, and I gazed from the heights of Oplenac to the villages beyond. Only the barking of dogs broke the silence. The wind refreshed me and I felt a little better. I went back to lie down, but my head was still heavy and my heart beating fast. I decided not to go to bed and turned away from the house, walking instead across the few yards to the church. I leaned on the leaden doors, barely able to move. Inside was darkness and silence, the smell of incense and burnt-out candles. I felt as though I were at the bottom of a grave. I groped my way along the wall and then sat down on the stone floor.

I do not know how long I stayed there. When I recovered consciousness it was already daylight. I recalled bits of conversation from the night before: I had dreamed I was talking with King Peter and King Alexander. The image of King Alexander had appeared before me as I had seen him when I was a boy of ten. He was visiting the home for war orphans in Selce, on the Croatian coast, and I had been chosen to greet him. The directress of the home made me repeat several times what I was to say until she was satisfied that I knew it by heart. But when the King appeared with his escort, in my confusion I could say nothing. His face was as black as earth. Now, in my dream, he was dressed like the medieval Serbian Emperor Dušan in the large painting in Skoplje of his coronation.

"What are you doing on my property? What kind of a communist are you, going around staying in imperial residences?" the King asked me severely.

"I am resting, I am sick, Your Majesty."

"This is all mine, and you are an intruder, you, the son of a peasant of Herzegovina. And you pay nothing!"

"I do pay, your Majesty. Comrade Blaško* set the price at one hundred dinars a day."

"A lot you pay, you and that Comrade Blaško of yours— one hundred dinars. That is not a fifth of what you eat. Ha ha ha, a fine lot of communists you are! You talk about the working people, and here you are on the royal premises. Now Stalin will come and chase all of you away. He is a wise man, even if he did kill the Grand Duchess in 1917. I hate you Yugoslav communists even more than the Russians."

Then appeared a figure like Jouvet's Don Juan hovering over us, attired in the uniform of a French Zouave. A metallic voice echoed deeply:

"I am Peter the First. I am listening to your conversation. My son is both right and wrong. He too had taken the wrong path. He chased his brother off the throne and shut him up in a lunatic asylum for no good reason. And he was not very kind to his old father either. I was a modest king, I gave away everything I had. I always knew the difference between my own pocket and the state treasury. But Alexander was greedy. He spent and wasted a great deal. Just look at this church he built."

"Yes, but I am a king," Alexander argued.

Then something seemed to snap and I heard cocks crowing in the distance. Both kings withdrew to their tombs. Then appeared the vampire Sava Savanović, from the story by Milovan Glišić, the nineteenth-century Serbian realist whose village was not far from Oplenac.

"Well," said the enormous red vampire, bloated with blood, "so here you are. I have been looking for you all night. Since that Glišić wrote about me, I have had no peace. I must find a new warped elm wood."

Vampire Sava then sat down, took out a small bag with

---

* Blagoje Nešković, then Prime Minister of Serbia.

some dry cheese, bread, an onion, and had his dinner, wiping the crumbs from his chest, on which shone the scar from the injury caused by a mill near which Glišić had killed him for the second time. He took out a copy of *Borba* and disappeared.

I kept to my bed the whole of the next day. Krcun came at dusk, and I told him something of my awful dream. I wept for Olga in the dark. He was silent, grasped me by the arm, and then went for a walk.

As soon as I could get up, I gathered my things together and went back to Belgrade. I was afraid of another dream like that one.

I was incapable of working for a few days but had recovered by May 1. It was a sad holiday without Tito, who was recuperating at Bled from a gallstone operation. It was obvious from the parade that he was not there, for there was hardly any applause.

An Instructive Tale ★

The surprise blow that Stalin struck at Yugoslavia in 1948 isolated the country economically and otherwise. Getting out of that ironbound circle was a matter of life and death.

In a talk which I recorded in my diary, Tito said that after 1948 Stalin continued the economic blockade of Yugoslavia "in order to create economic chaos in the country, so as to achieve his main goal the more easily. He exploited Yugoslavia's isolation by putting even more pressure on it and on the Party. He ordered all workers' and democratic organizations throughout the world to break off ties with Yugoslavia, as he wanted to isolate the country along these lines, too."

In 1949 the East stepped up its economic blockade. The East European countries refused to conclude new trade agreements and fulfilled the existing ones only in part. An agreement concluded with Russia on December 31, 1948, reduced our volume of trade with her to one-eighth the former level.

The official Tass communiqué said that the Soviet Union had decreased the volume of trade because of "the hostile policy of Yugoslavia toward the U.S.S.R." Thus did the Soviet Union publicly proclaim the political motives behind its economic discrimination against Yugoslavia. Then, in mid-1949, the East European countries stopped all deliveries to Yugoslavia. To do the greatest possible damage to the Yugoslav economy, they unilaterally either broke off or reduced communications and other ties. Rumania stopped postal and railway traffic; Hungary and Bulgaria reduced railway, road, postal, and telegraphic connections to a minimum; Albania severed all communications and barely kept the mail going; shipping was obstructed on the Danube; and Rumania made it impossible to regulate navigation along the Iron Gate (Djerdap) section. Yugoslav ships could not enter the Black Sea. The Soviet government violated the Danube Convention and tried to transform the Danube into a "Russian river."

And in the West, more difficulties. In his memoirs Svetozar Vukmanović-Tempo says the following:

Many people think that in those difficult days the West came immediately to our aid. That is not true. The Western countries took advantage of the situation to lay down such conditions as would actually mean continuing the plunder of our country. When we asked them to increase the volume of trade and credit, they told us everything would be all right if we undertook to pay them for the property we had nationalized without compensation (mines, plants, and so on) and to repay the debts which prewar Yugoslavia had contracted.

There was nothing for it but to accept both conditions, although the invested capital and loans to prewar Yugoslavia had been paid for many times over by the exploitation of our natural resources. The credit was extended under very difficult terms of repayment—a four-to-five-year term at an annual interest rate of 11 per cent. We agreed to such arrangements to be able to develop our economy, to put an end to our backwardness.

This reorientation forced us to redraft plans and build projects with Western equipment. The Western countries took advantage of this to put strong political pressure on Yugoslavia to resolve in their favor all the country's postwar problems. In Italy, especially, there were people who felt that Moscow's pressure on Yugoslavia would let the West apply pressure, too. This related above all to Yugoslavia's western borders—the questions of Trieste and Carinthia—and to relations between Yugoslavia and Greece.

Thus the most bellicose circles in the United States, Great Britain, and elsewhere strove to subordinate Yugoslavia's foreign policy to their own interests. There were also more farsighted individuals who perceived that Yugoslavia's struggle for equality with the Soviet Union was a call to all small and medium-sized states to achieve relations of equality in the Western hemisphere. Some of them, like General Franco, felt that Yugoslavia, together with China, was even more a menace than the U.S.S.R. *Le Monde* reported on March 15, 1950, that Franco had told the Mexican newspaper *El Universal* "that it was much more dangerous to extend a hand to the Yugoslavs, or to Mao Tse-tung, than to Stalin himself."

Some of the Western states which came into conflict with countries and national liberation movements in Africa or Asia tried to pressure Yugoslavia into not recognizing the governments of those newly liberated states—as for instance, in February 1950, the government of the Democratic Republic of Vietnam. Another example was the pressure put on Yugoslavia not to support Iran's Premier Mossadegh in the Security Council, in connection with his fight with British oil firms. In these two cases—and many more between 1949 and 1953—Yugoslavia refused to give in to this pressure bordering on blackmail, and maintained its position of principle.

On the other hand the U.S.S.R. also tried to complicate Yugoslavia's position, already difficult enough by any standards. The most tragic of these attempts revolved around the liberation movement in Greece. Yugoslavia had rendered assistance to the Greek liberation movement from its very inception early in 1946, despite Stalin's attitude that Greece was in the Western sphere of influence and not to be tampered with. When the Cominform resultion came, Stalin forced the leadership of the Greek Communist Party to take a stand against Yugoslavia, to brand us as imperialist agents, and so on. As Vukmanović-Tempo put it, "We had acted honestly. We gave them everything we could, but Stalin ordered them to slander us. . . . When they refused to stop, we closed our borders in 1949."

Lenin's foreign policy in the first years of the Soviet Union's existence served in many ways as an example for us during the Cominform blockade. Lenin had been forced to conclude the Treaty of Brest Litovsk to preserve the very existence of his country and revolution, and to disrupt the united front of the interventionist powers.

In the cold war, Yugoslavia was guided by the principles of the U.N. charter: equal cooperation among all states, opposition to blocs and aggression from any quarter. She was thus able to break through the wall isolating her and to establish good relations with a number of small and medium-sized states. This accelerated the process to which Kardelj had already referred in May 1944, in a letter to me with which Tito had concurred, to the effect that in the postwar period Yugoslavia should develop good relations not only with the big allied powers, but with small and medium-sized countries and liberation movements too. It was on the basis of this policy that after 1948 Yugoslavia continually stressed that she did not wish to join any bloc whatsoever.

We defended this position openly, everywhere. In January 1951, during our visit to Attlee and Churchill, Djilas and I explicitly stated that Yugoslavia could not join the Atlantic Pact, although she was willing to accept economic and military assistance for her defense. When we got back to Belgrade I told Kardelj, "We went to the mosque, but we did not bow."

When Cominform pressure built up, Yugoslavia established closer ties with Greece and Turkey for the purpose of creating a regional defense alliance. She also began receiving considerable economic and military assistance from the Western Big Three, which helped her consolidate her independence and pursue her struggle for equal relations in the world.

This policy yielded positive results. It is true that the decisive factor was the unity of the peoples of Yugoslavia and the readiness of the Yugoslav army, but international considerations also played a part: Stalin would have attacked Yugoslavia had he been certain that the local conflict would not escalate into world war.

Paradoxically, the infamous agreement to split Yugoslavia up fifty-fifty into spheres of influence had a favorable aspect in 1948, for neither Stalin nor the West could predict the other's reaction to an invasion of Yugoslavia, which was at the same time an East European and a Mediterranean country.

In 1956 a congress of the World Association for International Law was held in Dubrovnik, attended by prominent lawyers from all over the world. As was the custom, during the farewell banquet the toasts were laced with jokes. I requested the floor and asked those present if they knew of a state that had made war on itself. They all asked if I meant civil war and I said no, I was thinking of a real international war. No one knew the answer, so I told them a story:

"On the eve of the battle of Lepanto in 1571, this city-state whose walls surround us now was the vassal of the Sultan in Constantinople and, according to treaty, in case of war had to send its sovereign ten warships. When orders to this effect came from Constantinople, the men of Dubrovnik acted in accordance with the treaty. But they were Christians, and when their spiritual father, the Pope, formed a coalition against the infidels, he asked the people of Dubrovnik to do their Christian duty and send warships to the Christian side in the war. And so Dubrovnik, owing to its geopolitical position and its ideological loyalty, found itself at war with itself."

My story drew a good deal of applause, and I quickly added, when it died down, "The wind was not favorable to the Turkish side, so the Dubrovnik warships were three hours late in coming to the Sultan's help, while those on the Christian side were in time to share in a rousing victory."

Everyone laughed. Only Koča Popović, then Yugoslav Foreign Secretary, saw through my purpose and wagged his finger at me.

That night as I walked along the Stradun, Dubrovnik's main street, I wondered if perhaps the question of Carinthia and Trieste and our western borders generally would not have been better solved if we had emancipated ourselves somewhat earlier from rigid Stalinist dogma and blind fidelity.

Cooperation with Social Democrats ★

When the Russian Revolution was threatened by intervention of the bourgeois armies of eight states, the international working-class movement did its duty. The British trade unions, although differing ideologically from the Bolsheviks, organized successful strikes in British ports where men and material were being loaded for intervention against the young Soviet Republic.

We remembered these historic facts in 1948. But in our case our own dogmatism obstructed us. Even a year after the Cominform resolution, articles appeared in Yugoslav newspapers attacking social democrats and using the same vocabulary Stalin had employed when Hitler was coming to power—that is, calling them allies of National Socialism and fascism.

Apart from this, the Soviet intelligence service laid cunning traps of another kind for us. Fearing that Yugoslavia might establish ties with workers' parties—backed in various countries by the majority of the working class and thus able to influence affairs of state—Soviet intelligence tried to make us establish contacts with small dogmatic groups void of political influence. There were some honest people among these groups, but agents as well.

Initially these ties were maintained by officials in the Federal

Ministry of Internal Affairs, even after the founding of the International Commission in the Central Committee, of which I was secretary. Now in 1949 the Politburo of the Yugoslav Party Central Committee had assumed a position of principle: we were to establish ties with all mass workers' parties and try for free exchanges of views on theoretical and political questions of socialism. But it was difficult to implement this line: officials in the Internal Affairs Ministry considered that they had registered a great success in maintaining ties with the individuals concerned, and an open conflict was inevitable. I followed my Party instructions, promptly and energetically; we were really at loggerheads and no time could be lost. But certain police officials wrote me down in their black books and awaited a chance to get even with me personally—as sometimes happened in our country.

Contacts with the big parties in the West developed swiftly. We were visited by British Labour leaders, French and Belgian socialists, later by the Scandinavians and others. Long and fruitful discussions were carried on. We even suggested publishing a theoretical magazine for the free discussion of major problems facing us.

As time passed, elements in common between ourselves and the social democrats found expression, but so did the differences. In July 1951 I was invited by the Executive Committee of the British Labour Party to give two lectures on problems of socialism in the world and in Yugoslavia. For those lectures I also prepared a brief analysis of our relations with social democrats and a general outline of views then prevalent in the Communist Party of Yugoslavia. Milovan Djilas, then president of the International Commission of the Central Committee, read both of my lectures in advance and refined some of the passages relating to our position.

On July 15 I gave the first lecture in London, at a meeting chaired by Morgan Phillips, secretary-general of the Labour Party. Here are some of the highlights of those lectures, with Djilas' additions in brackets:

Against monopoly on ideology in the international working-class movement:

At its congress in Frankfurt early this year, the Socialist International condemned communism *per se*. On that occasion, I stated that Russian imperialism found it useful to be called communism by many serious circles in the West. But why attribute to Soviet expansionism that noble goal [toward which some of the greatest minds from Thomas More on have striven] which for millions of people throughout the world signifies a way out of the situation they find themselves in, and which is in any case identical with the concept of socialism? One thereby only helps the Soviet government to conceal its aggressive aims more easily [and to hide behind the mask of the greatest and loftiest ideas of mankind]. Why give the Russians a monopoly over communism, when so many contributions have been made to the idea of communism by other countries? Among them let us consider the case of England. The idea originated in that country with Thomas More and developed through Levellers and Diggers to Robert Owen and the Chartists. Had not the *Communist Manifesto* been proclaimed in London in 1848? . . .

Revolution or Evolution:

I think it is erroneous to give out [absolute] prescriptions of one kind or another, that is, to say that either the peaceful road or revolution is the only right one. This depends on the historical development of individual countries, the present objective conditions, the awareness of the masses, international cooperation, and so on. There are countries, especially economically developed ones, where the first socialist reforms were achieved by peaceful means; such was the case with England. As I see it [it is not impossible that] England will develop further along these lines, that is, by expanding the existing forms of democracy. But what would happen, for instance, if Vickers-Armstrong refused to agree to nationalization and started organizing an armed resistance? Naturally, for present-day England this is nonsense, but there is no doubt that the government would be compelled to use force to implement the nationalization law. And in essence that would mean using revolutionary means to defend the socialist reforms already achieved.

For instance, we in Yugoslavia have been compelled to take power by revolutionary means, not because we are a romantic Balkan people who like war and blood, but because there was no other solution.

Consequently, in my opinion it would be erroneous [and harmful] to preach that the peaceful way is the only way to socialism, or on the other hand that victory can be assured only by revolution. It would be erroneous and harmful to generalize the experience of economically advanced countries and apply it to the whole world, particularly the economically underdeveloped countries. Life itself has already demonstrated this.

One must take account of reality. You carried out your industrial revolution over decades, and peacefully. Backward countries, however, which for objective reasons have not been in such a position, must do quickly, in a few years, what you spent a hundred years doing. They are obstructed not only by remnants of feudalism and the domestic bourgeoisie, which is linked with foreign monopolies, but also by imperialism in various forms and all kinds of tendencies toward conquest. Therefore in backward countries revolutionary methods are still possible, even indispensable, and therefore justified.

In our relations with the Socialist International, we had difficulties because the Italian Social Democratic Party exploited its position in the International to try to force on us an unjust solution of the Trieste question. At one of its congresses the International appointed a commission on this issue —upon the demand of one side, the Italian. It was wrong not to inform us also and ask what we, the other party to the dispute, thought about it. The question of Trieste is an international question. Since 1946 we had presented Rome with nine different proposals for solution of the Trieste issue and it had rejected every one. They did not even inform us of the commission's terms of reference or manner of procedure, but simply asked for visas for commission members so they could visit the Yugoslav zone, Zone "B" of the Free Territory of Trieste. We said nothing for two months, then rejected the request without explanation. Three days later the request for the visas was repeated. We then submitted our position in principle, saying that we did not want unequal relations and would not accept dictates—sorry, no visas.

On the Trieste question I worked in close association with Boris Kraigher and Branko Babić. Our policy, in which we all concurred, was originally Tito's. Discussions on the most important issues dealt with by the International Commission involved Tito, Kardelj, and Ranković. They were held every few months and I always attended, gave my opinion when asked, then implemented the decisions. Sometimes, if the matter was urgent, I received instructions directly from Tito. On the eve of our delegation's departure for the U.N. session in 1951—where we lodged a protest against the Soviet Union—Bohumil Laušman, the socialist leader and former vice-president of Czechoslovakia, emigrated to Yugoslavia. This was considered a triumph for us. He visited me and advanced the idea that we ought to put a radio station at his disposal over which he could call upon the Czechoslovaks to resist the Stalinists. I did not like this idea. He was later received by Tito, to whom he presented the same notion. Tito's secretary, Branko Vučinić, called me to say that I would be visited by Laušman again and that Tito had agreed with his proposals. Laušman came, beaming with pride, to tell me that Tito had promised to let him have the radio station and publish a newspaper. I explained that I did not think his proposals could be carried out. An embarrassed silence ensued. He left, saying he would complain to Tito.

Tito telephoned me, furious. I tried to argue: "We complain about the Russians using their territory to propagandize against us, giving radio stations to our citizens there so they can work to bring down our social system, and now we want to make the same mistake. We are about to lodge a protest at the United Nations; agreeing to Laušman's proposals would jeopardize the very foundations of our complaint." Tito went on upbraiding me, though, and I kept quiet.

A friend later consoled me and said I should not be so stubborn. I proceeded to meditate on my attitude and my relationship toward Tito. Perhaps it was affected by the fact that I had first met him as an ordinary person without realizing he was Secretary-General of the Party. One spring day just before the war broke out, Djilas and Lola Ribar had brought him to my flat in Miloševa Street to hide out for a while. Into my tiny attic room came a slender, blond man of medium height. His index finger was scarred—probably in a foundry, I guessed, and concluded that he was a worker. We talked all night about Spain, Russia, the Red Army. It was only a few days later that he told me who he was and what position he held.

The easy feeling of being able to talk to him freely had remained throughout the years. He had a good habit: when he did not agree with someone, he might blow up, but if he saw some good in the proposal he would later ask for more details. That had happened to me a number of times, and it turned out to be the case with Laušman. Some months later, when I was at the U.N., I received a letter from Tito:

This is the way matters stand with Laušman. It is true that I said he could work and publish his newspaper in our country. But I did not think of our case before the United Nations and of how this would weaken our position vis-à-vis the Russians. Therefore I agree that for the present he should begin in a neighboring country, and later we shall see. I do not think he will have much luck abroad. I was thinking of the considerable national minority in our country from which he could get material for his work and his newspaper. Explain my position to him when he comes.

Best regards from
Tito

I thought, sometimes it is a good thing to sit tight and be stubborn.

Yugoslavia's Protest at the U.N. ★

The battle with Stalin lasted five years. Although pressure from the U.S.S.R. and other East European countries came in waves and in a variety of forms, its intensity rose steadily until the death of Stalin. For instance, statistics show that more than five thousand frontier incidents took place during those long years: in 1950, 937; in 1952, 2,390—or two and a half times more. Whether the incidents occurred on our northern border with Hungary, or on the eastern with Bulgaria and Rumania, or on the southwestern with Albania, it was obvious that all this seething activity was directed from one place. In analyzing the technique of those provocations, some future military historian will fully discover the drama in which Yugoslavia was involved during those thousands of nights and days when no one knew where the enemy would strike next. It was a true war of nerves.

The military pressures varied in form, from troop concentrations near the Yugoslav border to other kinds of military demonstrations. At the time, there were indications that these demonstrations might mean preparations for armed action. This was the situation, for example, in the autumn of 1949 and again in the autumn of 1951. Moscow well understood the gravity of our military position, especially as regards heavy armaments. Our faith in Stalin before 1948 had made us order our military supplies exclusively from the East. And we did not receive modern equipment—most of it had been captured from the Germans—and for it we had contracted a loan of ninety million dollars in the Soviet Union. In 1948 our army had sixty different kinds of mortars; we were not permitted to build munitions factories to make mortar shells, but had to import them from the Soviet Union. Big Brother's embrace was truly a bear hug.

Information reaching Belgrade showed that the military pressure was not being organized in the neighboring states alone, but that preparations were being made in depth, that they were part of a serious plan for military aggression against Yugoslavia in which not only Yugoslavia's neighbors were involved. It was learned after Stalin's death that Moscow had made a decision in principle to invade Yugoslavia, and that a number of motorized divisions were ready and waiting in all the East European countries. But there were differences of opinion among the policy makers in Moscow as to the strategic and political consequences if Yugoslavia put up a strong resistance and the war dragged on. One group warned Stalin of the possibility of a world war, whereas another felt that the war would remain a local conflict, as in Korea.

When Stalin died, Bulganin boasted that he had been one of the group that had advised Stalin "not to strike at a hornets' nest." True, Bulganin had made this statement in a gay mood: however, having heard of his boast, I looked carefully through our archives and found that he had thundered loudly against Yugoslavia, not only from Moscow but also from Sofia, as for instance on September 9, 1949:

> The Judas, Tito, and his assistants, the malevolent deserters from the camp of socialism to the camp of imperialism and fascism, have transformed Yugoslavia into a Gestapo prison where every expression of free thought and human rights is stifled, where the best representatives of the working class, the working peasantry and the intelligentsia are being murdered savagely for fighting for the cause of democracy and socialism.
>
> Severed from the Soviet Union and the people's democracies, each day Yugoslavia is being transformed further into a colony of international, and above all American, imperialism.
>
> All progressive mankind views with repugnance these scorned traitors, agents, and lackeys of imperialism who do the will of their masters. But the Yugoslav people will have their say. The traitors will not escape the terrible judgment of their people. They will answer for their bloody crimes, their repulsive deceits and treason to the Yugoslav people and the entire democratic camp.

One of the East European statesmen who publicly voiced his opinion in the fall of 1951 that aggression against Yugoslavia would remain a local war and would not escalate into a world war was Walter Ulbricht. Ulbricht's statement was the subject of much of an interview that Tito gave late in August 1951, at Brdo in Slovenia, to the American newspaperwoman Marguerite Higgins, a correspondent for the *New York Herald Tribune.*

Miss Higgins asked the first question: "In view of the intensified Cominform propaganda against Yugoslavia and in view of the recent border incidents and the arming of neighboring satellite countries, is the war danger to your country rising?"

Tito replied at length:

> I have always considered this propaganda campaign against Yugoslavia as a war of nerves—not as an immediate danger for Yugoslavia, but rather as a threat, as pressure. The arming of Soviet satellite countries, which has long exceeded the bounds permitted by the peace treaties, is a greater danger today than it was previously, and this danger increases to the extent that we are not yet sufficiently armed. As this arming concerns countries on our borders whose leaders do not have friendly intentions toward Yugoslavia, it represents a growing danger to our country. As to the border incidents, the whole thing is still a war of nerves, although elements in it already begin to give some cause for anxiety. These provocations are no longer so insignificant, but I still consider them a war of nerves to which the Soviet Union will continue to resort. It is hard to say if there is justification for the world press asserting that Yugoslavia has never been as menaced as it is now, for we do not know what they have in mind. If they are aware that a war could cause a world conflict, they will be less prone to resort to aggression; but if they do not believe this to be so, then there is a danger of aggression. But by indulging in those border incidents, pressure, and propaganda, they are counting more on our weakening internally, in the hope that they will be able to bring about internal changes in our country and win positions here.

Miss Higgins: "What chance would the satellites have of winning a decisive victory against Yugoslavia if they attacked you without the help of Russia?"

I think that in such a case we could handle them, even now, with what we have at the moment. But it would be impossible for that to happen without Russia, just as it would be impossible for an attack on Yugoslavia to remain isolated and not be transformed into a world-wide conflict.

Miss Higgins then told Tito that during her recent visit to East Germany she had heard German leaders, notably Ulbricht, say that the war against Yugoslavia could be localized, like the war in Korea. She observed that this was an interesting philosophy. Marshal Tito replied that the statement showed the truth of what we said about thinking in the East.

In the autumn of 1951, in fact, not only did the pressure on Yugoslavia unfortunately not let up, but threats were intensified. Before then we had appealed to the Soviet government to stop attacking Yugoslavia. For instance, at the U.N. in September 1950, Edvard Kardelj had declared:

The peoples of Yugoslavia have defended in the past and will defend in the future the independence and integrity of their country from all aggression and all attempts to undermine their right to make their own decisions inside their country. But they will not participate in any kind of aggressive war, and wish to live in peace and peaceful cooperation with all peoples, and above all with their neighbors.

In spite of its consistently peaceful stand, the Yugoslav government states that it is willing to conclude an agreement on lasting peace and nonaggression with each of its neighbors.

But in Moscow this appeal was interpreted as a sign of weakness and was followed by even fiercer aggressive pressure, instead of the hand of peace.

Then, in the spring of 1951, the Yugoslav government issued

a white paper on the aggressive actions of the governments of the U.S.S.R., Poland, Czechoslovakia, Hungary, Rumania, Bulgaria, and Albania toward Yugoslavia. This collection of official documents and materials listed evidence on the following violations of international law: political forms of aggressive pressure; economic aggression; direct espionage and terrorist actions; and recourse to military force on the Yugoslav borders. It also cited the Yugoslav government's efforts to find an honorable and peaceful solution to the dispute.

Until now, the paper stated, Yugoslavia had not submitted this question to the United Nations but had endeavored to solve it through diplomatic negotiations between the parties directly concerned. But, the paper went on, if the governments of the U.S.S.R. and other East European countries rejected a peaceable solution, the Yugoslav government would be compelled to bring the issue before the United Nations.

After this introduction we submitted concrete proposals on how relations could be normalized with the U.S.S.R. and the other East European states:

The government and peoples of Yugoslavia state once again that they have denied no one the right to criticize Yugoslavia, its policies, and its conditions, according to his own views. Naturally, the government and peoples of Yugoslavia consider that they have the same right in equal measure. However, as concerns the behavior of the governments of the Soviet Union and other East European states toward Yugoslavia, this is a question not of the right to criticize, but of aggressive pressure against a sovereign state, accompanied by warmongering propaganda, economic blockade, threats, and so on. Consequently, the peoples and the government of Yugoslavia would like to hear the answers of the government of the U.S.S.R. and East European countries to the following questions:

1. Are these governments going to stop their aggressive threats against Yugoslavia?

2. Are [they] going to renounce interference in Yugoslavia's internal affairs?

3. Are they going to stop their economic blockade of Yugoslavia?

4. Are they going to stop aggravating relations with Yugoslavia?

5. Do those governments truly wish to maintain peaceful and correct relations with Yugoslavia?

The peoples of Yugoslavia would like to hear answers to these questions from those who so frequently emphasize the pacific nature of their foreign policy.

It is in the highest interests of the freedom and peace of an independent country, in the highest interests of peace and security in the Balkans and in the whole world, for the governments of the U.S.S.R., Poland, Czechoslovakia, Hungary, Rumania, Bulgaria, and Albania to stop undertaking aggressive actions against Yugoslavia and to take into account the cause of international peace and security in this part of the world.

As there was no response to these questions and the pressure continued building up, in mid-1951 Belgrade decided to acquire heavy armaments wherever it could. Accordingly, negotiations began with Western states. At the same time another far-reaching decision was made: to bring the dispute before the U.N.

Our delegation to the autumn session of the U.N. was headed by Edvard Kardelj. Other members were Milovan Djilas, Aleš Bebler, Leo Mates, Miloš Minić, Boris Ziherl, Veljko Mičunović, Ivo Vejvoda, Milan Bartoš, Koro Hadži-Vasiljev, and myself. Our resolution, drafted in Belgrade, read as follows:

The General Assembly,
HAVING CONSIDERED the complaint submitted by the Yugoslav delegation in connection with the activities of the government of the U.S.S.R. and the governments of Hungary, Bulgaria, Rumania, and Albania, and the governments of Czechoslovakia and Poland against Yugoslavia,

OBSERVING with grave anxiety the evidence of tension, as submitted in the foregoing complaint,

CONSCIOUS of the goal of the United Nations to "develop

friendly relations between nations, based on respect for the principle of equality and self-determination of peoples and to undertake other measures necessary for consolidating international peace,"

CONSCIOUS of the right of the General Assembly to "recommend measures for the peaceful solution of any situation whatsoever, regardless of its origin, which it feels might harm the general good, that is, friendly relations among nations,"

ACKNOWLEDGES the statement by the Yugoslav delegation to the effect that the Yugoslav government is for its part ready to do everything necessary to implement the recommendations of this resolution,

RECOMMENDS that the governments concerned:

1. regulate their relations and solve their disputes in line with the spirit of the U.N. Charter;

2. synchronize their diplomatic contacts with the rules and practice customary in international relations;

3. solve their boundary disputes by way of mixed boundary commissions or other peaceful means that they themselves select.

It had been agreed in Belgrade that during the general debate, Kardelj should present the reasons why Yugoslavia had decided to submit the issue to the U.N., and this he did on November 15, stressing that the aggressive behavior of the governments in the Soviet bloc had become a source of grave danger to peace. The complaint itself was to be submitted in the Special Political Committee by my friend and immediate superior Djilas. As I recorded in my diary, we came into sharp conflict—neither the first nor last between us—over his statement.

As soon as the decision had been made in Belgrade, I asked Djilas if he had drafted his statement from the standpoint of international law, as we were submitting the matter to the U.N. from the aspect of interstate relations and establishing which principles and provisions of international law had been violated by the aggressive pressure on us. Djilas said that naturally he had this in mind and that a group in the Foreign Ministry was helping him with it.

Although I had my hands full in the Third Commission, where we were working over a draft of the Universal Declaration of Human Rights, I saw the text of Djilas' statement a few days before he was scheduled to give it to the Special Political Committee. Reading it carefully, I thought it would be inappropriate for what we wanted to achieve in the U.N. Instead of laying stress on relations between states, on violations of international law, this was a Marxist disputation on philosophy, with theological overtones as to who was right and who wrong, and falling just short of discussing how many angels could fit on the head of a pin.

Kardelj and the rest of us were accommodated on the upper story of our ambassador's residence at No. 1 Boulevard Delessert; we saw each other all day long, since we worked in our rooms. So Djilas and I went to Kardelj's room for Turkish coffee and I said what I thought of Djilas' statement: it was suitable for an underground Marxist cell but it would only do our counrty harm in the United Nations. Again I had made my usual mistake: my criticism was sound, but I had put it so clumsily that Djilas was furious.

He leaped to his feet: "Do you think I don't love my country? How can you say something like that—that is outrageous!"

Kardelj blinked, raised his hands, tried to calm us down. No luck. Djilas stormed out of the room, banging the door behind him without saying good-by. Kardelj was cross, but said he would have a look at the statement.

Bad luck dogged me the whole day. That evening President Vincent Auriol was giving a reception for the delegations at the Elysée Palace. Djilas and I had been invited. We put on tuxedos; mine did not fit well, and I looked like a doorman in a better-class cabaret. In the car on the way to the reception Djilas and I continued our quarrel. I refused to shut up. Even as we were entering the palace and a footman in livery announced "His Excellency Milovan Djilas and M. Vladimir

Dedijer," I said something nasty and Djilas turned on his heel and left, just as we were approaching Auriol. Flustered, I stood before the silver-haired M. Auriol, who shook my hand saying, "I am happy to see you, M. Djilas."

The next day Kardelj summoned me to his room. Djilas was also there. Kardelj told me he did not agree with the way I had put things but that he did agree with the substance of my criticism. He had read the report and found it inappropriate; it would have to be written anew. Djilas took this good-naturedly. We slept on it, and the next day I begged his pardon for being so clumsy. This ended the incident between us. He never mentioned it again, nor did he ever try to "get even." We continued working together—he as president and I as secretary of the Central Committee's International Commission. (Upon returning to Belgrade he even proposed that I become president, which I immediately turned down, not being interested in formalities.)

Working day and night with Kardelj, Bartoš and Veljko Mičunović, we made a new outline. We had to get fresh material from Belgrade by messenger. Bartoš, Mičunović and I got no sleep for twenty-eight hours, until the statement was ready.

Our complaint came up on the agenda of the Special Political Committee on November 27. It was divided up as follows:

1. The origin of the aggressive pressure. Here we argued that the open, unconcealed pressure had begun on June 28, 1948, with the Cominform resolution, but that the U.S.S.R. had initiated its hegemonistic policy toward us and Eastern Europe immediately after the war.

2. The forms of aggressive pressure.

A. Political pressure: interference in internal affairs; official threats; frustration of normal diplomatic communication; hostile propaganda and mobilization of nongovernmental organizations against Yugoslavia, with special reference to the staging of trials; cancellation of international treaties and agreements.

B. Economic pressure and blockade.

C. Terrorist and diversionary activities.

D. Violation of human rights.

E. Terror against citizens of Yugoslavia: forcible detention of Yugoslav children, and the persecution of Yugoslav national minorities. As regards the first, facts were submitted to show that 91 children between the ages of 9 and 12 had been sent to the U.S.S.R. for schooling in 1945. In 1947, 16 were returned, and in July 1948 another 12. 63 children were still in the Soviet Union in 1951, therefore, being brought up not just denationalized but in a spirit of hatred for their country. As for the Yugoslav national minorities in Bulgaria, Hungary, and Rumania, not only were they forbidden to use their mother tongue, but groups from the boundary areas were resettled. Such measures bore all the hallmarks of collective punishment bordering on genocide.

F. Provocation of border incidents.

G. Military pressure and violation of military clauses in the peace treaty.

The Yugoslav complaint was answered by Soviet representative Arkadiye Soboliev, who claimed that "the purpose of the Yugoslav complaint is to deceive public opinion. . . . These slanderous remarks deserve no attention whatsoever." Although Soboliev spoke for forty-five minutes, he did not go into any detail, saying only that Yugoslavia was provoking the incidents, particularly along the Albanian border.

It was all allegedly linked up with the Rajk trial in Budapest: "The far-reaching aim of the boundary provocations was to provide a formal pretext for military intervention against Hungary, for the military occupation of Hungarian territory!" The main part of Soboliev's address was therefore based on "elaboration" of the Rajk indictment in Budapest and the Kostov indictment in Sofia: "At the trial of the traitors László Rajk and his accomplices, it was proven that leading persons in the present Yugoslav government participated as instigators and organizers in the plot to overthrow the government of the Hungarian People's Republic, murder [the country's] leading statesmen, and establish a fascist regime."

Soboliev also referred to Traiche Kostov's trial in Sofia, at which it had been "proved" that Yugoslavia had wanted "to annex Bulgaria quickly, a plan approved by the Americans."*

In the ensuing discussion a number of delegates stressed the reasonableness of the Yugoslav resolution—notably the Brazilian representative, Ribeiro Kuoto, otherwise his country's ambassador to Yugoslavia:

> It seems to the Brazilian delegation that this proposal, which concerns political problems of unusual gravity, was submitted to the committee with extreme moderation—a sign of good will and wisdom. This moderation would be surprising if we did not know, as we do know, the efforts shown by the Yugoslav government to stifle its wounded pride, a national pride which in its political maturity it sacrifices to the interests of Balkan peace. . . . This wisdom can only give us cause for rejoicing. It demonstrates that the Yugoslav delegation is capable of distinguishing between what its government has the right and freedom to say when it courageously replies to its opponents, and what it asks that we say and recommend—we whose task it is to apply the legal and objective principles of the United Nations Charter.

The delegates in the Soviet bloc—Ukrainians, Byelorussians, Poles, and Czechoslovaks—submitted their "facts" on the second day of discussion, but without much success.

After the Byelorussians, Djilas asked for the floor:

> I should like to request the representative of the Byelorussian Soviet Socialist Republic to be kind enough to amplify some of his data. Perhaps he can do so immediately. I should like to ask him three questions:
>
> First, the Byelorussian representative mentioned that an airport is being constructed near the town of Bačka. As there is no such town in Yugoslavia, may I ask him from which geography book he took this information, from what source?

---

* World public opinion perceived the holes in the Soviet delegate's statement. The *Times* of London noted that Soboliev's anger only reflected the weakness of his words.

Second, he stated that the Kamnik mine in Yugoslavia is in the hands of the Americans. As there is no such mine in Yugoslavia, can he explain this matter with more concrete data?

Third, he stated that the Yugoslav government had withdrawn the Law on Nationalization of Industry and Trade. I am a member of the Yugoslav government and know nothing of any such decision. I know nothing about any withdrawal of a law on nationalization of industry. Perhaps he has such information available to him. We do not.

Also, what is the source of his statement that the mines of Trepča and Bor in Yugoslavia are owned by American capital? The Byelorussian representative mentioned a certain American firm. Can he tell us where he got his facts from?

The Byelorussian delegate said nothing in reply to these questions.

Finally, the Special Political Committee voted on our draft resolution. Fifty states voted for it and five against (the U.S.S.R., Poland, Czechoslovakia, Ukraine, and Byelorussia). Iran and Afghanistan abstained—both having long common boundaries with the Soviet Union and insufficient military forces to defend them.

On December 7 Edvard Kardelj gave an interview to U.N. correspondents in which he discussed the significance of this vote. An Arab news agency correspondent addressed him: "We listened with great interest to Mr. Djilas' address regarding the Yugoslav complaint against the Soviet bloc. But for all that, the complaint was mild. Can you tell us why?"

Kardelj replied:

The Yugoslav complaint reflects our efforts to reduce the Yugoslav-Soviet dispute to such dimensions that it will no longer be a threat to peace. In the United Nations our delegation stated that the peoples of Yugoslavia ask nothing of the Soviet government but to be left in peace. All it wanted to stress was its request that the Soviet government in its relationship with Yugoslavia show at least minimum respect for a country's sovereignty and independence, without which lasting world peace would be impossible.

We therefore limited the resolution to the minimum which could and should be accepted by any government that claims it supports peace and the principles of the U.N. Charter. Our resolution does not therefore ask for much. But if what it does propose were to be achieved, it would suffice to change the situation on our borders and remove one focus of international tension.

However, as you know, the Soviet delegation was violent in its attacks and slanders against even this resolution. It showed not the least desire to eliminate the tension on our borders—thereby showing once again that as far as it is concerned peace is only propaganda, false phrases concealing the aggressive, hegemonistic substance of its actual policy.

The voting on the Yugoslav resolution demonstrated, however, that the world unanimously condemns Soviet policy against Yugoslavia. Therein lies the significance of its success. The support received by the Yugoslav people from the United Nations will help them considerably in their further struggle to defend independence and peace.

9.

The Painful Road
to the Truth

Before 1949 I had always imagined that the worst situation we had ever been in was the battle of the Yugoslav partisans at the Sutjeska, but that long-drawn-out year of 1949 seemed to me even worse, with pressure from the Cominform, troop movements on the borders, mistrust in the West, and the economy in a state of crisis. Factories stood idle. At the same time, plagued by our own dogmatism, we started a wave of forcible collectivization. Compulsory purchase of agricultural products was introduced. We clashed with the peasants, our faithful wartime allies. In the cities food was rationed and people had to buy it in the villages, but the peasants would not give it up. They had had centuries of experience in dealing with the state—once a foreign one but now their own. Here and there some of the junior officials succumbed to this war of nerves and threatened them if they did not give up their wheat to the state.

The West laid down harsh conditions for our trade. We had to export as much ore as possible, and timber from our beautiful forests. We did not have enough manpower. When we had to meet a certain quota and were undermanned, the militia simply loaded trucks with everyone it could find and took them off to the mines, factories, and forests.

Still, if the people had not shown so much initiative and the youth so much self-sacrifice, we would never have survived the crisis. That was our real cultural revolution—solving economic problems by revolutionary methods. But there were excesses, as in all such movements. Most of the people volunteered, but some refused, in which case force was applied and a terrible mess resulted: university professors were hauled off to dig coal in Aleksinac. One zealous Front member in the Zapadni Vračar district of Belgrade, who wanted to get the better of the eastern Vračar district, issued a directive that an official summons be sent to all those who did not volunteer. He took the lists of tenants in each apartment house and notified every citizen to show up at such and such a time with a shovel. He forgot, however, that diplomats lived on one of the streets, so a summons for street work was also issued to Her Majesty Queen Elizabeth's ambassador, Sir Charles Pick. This distinguished diplomat promptly went to see one of our Deputy Foreign Ministers.

"I would gladly do the work," he said apologetically, "for I am fond of your country. But I have been a war invalid since Ypres and could never fill the quota."

Those responsible for such scandals were taken to task, but our Front members and young people continued to be suspicious of all who did not do their part. Staying in Belgrade at that time was a Yugoslav prima donna from the Metropolitan Opera House in New York, who had come to visit her husband. Front members were very strict about checking on those living in the Dedinje residential area to see who responded to the summons and who did not. (My wife Vera was pregnant at the time but regularly went out to work.) One day in the Agitprop section of the Central Committee we received a note from the city Party Committee on Zinka Milanov: "She does nothing but sing, and she refuses to join the volunteer labor drives."

The total mobilization of the country for construction of key projects went on during all of 1949. (The army, too, worked with all its might, though it was also guarding the borders. Twenty-two per cent of our national income went for the armed forces; we could not afford to neglect them for even a moment.) Processing industries were developing, but the food industry lagged behind. Enforced collectivization had complicated the situation, and the cities and towns had unwieldy bureaucracies charged with the task of food distribution. For this futile bureaucratic occupation, we stripped our plants bare of personnel.

From that economic necessity, from that misfortune, came the beginning of Yugoslavia's system of self-management. It developed as we gained in knowledge of the Soviet social system; criticizing the latter, we were constructively criticizing our own existing system. Norms on credit planning and the market had to be revised.

Discussion on all these issues continued far into the night—particularly among Tito, Kidrić, Kardelj, Djilas, and Tempo. Kidrić was particularly keen on having Yugoslavia find her own economic form. He had organized his sector in a modern and efficient manner—receiving reports from even the smallest factories, rushing around the country talking to people, returning to his office in Miloseva Street, discussing matters with his assistants. Whenever a new idea occurred to him he would telephone Kardelj and Djilas to exchange views, and then rush off to Tito with a batch of proposals.

I began to notice the works of Marx and Engels in the offices of Kidrić, Kardelj, and Djilas. I knew they had studied the Marxist classics while in prison, but now they were reading *Capital* again, comparing our reality with the positions of Marx. Vlajko Begović, a close associate of Kidrić, remembers those days and nights of discussion: "One night Boris said we could keep the proletarians on our side only if we expanded their rights: the factories to the workers and the land to the peasants."

Kidrić elaborated that idea in his public statements:

> Under our present planning and financial system, almost the entire surplus product has gone from the state enterprises to the state treasury. Actually, the enterprises simply distributed to the wages and salaries fund. However, the enterprises' hands have been tied. Of course in this people's state—under the leadership of the revolutionary Communist Party which has since the very establishment of the new Yugoslavia pursued a keen struggle against bureaucratic tendencies and those who perpetuated them—in this state, that surplus product has been distributed to meet the needs of the working people, that is, socialistically. But it had inherent in it all the potential and latent dangers which led long ago to exploitation of the working people in the Soviet Union.

Between 1949 and 1953, long discussions about the Soviet social system occurred among Tito, Kardelj, Djilas, Kidrić, and others. The theory arose that the society was socialistic in form only, in substance being state-capitalism. Djilas, in charge of agitation and propaganda, had more time and opportunity to put these new ideas on paper and was inclined to theorize anyway. I think he was the first to argue this thesis about the U.S.S.R., but others, too, advanced their own theories.

Party members were not accustomed to articles by individual leaders not representing the Party line. But Tito himself discussed the Soviet system on a number of public occasions. And in an address to the second Party conference of Guard units in Belgrade on February 17, 1951, he stated that "a single theoretical article does not represent the line of the Party." Then, in the summer of 1951, the plenum of the Central Committee passed a decision of historical significance:

> 1. The development of new theoretical views in the CPY is pursued on the basis of discussion and exchanges of views. On those grounds, members of the CPY elaborate their theoretical viewpoints. Members have the full right to freely

express their opinions, either verbally or in Party or other newspapers, on the theoretical views of individual Party members, irrespective of their positions.

2. Branch Party organizations are under the obligation to study only the decisions of Party congresses and forums, and the statements of individual leaders having the same official character. Works of individual leading members which are expressly theoretical are to be studied by branch Party organizations only if the Politburo of the Central Committee has explicitly passed a decision to that effect—that is, in cases when these works are the end result of exchanges of views and discussions, and have direct practical and ideological significance for the further work and development of the Party.

3. The present Party theoretical organs belonging to specific Party forums should be all-Party organs for Marxist theory in which all members of the CPY have the right to participate.

Thus the process of democratization in the Communist Party of Yugoslavia developed parallel with the growth of self-initiative in the masses. When writing about the history of self-management in Yugoslavia, it should not be forgotten how very difficult it was at first. A means was being sought for something which had not previously existed—apart from the experience of the Paris Commune and so on—and within the Party itself there was considerable resistance to the very idea of self-management. We were constantly suffocated by dogma.

Boris Kidrić was the most radical in searching for new ways, and he burned himself out in the process.

This chapter was not written at one sitting. I tired toward the end; it was one in the morning, and the chimes on the bell tower of the church on Vič were striking the hours. I slept heavily and leadenly. Again I was with the dead, this time Boris Kidrić. I stood beside his memorial in Presernova Street. He seemed sad. "Vlado, why did my collected articles of 1948 to 1953, critical of the Soviet Union, never appear? Why did my collected works stop there?"

I started in my sleep. It was two. A locomotive was hauling a long train towards Trieste. The noise woke me up and I sat down at my desk again.

The Failure of the "Vladimir Dedijer" Cooperative ★

As we have seen, the Cominform resolution against Yugoslavia was followed by a tidal wave of collectivization. The formation of peasant cooperatives was stepped up. On January 1, 1949, there had been 1,318 such cooperatives in Yugoslavia, and on December 10 of the same year there were 6,492; during the same period the number of families in cooperatives rose from 60,156 to 323,849, and the land included in them from 323,984 to 1,782,614 hectares.

Why did we do this? Out of dogmatism, which still ran strong in us? To prove to the Cominform that their accusations were ill-founded? Or because of the famous "objective difficulties" to which our bureaucrats ought to raise a monument: you do something stupid, do not have the courage to say so, blame it all on "objective difficulties," and sleep soundly.

I once asked Tito to answer this question for me. I was visiting him on Brioni Island in July 1952, and had asked my school chum Tiča Stojanović, then Tito's secretary, to take down steno notes of our conversation. Afterward I even succeeded in getting the notes from Tiča. (Rumor has it that he still has about a thousand untranscribed conversations with Tito in his notebooks.) The reader might keep in mind that Tito was not in a good mood that morning, and I had been as persistent as a bulldog. But it turned out to be an interesting conversation after all. We began with more incidental matters:

DEDIJER: Comrade Tito, I am interested in knowing how you work, how you prepare your speeches, how you deliver them.

TITO: You want to see and know everything. . . . First of all, when I am doing something I don't like very much, I try to read to make the time pass more quickly. . . . I never write my speeches, except when speaking in parliament or for the press. I did not write that big speech about Italy, or any other.

DEDIJER: I noticed that you made a great deal of progress as a speaker during the war.

TITO: One cannot be a "born" speaker. It comes gradually, for some slowly, for others more quickly. Some people can never be speakers and others are forever babbling. In my own mind I systematize what I am going to say. I think of the basic idea, then I ask myself two or three subquestions, think about them, arrange them in systematic order in my mind—then it's not hard to make a speech. The rest I make up as I go along, in direct relation to the people I am talking to.

DEDIJER: Why is it that speeches over the radio are not so effective?

TITO: Naturally, they can't be. When I speak I am really conversing with the people.

After this introduction Tito unwound, and we had a long talk about how he wrote his reports, what he read, which languages he knew, and how much of each (he had forgotten Kirghiz), and then painting. (DEDIJER: "What do you think of socialist realism?" TITO: "It's awful. As though it had been painted with a shovel. They put that difficult question to me in the Hermitage, and asked if I liked Gerasimov.")

Then we got on to serious subjects. Tito first explained his concept of the role of the individual in history, and gave his definitions of socialism and "Titoism," the nature of our revolution, and individual liberties in socialism. He went on to speak of collectivization:

DEDIJER: Do you feel that it was on the peasant question that the Russians had the most negative influence on us?

TITO: We made a major mistake in following the Russian

way of creating cooperatives. We gave them a different name, but the method was the same.

DEDIJER: But there wasn't as much coercion as in Russia.

TITO: There was at the lowest level, in the field. All sorts of things.

DEDIJER: But there was no Siberia . . .

TITO: We had no Siberia, but if we had had one, we would have sent people there. I think it was a great mistake for us to do as the Russians did when we knew that even after twenty odd years the kolkhozes were not working well. That meant the methods were no good. We did not draw the right conclusions. These erroneous practices should have made us stop short. And we still have not got rid of all that. Now we let the peasants do as they like, but we still haven't found the right type of cooperative. We must do some re-thinking about the whole matter and find a better way to promote agriculture. We must find a form suitable to the internal life of the cooperatives, because the peasants do not feel at home in them. We made a mistake in following the Russian way and the sooner we get rid of it the better. We cannot allow the cooperatives to be disrupted now, as that would influence the creation of peasant households in the villages. We must also frustrate our opponents, and there are many. On the one hand, there is the class enemy who wants to make things impossible for us at any price. The class enemy has lost his economic position, but he is hanging on in the villages for all he is worth. He relies on the villages and makes difficulties for us in proportion to his strength there. On the other hand, there are people who like socialism, like the new society, like our way, but cannot see anything in the actual situation that is attractive to them personally. Perhaps there is something for them in a few of the cooperatives.

We have a great deal to do in the cooperatives, to make their organization and life more acceptable. But we cannot be radical and do it all at once. We have switched over to the system of business accounting; it has turned out quite well and most of the cooperatives have accepted it, but they still do not perceive all the benefits. The cooperatives' internal organization must be placed on a different basis; the peasant must be an individual and not a number, for he fears being a number. There are still some Soviet methods we must erase. It sometimes happens that a cooperative is set up and within a year there is a strong bureaucratic apparatus in it, meaning also a bureaucratic attitude toward the cooperative members. The cooperatives must have the maximum amount of democracy. Democracy must prevail everywhere.

The talk turned to the war days, to the peasants' participation in the revolution, which was actually a merger of working-class ideology and the peasant masses in revolt. I reminded Tito of something he has told a number of French socialists: "If there had been no war, our revolution would have been the most bloodless one of all." Tito took up the subject:

It turned out that our revolution, in contrast to the Soviet one, had a much wider mass base. This is precisely the special nature of our revolution. The broad base of the revolution resulted from its twofold character as not only a liberation struggle against occupation forces, but also a struggle against the old social order. If we had pursued only a proletarian revolution, it would not have succeeded. Or perhaps it might have, but only at Soviet bayonet point, and that would not have been a revolution and we could never have acquired such a mass following. That is the basic thing, that is what is specific to the character of the Yugoslav revolution: it was both a liberation and a proletarian struggle.

We are always saying this and there is nothing new in it. As soon as a revolution has a mass basis, it becomes less bloody. The more narrowly concentrated a revolution, the smaller and narrower the striking power, the bloodier it is; for it is weak, and weakness demands a lot of blood because it must achieve by bloodletting what cannot be achieved by force of circumstances. Although we had this mass basis, our war was bloody because we were an occupied country. Had there been no occupiers, there would have been no

Pavelić, Nedić, or the other traitors, and the revolution would have been far less bloody. At the end of the war we had so enormous a material basis for the revolution that the class enemies did not dare make a move. We nationalized them, and they could not do a thing; not a single shot was fired. That was for the simple reason that our revolution was so broad, broader than any in the world so far.

"Well, you see, in the beginning you were cross with me for nagging you, but this has developed into a fine discussion anyway," I told Tito. He laughed, and I suggested five minutes of mental hygiene—that is, that I tell him some jokes.

"Do you know that Vladimir Dedijer has kicked the bucket?"

"What kind of idiocy is that?" replied Tito.

"I'm telling the truth! In the village of Draževac, the old partisan center near Obrenovac, a peasant cooperative named Vladimir Dedijer was formed in 1946. The idea came from Ranković's mother, Grandmother Daca. She was reading my published war diary and suggested to the peasants that the cooperative should bear my name. But while I am a big man, the cooperative was not a very lusty child. It languished; in fact there were only seventeen households in it, although the village is full of partisans.

"The key to the situation was Ranković's uncle. All the peasants said that if he joined, they would too. But the uncle refused. Three years ago, when we were setting up cooperatives all over the place, we all went there on St. George's Day; Ranković ordered roast lamb and we sat around under an elm tree—Kardelj, Djilas, Ranković, and I, trying to convince the uncle to join the cooperative. But the old man just stroked his long white whiskers and smiled politely."

"What happened then?" asked Tito.

"Kardelj explained it this way: 'The old man refuses to join the cooperative, Vlado, because it's named after you.' There was some truth in that. Anyway, as soon as pressure let up on our old allies, the partisan peasants, Vladimir Dedijer disappeared overnight from the face of the earth."

The Thorny Path to More Humane Relationships ★

In revolutions and great social upheavals such as occurred in 1941–1945 and 1948–1953, when the fate of Yugoslavia hung by a thread, can the individual expect complete justice and equal treatment? In that atmosphere of "to be or not to be," do the innocent suffer? I first began brooding on this problem upon my arrival in newly liberated Belgrade in the autumn of 1944, and I have been pondering it ever since.

In the autumn of 1941, I was political commissar of the Kragujevac detachment when it was joined by a former Party member who had been expelled for being an informer during raids on the Party in 1937. He told us he wanted to fight with us to erase the stain on his character. We gave him a rifle and that same night he went into action. The next day the group commander reported that when the fighting started he had thrown down his rifle and fled. He was caught by a patrol, brought before the detachment's tribunal, and unanimously condemned to death. Just then the Germans made a break-through at Milanovac. I was wounded and had no idea what became of the fellow, when he was executed, by whom, and so forth.

By the end of 1944 I had forgotten all about the case. One day I was in the National Assembly building with a group of officers who were being awarded the Order of People's Liberation by Ivan Ribar. My glance fell on one of the men in the group, wearing a major's uniform. I recognized him as the man condemned to death by our tribunal in 1941.

How many such terrible mistakes had we made then? What had happened? The man had been sent to the Second Battalion for execution. Meantime the Germans attacked the battalion and the senior officers were killed. The man took a rifle, started fighting, and also, since there was no one else left to do so, took command. The partisans realized they could no longer execute him. The next morning the German offensive continued. Little by little, the man developed into a good fighter.

Now here he was at the end of the war a major, and I, his would-be judge, a lieutenant colonel.

In 1948, when Stalin's intelligence service infiltrated key positions in our army, security forces, Party, and major ministries, again that question came to mind: were they guilty— all those arrested for working for the Russians? Were there differences among them in terms of motive? Some were agents working for money and position, whereas others were simply confused. Had we not trained them for decades to be loyal to Stalin and the U.S.S.R.? Many found it impossible to change overnight, to switch themselves on and off; they had to grope their way painfully, to think through on their own to the conclusion that they had erred.

I knew that both army and civilian investigators were up to their necks in work, on the job day and night, with no private life, that they were going at it just like partisans in the toughest offensives. But were their criteria always just? Did they also err, as I had erred toward that man in the Kragujevac detachment in 1941?

I was troubled by this problem particularly after the spring of 1949, when the Yugoslav security forces scored a signal success in cleaning out the Soviet network in our country. Had this success gone to their heads, had they not thereby acquired great power, were their motives in ordering arrests always just? Also, what *were* the methods used? Were they perhaps fighting Stalinism with neo-Stalinist techniques?

I posed this problem openly for the first time after receiving from the Cadres Department of the Central Committee certain materials about Lale Ivanović, former counselor in the Yugoslav embassy in Washington. In 1948 he had come out in support of the Cominform resolution and gone on to become one of its most outspoken propagandists. In the materials I received, it was stated that Ivanović had been a Soviet agent even during the war. I wondered if we had known that before, while he was still in the embassy in the United States, or if we had learned it later, after he had opted for the Cominform.

The discussion was painful. I was reproached for being an

overly suspicious intellectual. I was in a bad mood anyway and replied that the methods were precisely the same as those the Russians used. Stalin had pronounced all old Bolsheviks spies from the cradle; this was not exactly the same, but not too different either.

The next day I talked with a responsible official who told me not to interfere with the work of the security organs, which were fighting a life-and-death battle not only with the Russians, but with Western agents as well, and also the Ustaši and Chetniks. We were again involved in a full-fledged revolution, he said, and if we let up even for a second, the country would go under.

But the battle against Stalin developed according to its own laws, and another side to the process was revealed. The only support the government had was the people, and this led inevitably to democratization. It was the beginning of a more humanitarian socialism, as society started sloughing off Stalinist influences not only in the security services but in all walks of life. Thus it happened that in the years 1948–1953 we went through two parallel processes: the strengthening of power as such, and at the same time the ebbing away of absolute power.

I had occasion to feel the effects of this process personally. The publishing house Jugoslovenska Knjiga asked me to prepare a new edition of my wartime diary with the three volumes abridged into one. I accepted the offer and began work. But someone in Jugoslovenska Knjiga secretly informed the security services that my diary mentioned many people who had become Cominformists. One of the top men in the Internal Affairs Ministry phoned to tell me I would have to delete the names of all Cominformists from the diary. I countered by saying that this would kill the book, that these were Stalinist methods, that it would be scandalous to do so. But he would have none of it. "I am telling you for the last time that you must delete them. We are in this up to our ears, and there you go giving them publicity. Traitors must be called by their true names."

"But they were not traitors during the war!"

The matter went all the way up to Tito, to whom I repeated my arguments. He agreed with me, and I wrote in the foreword:

"In preparing this second edition, I have done some slight abridgement which I thought necessary, while taking care to preserve the historic accuracy of each event and not to change essentially the role of any person."

In the diary's index Tito is mentioned in twenty-seven lines; Djilas in eighteen; Ranković in fourteen; Žujović in twelve; Kardelj, Koča Popović, and Peko Dapčević in eight each; and Arso Jovanović in six. However, without my knowledge, certain references to Žujović and other Cominform followers were deleted. I was extremely upset by this, especially as it coincided with an incident involving one of my associates: a report had arrived from the security services saying that he was a foreign agent, but I defended him strongly, telling the investigators that I would bet my life on his honesty, and so just managed to save his skin.

The more successfully the battle against the Cominform was waged, the more I wondered if all the arrested communists— and their number came to several thousand—were really guilty, or if in some cases their only crime was confusion.

In the autumn of 1951 I received a strange letter, postmarked Rudnica, near Kopaonik Mountain, from my boyhood friend Dragoš Stevanović, whom I had recommended to a publishing house for a job writing tourist brochures:

Vlado,

I heard you were angry with me. You say I disgraced you. I did. I couldn't hold out in that publishing house. I took the job to write, not to play the bureaucrat, not to be a small-time white-collar worker who has to put up with the inhibitions of that old maid, that crow with a wrinkled neck. I have been an athlete, and a man with real backbone. And they want invertebrates, sycophants.

Well, I just couldn't do it. So I left the job and took off for the woods, to live far away from those bums. I have saved myself. And now you save the others who are left behind.

Regards,
Dragoš, your former comrade,
now a vagabond and fisherman

I barely succeeded in saving Dragoš. There was talk that he was under suspicion for having left his job, that he was a deserter. His brother Draško had died a heroic death in the war as a communist. Before the war Dragoš himself had been a Party courier traveling back and forth from Paris with suitcases full of illegal material. I knew him inside out.

He was experiencing in his own way the entire conflict with the Cominform. He was sick and tired of Stalin, and was sick and tired of the woman who ran his office. And since he was a person who acted on instinct, he responded to the situation in his own way. For four months he wandered about the woods far from towns, his only human contacts an occasional fisherman or shepherd girl. His main companions were animals. When I finally caught up with him, his first words were, "Animals are better than people. You should see how they help each other. Their life is not just a struggle for survival—they have their own ethics, there is mutual aid among them."

"You think you're telling me something new? Kropotkin found that out eighty-five years ago. You big jackass, come over here so I can give you a hug."

There is something quite profound in Dragoš' experience. We often forget that in human society the greatest value is man. During the battle against Stalin in 1948–1953 two processes were in evidence, humanization on the one hand, and on the other the strengthening of certain structures, particularly certain branches of the government's executive power. The internment camp on the island of Goli Otok, in the Adriatic, was the best proof of this contradiction. The severe conditions in the camp, a miniature model of Siberian camps under Stalin, were introduced by security people trained in

Russia after the war. At the time I did not know all the details of what was going on there, but that does not exonerate any of us who were intensively engaged in the struggle against Stalin and his system.

Stalin, Mao Tse-tung, and Yugoslav Soccer Players ★

At the very beginning of the struggle Stalin had ordered ties in the field of sports to be severed between Russia and Yugoslavia. As circumstances had it, however, and against his will, the state soccer teams of the two countries faced each other during the 1952 Olympic Games in the Finnish town of Tampere. Under normal political conditions that would have been an ordinary game. But in view of the conflict between the two countries, then at its peak, this game attracted the attention of all sectors of the populace in Yugoslavia, even those who hate soccer and consider it "the opiate of the masses." There is no authentic data as to the reaction the soccer game evoked in the Soviet Union, except for a few short and tardy notices. But the dramatic outcome raised temperatures in Yugoslavia to fever pitch.

The game began very well for the Yugoslavs, with Mitić scoring the first goal in the twenty-seventh minute, Ognjanov the second goal in the thirty-fifth minute, and Zebec the third in the forty-fourth. In the second half the Yugoslavs continued their vigorous attack, and by the second minute Mitić had already raised the score to 4:0. In the fifty-ninth minute the Russians retaliated with a goal by Bobrov, making the score 4:1. Fifteen minutes before the end of the game, Bobek scored for Yugoslavia, making it 5:1. It seemed that Yugoslavia had won the game hands down, but luck turned against us: during the last fifteen minutes the Russians scored four goals from four corners, evening up the score and missing victory by a hair's breadth.

The game was broadcast, and apparently all of Yugoslavia was glued to the radio. That Sunday in July I was in New

York, where I had gone to deliver Tito's biography to my publishers, but my friends in Belgrade told me that the atmosphere was one of national mourning when the Russians started scoring. I heard from a reliable source that the director of one of our radio stations so lost his head that he called Tampere and told our radio announcer there: "Say that the Russians are playing rough, that they are fouling, that the umpire is on their side. Otherwise the people here will never understand."

After a short recess the teams played another two games of fifteen minutes each, but both sides were so exhausted that no goals were scored and the game ended with the result 5 : 5 (3:0).

Two days later, on Tuesday, July 22, there was another game, again in Tampere. This time the Yugoslav players were more cool and collected. Although the Russians scored the first goal, we evened up the score and started leading by 2:1. Then came yet a third goal. The Russians did not rally as they had the first time, however, lost the game, and dropped out of the Olympics.

After this victory there were joyful manifestations in Belgrade and all other Yugoslav cities. The newspaper *Politika* wrote on July 23 that men of the Yugoslav navy had sent the following telegram to the Yugoslav soccer team in Finland: "All our ships sounded their whistles to salute your victory. This triumph is a significant success for the representatives of socialist Yugoslavia. We send you best wishes." The *Politika* correspondent in Sevojno, near Užice, where a new copper rolling mill was being constructed, reported that three thousand workers vowed to finish the factory ahead of time in honor of the victory.

The Belgrade correspondent reported on songs made up by demonstrators to celebrate the victory:

> Tito—the Party
> Our victory
> Rajko—Bobek

Tito's players are stronger
Ours are better
Than Stalin's stooges

Our soccer players
Real bombers
Ours are better
Than the Cominform boys

The manager of the Yugoslav team, Aleksander Tirnanić, sent me a postcard from Finland:

Dear Vlado,
This is my happiest day.
After our greatest and most wonderful victory, best regards
Fondly
Tirke

Later, when I saw Tirnanić, he told me about some of the strange goings on after that victory. The Soviet players had refused to salute the public or our players. The captain of the Yugoslav team, Horvat, had gone up to the Soviet captain to shake hands, but the latter turned his head. The Finnish spectators chanted their approval of the Yugoslav players and hugged them as they left the field.

Many European papers commented at length on the game. A number of them took the Soviet team to task for refusing to greet the public, and even *Unità* found it necessary to comment on Horvat's gesture: "Sports bring people closer together and reconcile them."

Some Yugoslavs thought this news item a Cominform trick. *Borba* even commented that *Unità*'s purpose had been to make the West think we could come to terms with the Russians. I did not believe this and said so at a meeting of *Borba*'s editorial board.

On July 25 *Politika* carried a warm and human editorial condemning, not the Soviet players, but rather Stalin and his desire to lord it over everyone in all respects, down to the very last detail, everything being subordinated to a single purpose. No one minded the Soviet players striving to win for the prestige of their country, but when they lost they should have taken it in good grace, like true sportsmen.

At the partisan tennis court I later met Miro Radojčić, who wrote this article, and we agreed that we were not very different from the Russians, we did not know how to lose well. Our people have a good saying for this: "The one who loses is the one who gets angry."

Some French papers published the fantastic news that after their defeat in Tampere, the Soviet team had been disbanded and each player sent to a small provincial town. Poor fellows —but they got off rather lightly—they could have ended in Siberia!

It seems that Stalin did not go in for sports as a young man, which is why he treated those Soviet players as he did. But Mao Tse-tung was different, or such, at least, is the Yugoslav experience. On February 5, 1956, a Yugoslav team played soccer in Peking against the Peking team. The Yugoslavs won by a score of 3:1 in full view of 40,000 spectators—the same score that had been chalked up against the Russians in 1952. But the next day Mao Tse-tung received our team and spoke kindly to them. In some archive or other I have found a note on that reception, describing how Mao Tse-tung met the team in a large hall where photographs were taken, after which they all went into a smaller room and sat down at a long table with place cards for all the players and game organizers.

The Yugoslav organizer, Branko Pešić, greeted Mao Tse-tung, after which the Chinese organizer replied: "I should like to greet your team and through it your lovely country. Your team won and we shall learn a lesson from our defeat. That is one experience more for us. We should like to send a team to your country and ask you to teach them so that the Chinese team can be better and win also." What a difference from

Stalin's primitive reaction! Mao Tse-tung spoke like a true mandarin from a country with four thousand years of culture.

Tito's Biography Is Published ★

On September 28, 1952, I finished writing Tito's biography. The work on it had taken almost three years. I celebrated the event by inviting my boyhood friend Dragoš Stevanović for a cross-country race over Banovo Hill and around Košutnjak Park. I ran furiously, branches whipping my face as we raced through the woods. After an hour's running, we went back to my house for corn-meal pudding and milk.

Dragoš started talking about Milovan Jakšić, the best goal-keeper at the world championship soccer games in Montevideo in 1930, also a bookstore owner and good friend of ours, who had died of a stroke. I agreed with Dragoš that he had been a great man.

"Just think of it, Dragoš," I said. "Jakšić was not even a Party member and yet in 1941 I was able to leave the entire archives of our Party cell in *Politika* with him, as well as our cash box and some other things. And when Belgrade was liberated, I went to his street [Georges Clemenceau—now Lola Ribar—Street], and he gave me the archives and the Party money. He had kept them four whole years, his life always in danger since the Gestapo often searched his place. That's what you call honesty."

We were interrupted by the appearance of Slavica Fran, who was working with me on the biography, and Dragoš started teasing me about exploiting so many associates. I laughed and replied that I did so whenever I could. In New York, when I was winding up work on the English edition of the biography, I was assisted in reading proofs by Ratko Pleić, Paja Gregorić, the sculptor Avgustinčić, and especially one of our prewar sympathizers from Zagreb, Lujo Vajsman-Goranin. The latter even wrote a poem about my exploitation of friends and associates. I found it among some papers and started reading it:

Vlado Dedijer is writing a book.
He gets his help by hook or by crook.
The most overworked is Lujo, and the saddest.
When the work is over, he'll be the gladdest.

The book is a good one, but no end in sight.
We're reading the proofs, with all our might.
We all of us say it's a damned fine book.
It will really get them up on the hook.

In the last verse, Lujo and the others are portrayed as exhausted by their labors, and he says appealingly:

We ask you, oh Vlado, as we heave a sigh,
When will your fountain pen run dry?

That evening Djilas and I went to see Tito. I proposed that
Tito should in some way dissociate himself from the book, and
stressed that final judgment on the events concerned could be
passed only from a later perspective. Tito agreed immediately,
and requested Djilas to outline a letter to that effect. He then
added a few more precise formulations:

Dear Comrade Vlado,
    It was with great pleasure that I read the account of the
talks which we had before the war, during it, and in recent
years concerning my life and political activities, and which
you have recorded in this book.
    This pleasure arose from the fact that in reading your
manuscript I revived memories of a life which, as the book
shows, was no easy one, but from which I derived such hap-
piness that I would not on the whole choose any other if
I had to make the choice now.
    I must say that not only have the talks been accurately
recorded, but the facts also correctly established and presented.
    But I am sure you will agree that the book's interpreta-
tion of various events cannot be considered as definitive, for

the simple reason that final judgment requires a longer perspective.

With comradely greetings,

Tito

It then occurred to me that Tito himself ought to write his memoirs, after all the pertinent documents had been sorted out. When I said so, Tito threw up his hands in despair: "How can I, when I am up to my neck in work?"

He then waved us to another table and took out a chess set. "I see you wrote for the American edition that I am such a bad chess player that even a poor player like yourself beat me 6 to 2."

"You'd better watch out, Stari. Do you know that at Hastings this summer I even beat a master, Miro Radojčić?"

The game ended in a draw. Tito was not pleased.

Before the biography appeared in book form, it ran as a series of articles in many magazines and newspapers throughout the world. I had an interesting discussion about this with Marko Ristić. He thought the series should be published in left-wing and progressive newspapers, whereas I was aiming at papers with a big circulation, regardless of political orientation. So I chose *Le Figaro* of Paris, the London *Sunday Times, Le Soir* in Brussels, and *Life* in America. Thus the book reached the reading public at large. It is not my fault if progressive papers in the West have small circulations.

The right wing started a campaign against the series everywhere. In the United States, *Life* was flooded with letters of protest, especially from European fascists who had fled to America after Hitler's collapse. For me the main thing was to see that the truth about Yugoslavia and Tito reached the American reading public. In France even King Peter joined the fray, writing an article for *Le Figaro*. But I did not reply. Another one to put in an appearance was Živko Topalović, a social democrat from Belgrade and a close wartime collaborator of Draža Mihailović.

After its serial publication in newspapers and magazines, it went through thirty-eight separate book editions in thirty-six languages.

Moscow reacted sharply. The Cominform paper *For Lasting Peace, For People's Democracy* reviewed it under the caption "The Biographer of the Hangman of Belgrade," and branded me a spy, murderer, and bandit. This was proof that the book had helped us break through the Soviet blockade. Moscow had a tremendous propaganda apparatus throughout the world, with powerful communist parties to help it, while we had nothing comparable and no money to finance such undertakings. We had to use our brains, our own resources. But even here we ran into difficulties. Our ambassador in Bonn cabled me: "Found progressive publisher to publish Tito biography 5,000 marks." I wrote back: "And I have found the biggest German publisher, Ullstein, who will pay us 25,000 marks."

The proceeds from the book were considerable. *Life,* for instance, had paid a higher fee only to Eisenhower, Churchill, and the Duke of Windsor for parts of their memoirs. I might have done better than these crowned and uncrowned heads, but Tito did not permit me to raise the price. (The battle for the highest possible fees was skillfully conducted by my literary agent, John Phillips, a journalist who had come to the Yugoslav partisans from Italy in 1944 and had personally photographed Slovene partisan attacks on the railway lines between Germany and Italy.) At any rate, the question came up of what to do with all this money—more than 150,000,000 dinars or, at the exchange rate of the time, somewhat over half a million dollars. Djilas thought I should give the entire sum to the Party, whereas I wanted to commemorate my late wife Olga, who had lost her life while heading the surgical team of the Fourth Montenegrin Brigade (later the Second Division). There were few hospitals in Montenegro, least of all in the Nikšić area, so why not a new hospital?

The final decision was made by Tito. He thought I should have my way, although Djilas teased me for being a petty bourgeois. So I sent to Montenegro the entire sum received thus far. The Montenegrin newspaper *Pobjeda* carried a news item that Vladimir Dedijer had sent the first installment of so many dinars for the construction of a hospital. However, the money kept coming in and I decided to send some of it elsewhere. When my wife Vera and I were in Slovenia, we heard that the Slovenian government had refused to continue subsidizing the theater in Postojna. This struck me as regrettable. The Slovenes had not been able to speak their mother tongue for a quarter of a century while under Italian control, and now the Slovenian government was refusing help to a theater fostering the Slovenian language and literature. I told Vera that all the money received in the following weeks would go to the theater in Postojna.

Vera's face lit up. As we were about to leave, I overheard a conversation in the other room between her and my mother Milica, who was trying to persuade Vera to keep some of the money for the family.

"Look, you don't have a refrigerator—and the state of the children's clothes! Vlado should really put aside something out of all those millions for the children and you. You know he is sick and if, God forbid, the worst happened, you would be left with five small children. I know what that's like, because I was left a widow with three."

But Vera would have none of it. "That's the way we are, we really don't need anything. Look at the way the people are living. Slavica, for instance. She worked twenty hours a day while the biography was being completed. Then when Vlado wanted to pay her for all that typing day and night, for keeping track of the materials, for the work she did on top of her regular job, she got so angry that she said she'd never help him again with any book if he persisted in trying to pay her."

The actors at the Postojna theater sent me a cordial reply, together with a leather-bound repertory of their performances and a beautiful stalagmite from the Postojna Caves. Nor did they forget me later, even after their theater was disbanded,

when my family and I fell on hard times. In October 1959 I
was taking a cure at the Lasko spa, after the suicide of my
son Branko. Vera and I were suffering from terrible depression. All night we would listen to the clock towers of the
churches of Lasko striking the hours. Vera said she envied
those mothers who believed they would see their dead children
again in an afterlife. One day we received a wonderful warm
note from two former Postojna actors who had heard of our
tragedy. We wept with gratitude at their helping us not to
lose faith in humanity.

I never received word from Nikšić as to what they had done
with all those millions I had sent. I could understand their
not writing, but Olga's parents waited and waited for word,
and finally died without knowing whether the hospital named
for their daughter had been constructed. I was wretched and
bitter about the whole thing. Not long ago I talked with the
Montenegrin author Miodrag Bulatović about it. "Look at the
difference between the Slovenes and the Montenegrins," I said.
"For the Slovenes, each dinar represents so much human labor,
so many drops of sweat. That is why those actors from Postojna
never forgot us. But for you Montenegrins, money is just a
subsidy. You got to be that way during the time of Peter the
Great."

Bulatović protested. "You are not objective about Montenegrins. You have to *understand* them. They are waiting for
you to send the second installment, and then they will inform
you what they have done with the first."

The Sixth Congress of the Communist
Party of Yugoslavia ★

The longer the battle with Stalin lasted, the more excited
and emotional both sides became. The atmosphere recalled
the religious conflicts of the Reformation. As time passed and
the Yugoslavs found themselves still alive despite Moscow's

anathema, they grew surer of themselves. This feeling was reflected in every plenum, every congress, every conversation with the man in the street.

The Sixth Congress of the Communist Party of Yugoslavia began in Zagreb on November 2, 1952. It dealt principally with the struggle against Stalin since 1948, and submitted a criticism of the Stalinist system. One innovation introduced at that congress was a new name for the Communist Party of Yugoslavia: the League of Communists of Yugoslavia. This meant that the Communist Party could no longer manage things directly, that the state could not be identified with the Party, and that the standard administrative methods for running the country had to give way to methods of ideological and political struggle. This decision was made at a time when the introduction of worker management had been designated as a turning point in the development of Yugoslavia's direct socialist democracy.

Koča Popović, who greeted the congress on behalf of the Yugoslav army, stressed that the struggle against Stalinism had thwarted the danger of degeneration of the revolution, that is, that conditions had been created permitting the unfettered promotion of socialist productive forces and socialist relationships in society. "This fact," he said, "is worth emphasizing, especially in view of the tragic fate of the masses in the Soviet Union and in the countries of so-called people's democracy."

In conclusion he referred to the role of the army in the country's defense: "We have referred here to the past four-year period during which aggressive 'Soviet' policy toward Yugoslavia suffered total defeat. But we harbor no illusions about the danger having passed. We know whom we are dealing with. The latent danger of aggression still exists. That is why we are continuing to strengthen our army."

Mika Tripalo spoke of the importance of young people's participation—first in the war and now in the resistance to the Cominform. He remarked that young Yugoslavs had constructed many projects with their bare hands: railway lines, the Brotherhood-Unity Highway from Belgrade to Zagreb, and so on. He read out the inscription on a plaque from one of those projects:

> To our homeland and Party—we have built into a better future for the working people a part of our own youth, a part of the springtime of our lives. If need be, we will give our whole youth to guard what we have achieved so far under the leadership of the Party and Tito, shoulder to shoulder with the whole nation. . . . And the machines humming in the new factories, the trains gliding along the new lines, the electric power bringing light to remote villages— let them too repeat: "The young hands that built this will know how to defend it with a hundred times more energy."

On the second day of the congress Tito submitted his political report. He began by referring to the roots of the basic conflicts besetting the world, especially condemning the spheres-of-influence agreements of Churchill, Stalin, and Roosevelt. No one was surprised that the Western representatives behaved according to "their usual old imperialist way of solving world problems," he said, but for all those "who had believed in the selflessness of the Soviet Union, who had believed in the U.S.S.R.'s reputation as a protector of small nations, this was the first moral blow, the first strong feeling of doubt in the U.S.S.R., in the rectitude of Soviet policy."

> Even before the war, during the war, and especially since Teheran, the Soviet Union abandoned the policy of protection and even respect for the sovereignty of small states and the will of small peoples. Why had it done so? Because it had betrayed socialist principles and gone the way of old Czarist Russia, the way of Great Russian state interests, the way of imperialist methods to achieve those interests, while endeavoring to conceal this behind the revolutionary cause of the international proletariat. . . .
>
> What are the reasons for such an unsocialist foreign policy? They lie in the Soviet reality, in the entire internal

structure of that country—economic, political, and cultural. Long ago the Soviet Union deviated, in its internal development, from the path of socialist development to the path of state capitalism with an unprecedented bureaucratic system. In the U.S.S.R., bureaucracy has become an end in itself. More and more it is being transformed into an exploiting power above society, which not only obstructs the further development of the revolution and revolutionary thought, but also gradually liquidates the attainments of the October Revolution and acquires an increasingly counter-revolutionary character.

Tito bore down hard on the theory of a "leading nation" within the U.S.S.R., which had, "in terms of the outside world, been transformed into the theory of the Soviet Union's leading role in the world."

Pursuit of the policy of a leading nation in the U.S.S.R.— that is, of the Russian nation—has had terrible consequences for the U.S.S.R.'s non-Russian nations. Once upon a time, before they were enslaved by Czarist generals, some of them had been not only ethnically compact but politically independent; today they have been wiped from the face of the earth in the most brutal manner possible—one that even Hitler might envy. The theory of a leading nation in a multinational state reflects the actual subordination, national suppression, and economic exploitation of that country's other nations by the leading one. Naturally, the non-Russian nations resisted this theory and practice and are still doing so today. Some of them, being small, were consequently resettled in the Siberian wilderness or exterminated, like the German republic on the Volga, the Tatar republic in the Crimea, the Kalmyks and the Chechens, the Tannu Tuva republic, and others; also the peoples of Estonia, Latvia, and Lithuania, who lost their independence by Soviet conquest in 1939 and who even today are being deported to Siberia by the tens of thousands, thus being liquidated not only as states but in terms of their existence as a people. . . .

Even today the world scarcely realizes that from 1935 on it was precisely the leading *communists* in those nations who offered determined resistance to such an imperialist policy on the part of the top people in Moscow. To some extent we do know the fate of members of the Central Committee and Politburo of the Communist Party of the Ukraine, headed by Secretary Postishev; he and members of the Central Committee—Kosyor, Chubar, Skripnik, Popov, and many others—were arrested and executed, allegedly for nationalist deviations, but actually because they resisted Moscow's imperialism. The same fate overtook leading communists from other republics in the U.S.S.R., as for instance in the Communist Party of Byelorussia, where 361 of the 421 middle- and top-level leaders, expelled from the Party in 1937–1938, were liquidated.

These brutal methods of destroying people, primarily the leaders, in the smaller national republics, were used by Stalin and his associates to bring those peoples under the yoke of Moscow's hegemony. Stalin also gradually liquidated all the old Bolsheviks of merit, not only removing them from their posts but doing away with them physically.

Tito went on to speak of Yugoslavia and international co-operation; relations with the international progressive movement in the world; decentralization and democratization in the management of the economy and the organs of government; Yugoslavia's economic development and the consequences of the economic blockade; the growth in defense expenditure; and finally the work and development of the Communist Party of Yugoslavia in the period since the Fifth Party Congress in 1948.

It was also at this congress that Boris Kidrić made his last speech before his death early in 1953. He spoke of the principles underlying the new Yugoslav economic system:

1. Management of the factories and enterprises was to be in the hands of the workers actually engaged in production.

2. The new economic system was to be based on objective economic laws, administrative strangulation of which would be avoided as much as possible.

3. Interference by society in the operation of those objective economic laws should be drastically reduced to the general guidelines which we, in our contemporary planning terminology, call the basic proportions of social plans—guidelines which prevent capitalist anarchy in social production and also set the direction of the country's economic growth. It is within these guidelines that industrial workers and the communes should develop the greatest possible initiative.

4. There must be genuine social appropriation of the surplus product, and socialist management of the same.

One of the oldest revolutionaries, Ivan Regent, a Slovene from Trieste, was given a warm welcome when he spoke of the reasons why the Communist Party of Yugoslavia had the courage to resist Moscow's policy. Then Edvard Kardelj spoke about international relations with East and West, stressing that Russia's aggressive policy was the main reason for present world tensions. On the proposal to change the name of the Communist Party of Yugoslavia, he said: "I think that the proposal submitted by Comrade Tito gives clear indication of the new and essential elements in the development of socialism in Yugoslavia: a final squaring of accounts with bureaucracy and state capitalism, and the affirmation of socialist democracy as the only possible form of power by the working class and working people generally."

Milovan Djilas spoke about the Party's program, and especially the program submitted to the Fifth Congress in 1948, which had been so full of illusions: "As far as I and many other communists are concerned, I did not see or guess at anything ominous in the reality of the U.S.S.R. until late in 1947 and early 1948. . . . To be sincere and honest and to be a revolutionary is always right even when it is naive. . . . We need not be ashamed of our revolutionary illusions . . . or of the 1948 program. Even such as it was, it should be dear to us, although mistaken and full of illusions."

The congress wound up on November 7, the day the October Revolution is celebrated. Djilas delivered what was perhaps the best speech in his life, stating that the Yugoslav revolution had taken over the banner of the October Revolution, which Stalin had cast in the mud.

The Sixth Congress was marked by a militancy amounting virtually to a spasm. An atmosphere very like it must have prevailed among the Cossacks of Zaporozhe when they wrote the Sultan a letter and threatened the scribe with dire consequences if he did not include the well-turned curses he himself was addressing to the ruler on the Bosphorus. In such an atmosphere, no wonder people went to extremes.

Thus it happened that accounts were squared with the Holy Father in Rome and with Ljubodrag Djurić. The Pope had raised Archbishop Stepinac of Zagreb to the rank of cardinal, and we decided to break off diplomatic relations with the Vatican just as Christmas, the day of peace and love, was approaching. As for the unfortunate Ljubodrag Djurić, commander of the celebrated Second Proletarian Brigade that had saved the day at the battle of the Sutjeska, he was smarting under the wrongs done him by certain persons in high position. He got drunk so as to screw up the courage to speak, then went out on the congress podium to tell the story of his woes. Poor fellow, he was removed and proclaimed a traitor—said to have received instructions from the enemy to scuttle the congress. Later it was ascertained to be a purely personal crisis that he could no longer bear. Injustice had really been done him.

The Death of Stalin ★

On March 4, 1953, news arrived that Stalin was on his deathbed—a report that aroused hope in Yugoslavia for better relations with the U.S.S.R. That day I decided to start making daily entries in my diary again, having done so only sporadically before.

WEDNESDAY, MARCH 4, 1953. I have started making regular entries again. It would be a pity not to record the events as they happen.

This morning the telephone rang around five. I could hardly make out who was calling me—someone speaking English who wanted a statement for the *Daily Express:* "Stalin is seriously ill and may already be dead. What do you have to say for the *Daily Express?*"

Stalin seriously ill—the words echoed through my mind. I had no idea what to say, so I mumbled something that went like this: "Interesting report, but at the moment I'm rather sleepy. No comment. And thank you for the lovely news."

Then I sat up in my bed and started looking through the books on the shelf above it when the phone rang again. Tanjug confirmed the report. I dialed Djilas. He knew nothing about it. He called Stari on the special phone, as well as Kardelj and Ranković. I got dressed and went straight to Tempo's house to tell him the glad news. He was not at home, so I went to his office and we embraced with joy.

Faces all over Belgrade were beaming. It is in poor taste to rejoice at the illness of a mortal enemy, but the people could not forget how he had tried to humiliate us.

Later Djilas came to my office. He said, "I am glad we struck out at Stalin while he was still in good form. I think his last thought before the stroke must have been: 'Ugh, Yugoslavia is not giving in.' "

I asked Djilas what he would give me for being the first to tell him the glad tidings. He took out a gold wrist watch, presented to him by Tito on February 22, the day the Fourth Front Congress was held, and said: "Tito won't be angry if I give you this watch, because the news is really big." He gave the watch to his secretary to send to the goldsmith for the following inscription: "To Vlado for the good news. Djido."

Then we read the official communiqué from Moscow. Djilas said, "They go into such detail they seem to have taken the whole thing out of a medical textbook. It looks suspicious."

Veljko Vlahović, Veljko Mičunović, and I had lunch at Djilas' house—corn-meal pudding with potatoes and buttermilk.

"In Stalin's honor!" I said. We talked of Stalin and what he had meant to us at various periods.

"He was a good wartime leader," Djilas said.

And we talked about the period just before the war. I blurted, "Well, let's not get sentimental about it."

Djilas: "For us Yugoslav revolutionaries, his name is linked with many periods of grueling struggle. For us he was the symbol of that struggle. But all revolutions have their illusions."

"Now it's clear how much historical credit we deserve for unmasking him," said Vlahović. "Imagine if there had been no conflict with us, how erroneous the impression of him would be and how much time would have gone by before a true assessment could be made."

THURSDAY, MARCH 5, 1953. Today Branko Vučinić [Tito's secretary] telephoned to ask me to be at the Košutnjak Railway Station at eight p.m. When I arrived I found Kardelj, Djilas, Ranković, Gošnjak, and a dozen or so people: Simić, Tempo, Stefanović, Mičunović, Popović, Bebler. Stari was leaving for England. He was in a good mood. I caught him for a second to ask him to read the message to the people of Great Britain which would be published in the *Picture Post*. As the train was leaving, Tito said jestingly: "Take care of Yugoslavia for me."

After he had left, we talked about the significance of his visit to England. It was timed perfectly—not only because of Stalin but because he was going to London with the Balkan Pact in our pockets. The pact was important in case of a possible attack from the East, but also because of Italian appetites in the West.

Djilas said it was a good thing my book came out before Stalin's death. We had told him the truth to his face while he was still alive. Kardelj added: "What's more, it will now be even clearer that our criticism was right."

I got home after midnight. Just as I fell asleep, the phone rang. It was Tanjug, telling me that Stalin had died.

SATURDAY, MARCH 7, 1953. We were at Djilas' house for lunch again, the two Veljko's and I, after a short meeting to study the list of the new Soviet leaders.

Djilas said that this was a matter of historical significance. First of all, in essence, an *anti-Stalinist coup* was taking place. Stalin had hardly been laid out in his grave, and already the decisions of the last Party congress were being changed as regards both Party statute and personnel. All of it was very meaningful.

I said that I had made a comparison of the Soviet press at Lenin's death and at Stalin's—much less homage in the latter case.

Djilas remarked that Malenkov's election was a surprise. He had thought Molotov would be the man. Then he smiled. "If Malenkov follows in Stalin's footsteps, how are they going to call him the Great Malenkov [malenkov means "small"]?"

Look asked me to write an article about Stalin's death— a thousand words for three thousand dollars. I refused. We are not Riga, living by anti-Soviet propaganda and offering analyses to the Americans.

FRIDAY, MARCH 20, 1953. Tonight Djilas gave a dinner for the Vilfans, who have just come back from India. Tempo and Ranković were there. We talked about Russia. Someone said the worst that could happen would be a takeover by the army, which would mean orientation toward military aggression.

I took an empty cigarette pack in my hand, tore out the back part, and wrote the following sacrilegious thought on it:
STATEMENT
The day will come when even we shall mourn Stalin and set up secret Stalinist cells in the Soviet Union.
March 20, 1953   Vladimir Dedijer
I read my solemn statement aloud. Ranković took it and wrote: "I am confiscating this piece of paper," laughed, and handed it back to me. I added "Approved by V.D."

Stalin lost the battle not on the day he died but much earlier. Sometime in the autumn of 1949 I had firmly come to the conclusion: God has disappeared and I have no more gods. "The honest fools"—many of them, anyway—were coming to their senses. But it was not only in men's minds that Stalin had lost the battle. His unsuccessful attacks on Yugoslavia had revealed the following *urbi et orbi:*

1. Soviet society under Stalin had been full of contradictions —not contradictions inherited from the society that the revolution had destroyed, however, but ones generated by the new socialist structure.

2. A socialist state can engender hegemony, strangle other states (even socialist ones), and furthermore aggress against them.

Stalin died in 1953, but Stalinism remained. True, it was dormant for a while, but the summer of 1968 demonstrated just how tenacious and dangerous it could be.

Ethics—abstract, class ethics? To solve all the problems in human relations one must create the awareness that ethics are universal, that you cannot throw out the baby with the bath: the revolutionary class should take what is best from the past and raise it to a higher level for the sake of progress. Socialism's goal cannot be mere industrialization but the raising of human values to a higher level. That is one of the great experiences of Yugoslavia's struggle against Stalin. At the end of Tito's biography I summed up Tito's vision of socialism as follows:

> This, in summary form, is the attitude of the Yugoslavs toward their main internal and international problems. It is the attitude of a people striving in its *own way* to build a society in which there will be no exploitation of man by man, in which an individual will be freed of the fetters of the state, in which he will fully enjoy all economic, social, and political freedoms. That is what Tito calls socialism.

It is true that in 1948 Stalin sullied the banner of socialism; that banner fell, and we picked it up. But we do not have a monopoly over socialism, nor is the Yugoslav way the only one. Like every revolution in the twentieth century, ours had its own specific features and cannot serve as a model for others, except as an example of revolutionary self-sacrifice and achieving the impossible—proof that there are no barriers the awakened masses cannot bring down.

At one point in my ceaseless meditations I wrote down something which became the theme for a study of ethics in the Yugoslav revolution, examining the relationship between spontaneity and ideology in revolutions, and the indispensability of the ethical basis.

"Our revolution succeeded only insofar as it was able to identify itself with the genius of the people, reflected in the basic self-initiative of the masses. The greatness of the Yugoslav revolution therefore consisted in its democracy, and the revolutionary leaders were great to the degree they realized they should not go against that national genius, that the revolutionary initiative of the masses should not be curbed by a desire to centralize the war unduly or in a way at variance with the nation's moral and spiritual framework."

In writing this down I believed I had found the formula which—at least for the present stage of my deliberations—best expressed my belief about the secret of the Yugoslav revolution. Guided, but only along general lines, by the idea of revolutionary ideals, the revolution developed on its own and gained in power as it went along through direct and applied democracy. Carried out during a cruel and terrible war, our revolution nevertheless acquired certain elementary forms of broad popular democracy, and yielded incredible examples of self-initiative, not only within the framework of the various nationalities of Yugoslavia, but also in terms of local self-government. Later developments not in keeping with this initial spirit weakened and violated it.

The Yugoslav revolution, with its many components and organizational forms, could not but have its ups and downs, and the heroism—itself the most striking expression of the revolution—was a simultaneous proof of the complexity of the motives behind it.

"I am proud of following in the footsteps of men; freedom will spring from my blood," said a Montenegrin peasant woman from Andrijevica on her way to execution for having sheltered wounded partisans in her home. But do these words reflect only a forced heroism? No, and no again. They reflect a socially and emotionally developed attitude. That cry of the Montenegrin peasant woman, her people oppressed for centuries by a primitive and patriarchal environment, expressed also the deepening of an altruistic ethic, the strongest and most basic component of European civilization: *a desire for social equality.*

I saw similar strivings every single day during our revolution. *Borba,* printed in the midst of the grueling Fourth Enemy Offensive in the snows of the Bosnian mountains in 1943, once carried news that an enemy officer had been executed and his seven-year-old child captured. The headline read: "The Child is not to Blame."

Or again, at the time when Ilya Ehrenburg was writing articles in *Pravda* entitled "Kill the Germans" and Stalin was resettling the German republic from the Volga, a different awareness prevailed among most Yugoslav partisans: "Kill only the German who attacks your people with gun in hand; extend your hand to the German who wants to be a man." That same year the first German detachment of our army, called the "Karl Liebknecht," was formed in Slavonia.

Or to take another example: the old government was brought down in battle and a new revolutionary one created on its foundations. But it was infected from the outset by a doubt: would the soldier, the servant of the revolution, be transformed into the master of society? This problem revealed itself in minor matters, and the revolutionary had to attend to them immediately lest they grow like a malignant disease that begins innocently and silently enough, only to explode later and destroy a powerful organism. Would the revolutionary, because of his position, because of the power he exercised in the name of the revolution, have a greater right to material things—to food, accommodation, horses, etc.—than others who were fighting beside him? The temptations were great. But a good prescription against the disease was given by an old Serbian peasant, a communist for decades, who in 1941 commanded the Valjevo Partisan Detachment, the most celebrated unit in Serbia during the first year of the revolution. Here is what that man, Dudić by name, wrote in his diary: "The evening meal in the field at night. We had cooked food. But I cannot say what it was like, as there was not enough for me. In our detachment, the rule is that the leaders come last in terms of rights and first in terms of responsibilities."

I have already made mention of this diary, but the problem Dudić resolved in 1941 (before he was crushed to death by a German tank in Užice) was raised again for us in 1948–1953. In many ways this later battle had deep roots in the revolution and war of 1941–1945, at least on the moral level. The battle against the Cominform was not just one big "Hurrah!" Not everything progressed in a straight line, in black and white. The key questions of socialism were posed again just as they had been in the early days of the uprising. The initiative of the masses was powerfully expressed again, after having receded between 1945 and 1948, and the first seeds of the system of self-management, of collective participation, were planted. Social changes took place in which two opposing processes were developed: on the one hand, the humanizing of socialism, the harmonizing of the relationship between the individual and society, the state and society—the first signs of freedom from fear and pressure; and on the other hand, the strengthening of the executive authority, a certain complacency about the victory over the Soviet agents, a certain smugness, indications of which we had noticed at the start of the revolution.

A terrible nightmare oppressed all of us: was it possible to fight Stalinism not with Stalinist but with other means? For the process of liberation from Stalin as a god did not proceed evenly, equally, and simultaneously for all. There were some who became demoralized, in the full sense of the word, although they did not come out in support of the Cominform. The revelation of what Stalin really stood for left an emptiness, a vacuum which they filled with the worst type of philosophy, summed up in the words: "We shall not live long, so let's make the most of it."

Another development appeared: some of those fighting the Cominform felt their strength and power growing as Stalin lost one offensive after another. Were they always being truly revolutionary when deciding the fate of people at their mercy? Were they precise in differentiating between real agents doing what they did for money, and confused persons who were ideologically at sea? Decisive action was required on the part of the executive authorities and their superiors. But were there not subjective errors too, and even self-will? Were all ten thousand communists involved with the Cominform guilty in the full sense of the word? I have received countless complaints about unjust procedures during that period of struggle, some of them offering proof of miscarriages of justice.

One cannot rest easy in the face of these facts. But one must touch all the sore spots, delve into all the hidden corners, for only then can one first see oneself in perspective, against the framework of history.

Intellectuals must be suspicious of everything, above all of themselves. This soul-searching is a tough discipline, but it is the only sure way if man is to clear the thorny path to the future.

It is important to avoid conforming, to avoid being mired down in a petty-bourgeois mentality, to react as your conscience tells you. I myself have often faced temptations along these lines. The atmosphere was not pleasant in early November 1952 in New York. The Republicans had won the elections. Did that mean the triumph of the appalling Senator McCarthy and his inquisition? An official of the United Nations committed suicide. With little fanfare Mrs. Roosevelt was replaced as her country's delegate in the Third Committee. Charles Sprague, the delegate who replaced her, took the floor in a discussion on a Soviet draft of the resolution on "Measures to Suppress War Propaganda." Equating the Soviet Union with communism, he remarked that the countries of Eastern Europe were "under the yoke of communism," that the U.S.S.R. was spreading "communist propaganda" abroad.

I outlined a reply, and in the right-hand corner of my notes wrote: "In honor of the Sixth Congress of the Yugoslav Communist Party [then meeting], let at least one voice be heard in this mad America against the witch hunt conducted against communism."

I addressed three remarks to Sprague:

The distinguished delegate from the United States has submitted his opinion, but I feel it is a great blunder to say that the countries of Eastern Europe are under the yoke of communism. We in our part of the world do not feel this way for, as we see it, the idea of communism has nothing in common with the hegemonistic tendencies of the Soviet system, and is not the motor force behind Soviet expansionism.

Secondly, not only in our part of the world but in many other parts, communism is considered not as the monopoly of one country, but as a goal toward which the greatest minds of mankind have been striving for centuries—Thomas More and Robert Owen of England, Saint-Simon and Fourier in France, Marx and Engels in Germany, Lenin in Russia. Every country has the right to choose its own way of life and to hold its own views of the world.

I should like to call the attention of the American delegate to the fact that, by calling the hegemonistic tendencies of the Soviet Union in Eastern Europe "the spreading of communism," he is confusing the issue and thus assisting the Soviet Union in its aims in Eastern Europe.

Our delegation took a mixed view of my statement. The "professional diplomats" were very much against it, feeling that I had gone too far and that what I had said would obstruct relations with the new American administration. Only Veljko Vlahović, head of the delegation, took up my defense: "A man cannot act against his revolutionary conscience."

That was my last appearance at the rostrum of the United Nations. But I kept to a sacred rule: never denounce Saint

Nicolas because of a Nicolas, either domestic or foreign.

This pursuit of the voice of my conscience, this constant soul-searching, this restlessness that seems always to pursue me, brought me to Stockholm in 1967, to the Russell International Tribunal for Inquiry into War Crimes in Vietnam. As chairman, I asked for permission to make a few personal observations at the end of the session:

> I know we are all aware of the tremendous support our tribunal has won in the world, attested by the enormous number of telegrams [we have received]. But we should not forget that powerful institutions and structures are hostile to us and the truth we proclaimed.
>
> Some of us will be subjected to pressure because of this, particularly in the United States of America. I know that my fellow judges on this tribunal from America, David Dellinger, Courtland Cox, and Carl Oglesby, are men with love in their hearts, men of great personal integrity who will bear up under all trials and tribulations.
>
> You are the defenders of all that is best in the tradition of your country, you are the guardians of the bonds that must be established among people on all continents, among men of various colors, cultures, and religions.
>
> We can never forget that a small nation of peasants, the Vietnamese, have been subjected to the fury of the military machine belonging to the mightiest power in the world.
>
> We can never forget that the same weapons brought before this tribunal today, those terrible bombs used against civilians, are at this very moment being dropped on Hanoi, on other Vietnamese towns and villages, that hundreds of thousands of little shepherds like the young Do Van Ngoe, with his horrible burns from napalm bombs, have been doomed to a premature death.
>
> Let us swear by our conscience as free and independent men, that we will do everything in our power to stop these mass murders. The legitimacy of our tribunal is based on human will, on the consciousness of the masses throughout the world, and that consciousness is slowly being transformed into a powerful physical force.

Our session ended like no other court in the world. We were a revolutionary tribunal. The first to leap to his feet was Colonel Han Van Lau of the North Vietnamese army, who embraced us and wept, followed by others in the hall, filled to overflowing with Swedish citizens.

The sky was blue. I went to the harbor, sat on a bench, and took out of my pocket Andrić's *Story from Japan*. Never had I read with a fuller heart:

Among the Three Hundred and Fifty Conspirators banished under the rule of the Empress Au-Ung was the poet Mori Ipo.

He spent three years on the smallest of the Seven Isles in a hut made of reeds. But when the Empress fell ill and her power started to fade, he, like most of the Three Hundred and Fifty, succeeded in returning to the capital city Jedo. He lived on the outskirts of the city in a wing of a temple.

The citizens, sickened by the bloodthirsty tyranny of the mad and cruel Empress, grew to love the poet more and more, and the Three Hundred and Fifty were his inseparable companions. His short verses about heroism and death were passed secretly from hand to hand, and his kind smile often settled the disputes of his comrades.

It happened that the Empress died unexpectedly from the poison of general hatred. Her corrupt chamberlains ran away, and she lay ugly and swollen in the deserted palace, with no one to bury her.

The Three Hundred and Fifty Conspirators quickly assembled and seized power. They divided the ranks and honors among themselves and began to rule over the unified Empire of the Seven Isles.

When the first ceremonial meeting was convened in the palace of the late Empress, it was discovered that one of the Three Hundred and Fifty was missing. And when the list was read aloud, it was found that the poet Mori Ipo was absent. They refused to deliberate without him and at once a slave with a rickshaw was dispatched for him. After a time the slave returned with the empty rickshaw: he was told that Mori Ipo had gone and that he had left a written message for the Council of the Three Hundred and Fifty. The oldest in the Council took the folded paper and handed it to the Chief of the Official Learned Ones, who began to read aloud:

"Mori Ipo extends his greetings to his comrade conspirators, at this hour of departure!

"Profound gratitude from my heart, my comrades, for the common sufferings and for our common faith and victory. I beg you humbly to forgive me because I cannot share authority with you as I shared the struggle. Poets—unlike other men—are faithful only in the hour of calamity and leave when there is well-being. We poets are born for struggle; we are passionate hunters, but we do not eat the prey. A thin, almost invisible barrier stops us; it is not so keen as a sword edge, but just as lethal. Without damage to my soul I could not cross this line, because we can endure everything but authority. This is the reason I am leaving you, my comrade conspirators. I am going to see if there is somewhere a thought which has not yet been realized or a cause unfulfilled, but if any calamity or danger should befall our Empire of the Seven Isles and the need comes for struggle and succor, then seek me out."

At that moment the chairman of the Council, who was a little deaf, interrupted the reading, and with the impatience of an old man and with disapproval in his voice, said, "No calamity can befall the Empire during the just and enlightened rule of the Three Hundred and Fifty."

All the counselors nodded, and the older ones smiled with disdain and pity. "What nonsense!" The reading was discontinued and the bill on customs taxes was taken up instead.

Only the Chief of the Official Learned Ones read the poet's message to the end, to himself, after which he wrapped it up and deposited it in the archives of the late Empress.

Index

Adamic, Louis, 234–48; and Cominform, 242, 243, 244; letters to Dedijer, 242, 243, 244; death, 246–48; and Roosevelt, 60; in Yugoslavia, 239–42
Adamic, Stella, 236, 238, 244, 247
Albania, 31, 33, 56, 59, 114, 193–96, 207, 218, 220, 230, 268
Apró, Antal, quoted, 224
Arabjac, Svetolik, 157
Arbeiderer, 20
Association of Friends of Yugoslavia, 164
Atlantic Pact, 270
Attlee, Clement, 62, 270
Auriol, Vincent, 285, 286
Austria, 44, 93, 118, 124, 193, 209, 210–212, 215, 230

Babić, Branko, 276
Bakarić, Vladimir, 14, 33, 68, 101, 111, 183
Balkan Pact, 323
Baloković, Zlatko, 234
Bartoš, Milan, 221, 253, 258, 283, 286
Bebler, Aleš, 142, 143, 220, 221, 244, 255, 283
Begović, Vlajko, 293
Belgrade, 5, 11, 22, 26, 33, 78, 79, 83, 93–94, 98, 113, 118, 128, 134, 141, 159, 292; Adamic's visit to, 239–42; Cominform headquarters in, 119, 125, 128
Bentley, Elizabeth, 243, 244, 248
Berezin, General, 75–77, 83

Beria, Lavrenti, 108, 161, 180, 188
Bevan, Aneurin, 24–25
Bhose, Chandra, 18
Birčanin, Ilija, 61
Biro, Zolton, 119
Blažević, Jakov, 122
Bohlen, Charles, 198
Bolshevik (Moscow), 113, 154, 204
Borba, 55, 132, 191, 204, 207, 225, 308, 327
Bosnia, 5, 19, 54, 87, 89, 115, 214
Božović, Saša, 44
Brankov, Lazar, 218
Brest Litovsk, Treaty of, 270
Brilej, Jože, 63, 64
Broz, Josip, *see* Tito, Marshal
Bucharest, 35, 128, 129, 132, 154
Budapest, 87, 121, 123, 154, 199; Radio, 263; Rajk trial in, 217–18, 221, 223, 227, 254, 287
Bugarčić, Vuka, 263
Bulatović, Miodrag, 315
Bulganin, Nikolai, 104, 188, 225, 279
Bulgaria, 13, 32, 33, 34, 59, 65, 67, 101, 102, 104, 110, 111, 114, 186–92, 193, 207, 220, 230, 268, 288; cancels treaty of alliance with Yugoslavia (1949), 218
Burma, 9, 18, 22–23, 24

Cachin, Marcel, 172, 173
Cairo, 55, 61
Calcutta, 9, 15–18, 24–27, 29, 144

Cankar, Ivan, 45
Capital (Marx), 293
Carinthia, 44, 209–12, 269, 272
Cassin, René, 164–65
Castle, Barbara, 227–28
CDKA, 161
Chambrun, Gilbert de, 176
Chang Han-fu, 23
Chartorisky, Adam, 117–18
Chetniks, 7, 61, 147, 194, 256, 303
Chiang Kai-shek, 6, 8, 22, 68–69, 183
China, 3–9, 22, 23, 66, 68–69, 104, 182–185, 269; casualties in World War II, 39; Communist Party of, 6, 8, 122, 182, 183, 185; guerrillas in, 5, 9
Chou En-lai, 8
Churchill, Randolph, 58–59
Churchill, Winston, 59, 62–70, 237–38, 270, 313, 317
Çitizen Kane, 256
Čolaković, Rodoljub, 223
Cominform, 27, 35, 105, 118–21, 122, 125–132, 142, 164, 175, 179, 200, 204, 328–29; and Adamic, 243, 244; and biography of Tito, 313; resistance to, at Fifth and Sixth Congresses of Yugoslav Communist Party, 143, 316–317; Yugoslavia anathematized by (1948), 35, 129, 130, 132, 134, 140, 175, 177, 263
Comintern, 5, 8, 24, 32, 47–52 *passim*, 54, 116, 118, 127, 155, 156, 187
Communist Manifesto, 274
Cot, Pierre, 176, 177, 178
Cox, Courtland, 331
Crnobrnja, Bogdan, 102
Croatia, 59–61, 129n.
Cvijić, Jovan, 14, 208
Czechoslovakia, 34, 38, 71, 101, 114, 133–36, 138, 182, 193, 199, 200, 224, 231, 254–57, 262; cancels treaty of alliance with Yugoslavia (1949), 218; Soviet invasion of (1968), 191, 224, 231; Stalinist purges in (1948–53), 224

Daily Express, 322
Dalmatia, 56
Danube Conference, 153, 154, 159, 163
Danube Convention, 158, 268
Dapčević, Peko, 61–62, 206–207, 304
Dapčević, Vlado, 158
Decree on Peace (1917), 66
Dedijer, Olga, 41–45, 239, 264, 313, 315
Dedijer, Vera, 9, 10, 37, 196, 239, 240, 241, 292, 314, 315
Dedijer, Vladimir: addresses United Nations, 259–61, 262; as director of Information Office, 153, 203, 228, 240; in Great Britain, 62–65, 270,

273; in India, 15–19, 21–23, 26; joins Communist Party, 38; in Kiev, 164; lectures to British Labour Party, 273–75; on Negro rights, 165–66; in New York, 221, 234–35, 249–53, 306–307; and nightmare at Oplenac, 263–267; in Paris, 163–66, 167–68, 198; as president of Physical Culture Federation, 160–61; Russian attacks on, 44–45; in San Francisco, 6, 256; Tito's biography by, 107, 169, 252–53, 310–313, 325; United Nations as his university, 258–62
Dedinac, Mima, 168
Dehouse, F., 259
Dellinger, David, 331
Dimitrov, Georgi, 12n., 31–33, 48, 68, 101, 127; and Stalin, 186–92
Disraeli, Benjamin, 63
Djerdja, Josip, 189, 258
Djilas, Milovan, 9, 14, 26–27, 31, 33, 62–65, 68, 101, 102, 106–108, 111, 130–131, 134, 149, 183, 205, 207, 213, 221, 255, 273, 283–86, 293–94, 304, 313, 320, 322–24; quoted, 130, 149, 185, 190, 194, 288–89, 320, 323
Djurić, Ljubodrag, 321
Djurić, Stanojko, 44
Documents from the People's Liberation War, 99
Drašković, Juraj, 129
Dubrovnik, 271, 272
Dudić, Dragojlo, 146, 328
Dutt, R. Palme, 10
Dzhumaya, Gornya, 139

Eagle and the Roots, The (Adamic), 239–42
Eden, Anthony, 60, 65
Ehrenburg, Ilya, 327
Eisenhower, Dwight D., 58, 313
Encyclopedia of Yugoslavia, 143
Engels, Friedrich, 198, 293, 330
Estonia, 318

Farge, Yves, 176
Fedoseyev, P., 154
Ferdinand, Archduke, assassination, 124, 132
Figaro, Le, 312
Fischl, O., 219
For Lasting Peace, For People's Democracy, 27, 111, 126, 154, 313
Fotić, Konstantin, 60, 138, 234, 257
Fran, Slavica, 130, 263, 310, 314
France, 56, 71, 164, 172, 211; Communist Party of, 20, 114, 169–78 *passim*; at Danube Conference, 153
Franco, Francisco, 213, 269
Frank, Jozef, 219

French Revolution, 25
From Trotsky to Tito (Klugman), 221

Gandhi, Mahatma, 18
Geminder, Bedrih, 219
German-Soviet pact (1939–41), 20, 56, 57
Germany, 59; in World War II, 20, 40, 48, 115, 301
Gestapo, 45, 212, 220, 310
Ghese, Bhadmadhab, 18
Gligorov, Kiro, 74
Glišić, Milovan, 266, 267
Goli Otok island, internment camp on, 305–306
Golubović, Radonja, 157
Gomulka, Wladyslaw, 126
Gošnjak, Ivan, 220
Great Britain, 49, 55, 56, 59, 62, 93, 164, 211, 269, 323; casualties in World War II, 40; Communist Party of, 221; at Danube Conference, 153; Labour Party of, 273
Greece, 65, 67–69, 71, 193, 213, 220, 269–70
Gregorić, Paja, 310
Guindev, Panayot, 192
Gunther, John, 246

Hadži-Vasiljev, Koro, 283
Hajd, Vavro, 219
Han Van Lau, 332
Hapsburg, Otto, 60
Hearst, William Randolph, 256
Hebrang, Andrija, 34, 83, 111, 123–24, 141, 157, 188
Hervé, Pierre, 177
Herzegovina, 19, 22, 63, 87, 214
Higgins, Marguerite, 280–81
History of Diplomacy, The, 67
History of the Soviet Communist Party, The, 112
Hitler, Adolf, 20, 34, 39, 40, 41, 46, 47, 51, 54, 56–57, 59, 109, 132, 210, 272
Hoxha, Enver, 163
Humanité, L', 172, 174, 175
Humo, Avdo, 22
Hungary, 34, 59, 67, 75–76, 86, 101, 122, 125, 133–34, 219, 224, 268, 287; cancels treaty of alliance with Yugoslavia (1949), 218; Communist Party of, 114, 122–23

India, 10, 14–26, 144; and British imperialism, 16, 18; Communist Party of, 9, 10, 17, 19–25, 27–29, 167–69; Congress Party of, 18, 20
Inprecor, 5
Iran, 86, 269
Istria, 56, 88

Italy, 55–56, 59, 71, 93, 115, 193, 269, 313; Communist Party of, 114, 126, 178–80
Ivanović, Lale, 27, 137–38, 302
Ivković, Milutin, 5
Izvestia, 204

Jager, Vili, 9, 204, 242–43, 263
Jakšić, Milovan, 5, 310
Jakšić, Pavel, 83
Japan, 8, 18, 69
Joint-stock companies, 73–95 *passim*, 102
Joshi, J. P., 18, 21, 28
Jovanović, Arso, 35, 157–59, 304
Jovanović, Dragoljub, 138
Jugoslovenska Knjiga, 303
JUSPAD, 75–83
JUSTA, 75–83

Karaivanov, Ivan, 48, 155, 156, 228
Kardelj, Edvard, 14, 28, 33, 68, 74, 93, 95, 101, 107, 108, 111, 112, 114, 131, 139, 155, 163, 164, 165n., 183, 202, 211, 213, 214, 221, 255, 270, 276, 283–286, 289, 293, 304, 322, 323; quoted, 70–71, 184–85, 205, 254–55, 281, 289, 320
Kavran, Božidar, 147
Kennedy, John F., 230
Kersnik, Janko, 14
Khrushchev, Nikita, 225, 231
Kićevac, Milan, 93
Kidrić, Boris, 74, 77, 84, 85, 100, 103, 107, 197, 205, 213, 293, 295, 319; quoted, 74–75, 294
Kirov, Sergei Mironovich, 223
Kiš, Egon Ervin, 226
Klementis, Vladimir, 136, 219, 223, 224, 227–28, 256
Klugman, James, 221
Kocbek, Edvard, 41
Kolarov, Vassil, 32
Kolo, 135
Kommunist, 28
Korea, 66, 69, 279, 281
Kosanović, Savica, 60, 258
Kostov, Traiche, 32, 129, 139–40, 189; indictment and trial, 218, 220–21, 223, 228–29, 263, 287; quoted, 139, 228; rehabilitation, 224, 230
Kovačević, Nikola, 9
Kraigher, Boris, 276
Križman, Ivan, 36
Križman, Lado, 36
Križmančič, Andrej, 237–39, 244
Kruševac, Čedo, 22
Kulaks, 112, 205
Kuomintang, 8
Kuoto, Ribeiro, 288

Latvia, 318
Laušman, Bohumil, 276–77
Lavrentyev, Ambassador, 100, 107–108, 111
League of Communists of Yugoslavia, 316
League of Nations, 164
Left Book Club, 10
Lenin, Nikolai, 24, 37, 56, 66, 114, 198, 203, 204, 208, 260, 270, 324, 330
Life, 312, 313
Life of Josip Broz, The (Vinterhalter), 224
Li Li-san, 185
Literary News, 214–16, 246
Literaturnaya gazeta, 191
Lithuania, 318
Little Soviet Encyclopedia, 67
Liu Shao-chi, 184
Ljubljana, 37, 88, 133, 209
London, Artur, 219
London Treaty (1915), 56
London Tribune, 166
Long March, Chinese communists', 8
Look, 324
Luka, Vasili, 129
Lupescu, Madame, 155, 156

McCarthy, Joseph R., 329
Macedonians, 18, 37, 93, 140, 193–94, 209, 220
MacNeil, Hector, 227
Malaya, 23, 24
Malenkov, Georgi, 69, 188, 324
Maljcev, Orest, 45
Manchester Guardian, 137
Manuilsky, Dimitri, 6, 48, 52, 164
Mao Tse-tung, 5, 9, 69, 182–83, 186, 269, 309–10
Margelijus, Rudolf, 219
Marković, Svetozar, 45
Marshall Plan, 198
Marx, Karl, 56, 198, 203, 293, 330
Maslarić, Božidar, 220
Masleša, Veselin, 39
Mates, Leo, 258, 283
Mayhew, Christopher, 165
Menon, Krishna, 25
Mičunović, Veljko, 221, 251–52, 283, 286, 322
Mihailović, Draža, 7, 49, 51, 61, 62, 234, 264, 312
Mikoyan, Anastas, 102
Milanov, Zinka, 292
Minić, Miloš, 283
Mitić, Rajko, 160, 162, 306
Mitrović, Dojčilo, 263
Molotov, Vyacheslav, 6–8, 53, 61, 65–66, 95, 115, 120, 126, 140, 163, 194, 204, 211, 324; sends ultimatum to Yugoslav government (1949), 212–14, 254

Monde, Le, 153, 204, 206, 207, 250, 269
Montenegrins, 14–15, 42, 149, 315
More, Thomas, 274, 330
Morić, Zvonko, 74; quoted, 83–84
Moscow, 32–33, 65, 102, 112, 113, 211; Foreign Languages Publishing House in, 113; Radio, 49, 122; Yugoslav military delegation in (1948), 31; see also Soviet Union
Mossadegh, Mohammed, 269
Mrazović, Karlo, 219–20
Mukherjee, Sushil, 18
Murphy, Robert, 58
Myrdal, Gunnar, 25

Nadj, Kosta, 61–62, 220
Naples, 55
Nasyetnik, Filip, 113
Nedić, Milan, 59, 300
Nešković, Blagoje, 61–62, 100, 206, 266n.
New China Daily News, 23
New York Times, 137, 184, 247, 249, 252, 257
Neychev, Minche, 189–90
NKVD, 107, 110, 156
Norway, 59, 208; Communist Party of, 20
Notes on America (Dedijer), 239
Nyeftanoe Hozyaystvo, 86

Oglesby, Carl, 331
Olympic Games, 5, 130, 162, 306–309
Oplenac, Dedijer in, 263–67
Oranski, Petar, 212
Oswald, Lee Harvey, 230
Owen, Robert, 274, 330

Palfi, Gyorgy, 218
Panyushkin, Ambassador, 250–51
Paris, 163, 164
Paris Express, 166
Paris Peace Conference (1946), 3, 93, 153, 163, 226, 227
Partisans, Yugoslav, 40–44, 51, 61, 94, 98, 109, 146, 327; opposed by Mihailović, 49; Supreme Headquarters of, 39, 47, 49, 54, 98, 99, 110, 210
Pauker, Ana, 129, 138, 155–56, 158–59
Pauker, Marcel, 155–56
Pavelić, Ante, 59, 147, 300
Pavlov, Todor, 141–42, 148, 164, 233n.; quoted, 142, 233
Peasant Portraits (Kersnik), 14
Penezić, Krcun, 264, 267
People's Liberation Army, founding of, 49
Perović, Puniša, 141
Pešić, Branko, 309
Peter II of Yugoslavia, 51–53, 138, 147, 312
Petrićević, Branko, 158

Petrović, Rastko, 168
Phillips, John, 313
Phillips, Morgan, 273
Physical Culture Federation of Yugo-
slavia, 129, 133–36, 160–63
Pick, Charles, 292
Pieck, Wilhelm, 127–28
Pijade, Moša, 42, 47, 52, 54, 65, 93, 122,
129, 205–207, 216, 222; quoted, 65–
66, 124, 187–89, 199, 207, 212, 214–
215
Pittsburgh Press, 243
Pleić, Ratko, 249–52, 310
PM, 237
Pobjeda, 314
Poland, 14, 34, 101, 138, 193, 250; can-
cels treaty of alliance with Yugoslavia
(1949), 218; casualties in World War
II, 39; Communist Party of, 114, 126
Politika, 18, 22, 168, 207, 307, 308, 310
Popara, Miro, 22
Popivoda, Krsto, 115
Popović, Brana, 138
Popović, Koča, 100, 168, 272, 304, 316
Popović, Vladimir, 100, 102, 194
Postojna theater, 314
Potsdam Conference, 210
Pozganica (Voranc), 210
Prague, 129–30, 133–36, 139, 140, 141,
159, 200, 220; trials in (1952), 218–19,
223, 227
Pravda, 32, 115, 144, 154, 157, 184, 204,
222, 229, 327
Princip, Gavrilo, 132, 230
Puhalo, Dušan, 18

Radojčić, Miro, 309, 312
Rajk, László: indictment and trial, 217–
220, 221, 223, 227, 231–33, 254, 263,
287; rehabilitation of, 224
Rakosi, Matias, 119, 121–22, 138, 145,
224, 231
Ranadive, B. T., 21, 23–24, 27–28, 167–
168
Rankovic, Aleksandar, 32, 42, 74, 79,
100, 107, 108, 198, 219, 228, 264, 276,
300, 304, 322, 324
Regent, Ivan, 320
Reicin, Bedrih, 219
Ribar, Ivan, 301
Ribar, Lola, 38, 221, 277
Ribbentrop, Joachim, 20
Ristić, Jovan, 168
Ristić, Marko, 168–69, 312; quoted,
169–78
Ristić, Seva, 168
Rokossovski, Marshal, 249–51
Roosevelt, Eleanor, 60, 66, 164–66, 329
Roosevelt, Franklin D., 60, 66, 69–70,
198, 237, 317
Roosevelt, Theodore, 96

Roosevelt and Hopkins (Sherwood), 60
Rude Pravo, 219, 226
Rumania, 12, 31, 34, 65, 67, 75–76, 101,
138, 155–56, 159, 193, 195, 207, 268;
cancels treaty of alliance with Yugo-
slavia (1949), 218; Communist Party
of, 12*n*., 114
Russell, Bertrand, 191
Russell International Tribunal, 331–32
Russia, *see* Soviet Union
Russo-Japanese War (1904), 69

Salaj, Djuro, 52, 54
San Francisco, 6, 8, 163
San Francisco Chronicle, 248
San Francisco Examiner, 256
Sarajevo, 124, 200, 215, 230
Sartre, Jean-Paul, 191–92
Schwartz, Laurant, 191
Serbia, 49, 59–61, 99–100, 109, 112, 118,
124, 146, 187, 193, 215, 328
Servan-Schreiber, Jean-Jacques, 207
Sharkey, L., 23–25
Sherwood, Robert E., 60
Siberia, concentration camps in, 47, 318
Simić, Stanoje, 65, 173, 202, 234
Simon, André, 219, 226–27
Slansky, Rudolf, 129, 218–19, 223, 224,
229
Slovenia, 37, 41, 60–61, 93, 129*n*., 237,
242, 314; Communist Party of, 20–21
Smedley, Agnes, 5
Snow, Edgar, 5
Soboliev, Arkadiye, 287–88
Socialist International, 274, 275
Sofia, 127, 141, 191, 218, 220, 223, 228–
229, 287
Soir, Le, 312
Sokol games, 130, 133
South Slav federation, 186, 220
Soviet-German pact (1939–1941), 20,
56–57
Soviet Union, 5, 9, 13, 15, 32, 33, 34,
45, 46, 47, 49, 55, 56, 57, 66, 73, 93,
94, 183, 184; bureaucracy denounced
by Tito, 318; cancels treaty of friend-
ship with Yugoslavia (1949), 217–18;
casualties in World War II, 39; Com-
munist Party of, 112, 114, 121, 122,
125; constitution, 261; at Danube
Conference, 153; Dedijer's early views
on, 37–38; destalinization, 46; joint-
stock companies in Yugoslavia proposed by, 73–95 *passim*, 102; national
question in, 260–61; and ultimatum
to Yugoslavia (1949), 212–14, 254; in
World War II, 20, 39–41, 48; *see also*
Cominform; Comintern; Moscow;
Stalin, Joseph
Spain, 38, 180, 213, 219–20
Sprague, Charles, 329–30

Stalin, Joseph, 12n., 13, 15, 31, 32, 33, 45, 46, 48, 52, 56, 57, 59, 66, 67, 94, 95, 96, 102, 141, 183, 198, 204, 208, 263, 306, 308–309, 328, 329; and Albania, 193–94; and Churchill, 59, 62, 64–68; death, 321–25; and Dimitrov, 186–91; Eastern Europe, plans for, 33–34, 67, 101; and East European trials (1949–52), 217–34 *passim;* and Fifth Congress of Yugoslav Communist Party, 149–50; first misunderstanding with, 46–50; Great Russian sentiments of, 208; heretics, treatment of, 124–26, 166; on "honest fools," 94, 108; lies spread by, 45, 144, 221; his model for Yugoslavia, 97–100; obedience to Party, demand for, 232; offensives against Yugoslavia (1948–53), 34–35, 45, 46, 144, 147, 154, 156–57, 159, 212, 217*ff.*, 233, 267, 278–83; "opening gambit" against Yugoslavia, 104–32 *passim;* Pavlov's view of, 142; and Pijade, 187–89; purges by (1936–38), 37, 46, 47, 125, 220–21, 223, 226; quoted, 55, 68–69, 105–106, 113–15, 211–12; Renner's letter from (1945), 211–12; secret treaties on spheres of influence, 54–66 *passim,* 255, 271, 317; "silent strangulation" policy, 101; as symbol of resistance to Hitler, 41, 43; and Tito, 74, 114, 126, 142, 150, 151; at Yalta Conference (1945), 69, 70; and Yugoslav revolution, 50–52, 54
Stalingrad, 46
Stanovnik, Janez, 221
Stepinac, Archbishop, 321
Stevanović, Dragoš, 5, 27, 304–305, 310
Stevanović, Svetislav, 220
Stilinović, Marijan, 135–36
Stojanović, Tića, 296
Story from Japan (Andrić), 332
Story of a Generation, The (Čolaković), 223
Strong, Anna Louise, 5
Šubašić, Ivan, 6, 70
Sunday Times (London), 312
Suslov, Mikhail A., 125
Svab, Karel, 219
Šverma, Jan, 227
Switzerland, 144
Szónyi, Tibor, 218

T and T, 243
Tanjug, 12n., 130, 134, 140, 246, 322
Tarisznyás, Györgyi, 219
Tass, 61, 208, 268
Telingana, India, 21, 23, 25
Téry, Simone, 174
Thirty Days, 9, 10

Thorez, Maurice, 169–75, 178
Times (London), 137, 170, 242, 288n.
Timotijević, Dušan, 168
Tirana, 195, 220
Tirnanić, Aleksandar, 5, 162, 308
Tito, Marshal, 3, 4, 10–15, 22, 26, 28, 31–37 *passim,* 41–42, 48, 49, 51–52, 63, 70, 74, 100, 104, 111, 115, 139, 147, 171, 174, 196–97, 240, 253, 294, 304; biography of, 107, 169, 252–53, 310–13, 325; and Churchill, 63, 64; on ethics, significance of, 200–201; in Great Britain, 323; and Laušman proposal, 276–77; in Moscow, 108, 225; and Pieck, 127–28; quoted, 36, 49, 50, 70, 95, 107–108, 117, 147–48, 151–52, 199, 200–201, 202, 267, 277, 280–81, 297–300, 311–12, 317–19; and Stalin, 74, 114, 126, 142, 150, 151
Tito-Šubašić agreement, 62, 70
Togliatti, Palmiro, 154, 179–82
Topalović, Živko, 312
Trieste, 63, 93, 179, 237–38, 269, 272, 275–76
Tripalo, Mika, 316
Trotsky, Leon, 106, 222
Trotskyism, 177
Tun, Thakin Than, 22, 24
Tung Pi-wu, 6–9
Turkey, 118, 121, 208, 270

Ukraine, 125, 129, 319
Ulbricht, Walter, 127, 280, 281
Unità, 308
United Nations, 6, 44, 163–66, 167, 184, 198, 202, 221, 227, 234, 249, 254–62, 270, 276, 329, 331; Yugoslavia's protest at, 282–90
United States, 49, 66, 93, 164, 183, 198, 211, 269; casualties in World War II, 40; at Danube Conference, 153
Universal Declaration of Human Rights, 165, 285
Uruguay, 5
Ustaši, 147, 246, 303

Vajnberger, Dragica, 130
Vajsman-Goranin, Lujo, 310–11
Valjero Partisan Detachment, 146, 328
Vatican, 321
Vejvoda, Ivo, 5, 9, 212–13, 283
Velebit, Vlatko, 52, 74, 83, 107, 116; quoted, 75–77
Vermeersch, Jeannette, 172–73
Vietnam, 166, 269, 331
Vilfan, Jože, 140, 243
Vinterhalter, Vilko, 224
Vlahović, Veljko, 52–54, 61–62, 122, 191, 322–23, 330
Voranc, Prežihov, 210

Voroshilov, Kliment E., 224–25
Vučinić, Branko, 10, 276, 323
Vujović, Rade, 223
Vukmanović-Tempo, Svetozar, 78–79, 106, 108, 160–61, 205, 213, 214, 220, 268, 270, 293, 322, 324
Vukmirović, Dimitar, 158
Vyshinski, Andrei, 142–43, 148, 156, 163–64, 188, 211, 223, 254–57

Wallace, Henry, 203
Wang Ming, 185
Webb, Sydney and Beatrice, 38
Welles, Orson, 7, 256
World Association for International Law, 271
World War I, 7, 17, 19, 56, 66, 186, 215
World War II, 20, 39–45, 47, 66, 68, 70, 103, 115, 186, 259, 301
Wrangel, Pëtr N., 109

Xoxe, Koci, 218, 221, 230

Yalta Conference (1945), 69–70
Young Slovene, 36
Yudin, Pavel, 27, 108, 111, 119, 122, 125, 126–27, 138, 154
Yugoslav-Albanian Relations (Dedijer), 196
Yugoslav Communist Party, 9, 20–21, 22, 28, 34–35, 45, 47, 99, 101, 105, 106, 108, 114, 117, 122–23, 126–32, 175, 179; democratization in, 295; and dogmatism, 291, 295, 296; Fifth Congress, 141–45, 148–50, 152, 167, 205; new theoretical views, 294–95;

Sixth Congress, 316–21, 330; and socialist parties in the West, 272–75
Yugoslavia, 5, 9, 13, 31, 33, 36, 38, 48, 55, 67, 68, 70, 73, 197; banking, 91–92; blockade of, economic, 101–104, 159, 197, 199, 202, 267–68, 270; casualties in World War II, 39, 40; Communist Party of, *see* Yugoslav Communist Party; and communist parties of world, enmity of, 167–84, 201; constitution of, first, 100; democratization, 319; elected to U.N. Security Council, 254–58; forecasts of doom of, 137–40; foreign policy principles, 202–203, 270; mineral resources, 87–89; peasant cooperatives, failure of, 296–99; policy on national question, 259; raw materials, fight for, 84–90; revolution, 47–54, 73, 97–98, 151, 299–300, 325–27; and secret treaties on spheres of influence, 54–66 *passim*, 255, 271, 317; self-management system, 205, 293, 295; and south Slav federation, 186; Western attitude toward, 268–69; Western help for, 271, 283
Yugoslav Tragedy, The (Maljcev), 45

Zagreb, 48, 107, 116, 161
Zečević, Vlada, 109
Zhdanov, Andrei, 13, 103, 121–22
Zhivkov, Todor, 224
Ziherl, Boris, 27, 283
Zilliacus, Koni, 104
Žogović, Radovan, 9, 18, 27
Žujović, Sreten, 6–8, 34, 111, 116, 123–124, 141, 157, 234, 304